Anke Strüver, Sybille Bauriedl (eds.)
Platformization of Urban Life

Urban Studies

Anke Strüver is a professor of human geography with a focus on urban studies at the University of Graz (Austria). In 2004 she completed her PhD at Radboud Universiteit Nijmegen (Netherlands) on the socio-cultural production of cross-border spaces and their effects on everyday practices. Her research focuses on embodied human-environment relations in the city, especially along the themes of health, food, and active mobility, as well as digitalization and sustainable co-laboration.
Sybille Bauriedl is a professor of integrative geography at Europa-Universität Flensburg (Germany). She has been researching and teaching sustainable urban development and global environmental conflicts since the 1990s. She is engaged in scientific networks of political ecology and feminist geography and is involved in the right to the city movement. Current research projects deal with local energy transition, smart urbanism, colonial infrastructure in European port cities, and climate justice.

Anke Strüver, Sybille Bauriedl (eds.)
Platformization of Urban Life
Towards a Technocapitalist Transformation of European Cities

[transcript]

The publication of this book was supported by Elisabeth List Fellowship Program for Gender Research at the University of Graz.

**Elisabeth-List-
Fellowship-Programme
for Gender Research
University of Graz**

Bibliographic information published by the Deutsche Nationalbibliothek
The Deutsche Nationalbibliothek lists this publication in the Deutsche Nationalbibliografie; detailed bibliographic data are available in the Internet at http://dnb.d-nb.de

This work is licensed under the Creative Commons Attribution-NonCommercial-ShareAlike 4.0 (BY-NC-SA) license, which means that the text may be shared and redistributed, provided credit is given to the author for non-commercial purposes only.
Permission to use the text for commercial purposes can be obtained by contacting rights@transcript-publishing.com
Creative Commons license terms for re-use do not apply to any content (such as graphs, figures, photos, excerpts, etc.) not original to the Open Access publication and further permission may be required from the rights holder. The obligation to research and clear permission lies solely with the party re-using the material.

**First published in 2022 by transcript Verlag, Bielefeld
© Anke Strüver, Sybille Bauriedl (eds.)**

Cover layout: Maria Arndt, Bielefeld
Copy-editing: Mariëlle S. Smith
Proofread: Vivien Breinbauer
Printed by Majuskel Medienproduktion GmbH, Wetzlar
Print-ISBN 978-3-8376-5964-1
PDF-ISBN 978-3-8394-5964-5
https://doi.org/10.14361/9783839459645
ISSN of series: 2747-3619
eISSN of series: 2747-3635

Printed on permanent acid-free text paper.

Contents

THANK YOU! 9

Platformized Cities and Urban Life
An Introduction
Sybille Bauriedl & Anke Strüver 11

CONDITIONS OF PLATFORMIZATION OF URBAN LIFE

Platforms Becoming Infrastructural?
Mapping Socio-Spatial Transformations
Rabea Berfelde & Vicky Kluzik 39

From Smart to Platform Urbanism to Platform Municipalism
Planning Ideas for Platforms in Toronto and Vienna
Astrid Krisch 53

The Politics of Geodata in Urban Platform Capitalism
Boris Michel & Susanne Schröder-Bergen 73

Looking for Glitches in Mobility Platforms
Henk Wiechers 85

PLATFORM-MEDIATED CARE-WORK IN CITIES

Platform Care as Care Fix
Emma Dowling 103

Second Shift 2.0
Intensifying Housework in Platform Urbanism
Maartje Roelofsen & Kiley Goyette 119

"When Clean Angels Calls, I Run"
Working Conditions of a Gigified Care-Worker
Marisol Keller 135

Platforms for Basic Needs
Rethinking their Infrastructuralization as Reflective of Elsewhere
Christiane Tristl & Anke Strüver 149

SPATIAL AND SOCIAL EFFECTS OF PLATFORMIZATION

#FairDelivery?
Potential for and Limits to Alternative Platformization
Yannick Ecker 171

Riders United Will Never Be Divided?
A Cautionary Tale of Disrupting the Platformization of Urban Space
Barbara Orth 185

<title>"Processed Food on the Urban Data Highway. Food Delivery Services as In_Visible Infrastructure in the Production of Urbanity" </title>
<meta name="EmergeError">
<!— *Akteurinnen für urbanen Ungehorsam* 205

Ordinary Invitations in Spaces of Everyday Life
Arriving in Neighborhood Life through Analogue Platforms
Yvonne Franz 217

PLATFORM CAPITALISM IN NEOLIBERAL TIMES

Echo Chambers of Urban Design
Platformization in Architecture and Planning
Cordula Kropp, Kathrin Braun & Yana Boeva 239

The Financialization of the Housing Market in the Digital Era
Airbnb in Berlin
Katalin Gennburg 259

Smart Ambivalences
Social Economy and Capitalist Rationalities
Intersecting in the Field of Sharing
Andreas Exner & Thomas Höflehner 269

Platform Urbanization and Citizenship
An Inquiry and Projection
Filippo Bignami & Naomi C. Hanakata 281

Biographies 297

THANK YOU!

This anthology is the result of a longstanding collaboration between the two editors researching digital socio-spatial structures on the one hand and urban alternatives located in everyday practices on the other from a feminist geography perspective. The intensification of our collaboration on current dynamics of digitalization and platformization of urban infrastructures, labor relations in the care sector, and urban life was made possible by the Elisabeth List Fellowship Program for Gender Research at the University of Graz, Austria. Our project *Gender just urban development in smart city contexts* included the research leave of Sybille Bauriedl from her professorship at the Europa-Universität Flensburg, Germany. The fellowship has provided us with (1) time to work on the state of the art and to do empirical research on care platforms in Europe, (2) funding for three outstanding junior fellow researchers (Yannick Ecker, Henk Wiechers and Marcella Rowek), and (3) resources to organize an international conference.

The fellowship started in March 2020, right at the moment when the spread of the Covid-19 virus turned into a pandemic. Unexpectedly, we were forced to get going not face-to-face, but online only and to collaborate out of the respective home offices in various cities. However, the objective of the research, to investigate the trends of digital infrastructures in European cities, got a new dynamic and public relevance over night when the first lockdown kicked-off in Austria on March 16, 2020. The demand for delivery services increased by leaps and bounds, while the demand for intimate domestic services, short-term rentals, and ridehailing collapsed. Despite being bound to our respective homes, we found ourselves right in the research field, a very ambivalent experience that continues to influence our lives.

We would like to thank the junior fellows of the project and the coordinators of the fellowship program in particular for their extremely flexible response to the changing situation of the research subject and the work situation. Our originally planned critical reflection on smart urbanism in relation to gender relations had been shifted to the examination of platform urbanism and digitized urban everyday life.

We are also grateful to all participants of the international conference *Platform Urbanism – Towards a technocapitalist transformation of European cities?* in March 2021. Despite being still – or again – in locked down life, we had the chance to discuss face-to-zoom and via various other communication platforms intensively. After the conference, transcript publishing immediately made us an offer for a book publication, which we were very happy to agree on. In the last years the publisher has become specialized on the nexus of society, technology, and space in the field of cultural studies. In 2018, we have already published the anthology *Smart Cities. Critical perspectives on digitalization in cities* with transcript. For this current volume, some of the conference participants have contributed their papers in more detail and we were able to engage additional authors. We would like to thank all of them for the inspiring discussions of their drafts and the excellent revisions.

Last, but not least, we would like to extend our gratitude for the technical support of the conference warranted by Luca Braun, Theresa Bürstmayer, and Mario Diethart and to Vivien Breinbauer for preparing the final book manuscript. We also thank Marielle Smith for her professional proof reading.

In nearly every end there is a new beginning: in the aftermath of the fellowship, we were working on a project proposal together with labor and feminist geographer Karin Schwiter from the University of Zurich, Switzerland. And right at the moment when this book's manuscript was finished, we got the approval for the follow-up project *Urban Platform Economies: Transformations of labour and intersectional inequalities in care services (TICS)*, which is funded by the German Research Foundation, the Swiss National Science Foundation, and the Austrian Science Fund. We are very excited about further collaborations and debates on digitized urban futures and critical, feminist reflections on technocapitalism, racialized labor relations, and gender justice.

Sybille Bauriedl, Flensburg & Anke Strüver, Graz, April 2022

Platformized Cities and Urban Life
An Introduction

Sybille Bauriedl & Anke Strüver

The increasing platformization of everyday life has recently become a subject of research across the social sciences. This edited volume aims at collecting and strengthening critical research on platform urbanism. Urban scholars have advanced this concept to examine the significance of changing everyday practices and power shifts brought about by the expansion of platform operators into all areas of urban life, such as domestic and rental services, deliveries of meals and groceries, and mobility. Platform urbanism can thus be understood as a special mode of using and producing urban spaces as its inherent mechanisms take on an increasingly central role in refashioning relational dynamics between code, commerce, and corporealities (Barns 2019; Sadowski 2020a; 2020c; Lee et al. 2020).

The task of critical platform research lies in engaging with the socio-spatial and normative implications of platform-mediated urban life. Platformization reconfigures existing digital socio-spatial orders and exacerbates inequalities in cities (Elwood 2021). Moreover, platforms do not only challenge existing regulatory frameworks (Graham 2020); they also increasingly shape ways of imagining urban futures and experiencing urban space in what may be called platform-mediated practices of placemaking. Hence, the inclusion in or exclusion from the newly created networks of data, value, and work produces new forms of precarity, injustice, and (in)security.

However, beyond a mere 'techno-dystopian' stance, critical platform research also needs to emphasize the call to understand platforms as well as contested sites of social creativity and everyday appropriations (Leszczynski 2020; Elwood 2021; Richardson 2020; Pentzien 2021). Rather than yet another critique of *Uberization* or *Airbnbization* in cities, this volume comprises critical debates of the actual consequences of digitalization for socio-technical relationships between citizens, cities, and urban infrastructures with reference to platform urbanism and beyond. In this introduction, we summarize these trends along four themes: practices of platformization, platform-mediated work, spatial dimensions of platformization, and an outlook on alternatives to platform capitalism.

Practices of platformization of urban life

In this book, we focus on *lean platforms* because this is the fastest growing platform type in recent years and they radically transform urban everyday life, labor conditions, and relations. Lean platforms such as Airbnb and Care.com have strongly transformed the supply of public and private services, especially in cities. In contrast to product platforms (such as Amazon and Zalando), lean platforms do not provide goods but services on demand. They are 'lean' in the sense that they seem to rely not on material infrastructures but capitalize from software and data analytics. Most of the workforce of these companies are freelancers. With the spread of lean service platforms in urban spaces, they have a massive short-term and long-term impact on urban economic and social relations, urban consumption patterns, supply infrastructure, and working conditions.

By lean platforms, Nick Srnicek (2017) refers to a distinction between four types of platforms: (1) advertising platforms that offer information for free and sell income to other companies, such as Facebook and Google, via the placement of advertising and the sale of personalized data, (2) cloud platforms, such as Google, that provide IT infrastructure rental to ensure digital communications, (3) product platforms that offer physical or immaterial goods such as music, movies, or cars on demand (e.g., Spotify, Netflix, DriveNow), (4) lean platforms that, unlike product platforms, do not appear to own any goods, and thus no capital, but nevertheless control the availability and the selling and sharing mode, such as Uber, the world's largest taxi company, which owns no vehicles, and Airbnb, the world's largest accommodation provider, which owns no real estate. These platforms own as little as possible and try to outsource costs as much as possible. The only asset of lean platforms such as Uber and Airbnb is the software they use to mediate the work of independent contractors. The core of lean platform business models is based not on strategies of superabundance but of depletion. The goal is the rapid flow of goods and labor when they are needed (called *on-demand services*). Lean labor workers are more often freelancers than employees, which represents huge savings in labor costs to these companies. Lean platforms generate informal as well as precarious work that is offered, coordinated, and monitored online.

Digital-savvy people often view the promise of flexibility, low-threshold availability, and multiplication of services of lean platforms positively. However, this assessment depends on digital competence and equipment with digital devices. The barriers to using platforms reflect the digital divide based on age, knowledge, income, and access to the labor market. When van Dijck, Poell, and de Waal (2018) describe platformization of everyday urban life as part of an evolving *platform society*, this does not apply to the entire urban society. Not everyone uses digital platforms mediating information, goods, and services, but everybody is influenced by the implications of service platforms on the housing and labor market and the use of public space. We call this phenomenon *platformized urban life*.

The term *platform* thus expands beyond its technological definition as a programmable interface to encompass the platform as an organizational form for a data-based business model (Srnicek 2017; van Doorn/Badger 2020) and a mode of governing (Barns 2019). Platforms are quasi-commodities that appear in the form of undemocratic institutions under corporate control. Platforms as intermediaries and infrastructures are positioned to capture and control data. Globalized companies use the internet to access people and their digital devices, which are available almost always and everywhere. There are intermediary platforms that exclusively provide digital content and do not offer any products or services of their own, whose business model is based solely on data extractivism and personalized advertising, and there are platforms that offer goods and services themselves. Data has become the central source of profit for all these platform companies.

In his book *Platform Capitalism*, Nick Srnicek (2017) describes platforms as large monopolistic companies that focus their attention on data to extract, use, and control them on a large scale and thus achieve dominance in the trade of personalized information. The platform itself is the economic asset of these companies. Platform companies are focused on rapid growth through network effects and venture capital and seek to evade government regulation (see Gennburg in this volume). The economic interest is aimed at network effects through the expansion of services, brand dominance, and the marketing of by-products (especially personalized data on consumption behavior).

The foundation of the growth of platform companies are the increasingly inexpensive digital technologies of the 21st century, the ever-increasing amount of data through digital communication, and the enormous demand for data to optimize production processes or to predict and influence consumer preferences. In addition to these material conditions, however, the neoliberal framework was crucial for the development of a booming platform economy. The digital economy developed in an economic period characterized by international competition, overproduction, and price pressure. The global financial crash in 2008 was a driver for platform companies. The post-crash landscape of austerity, entrepreneurialism, and privatization in many urban sectors has provided the perfect conditions for new flows of (venture) capital to start digital platforms that want to operate core services in terms of living, working, traveling, and consuming. The low interest rates on the capital market gave start-ups access to capital and many people were involuntarily self-employed due to job loss or debt and had to rely on informal work or micro-tasking. Moreover, in response to the financial crisis, many national governments implemented a neoliberal restructuring that led to intensified precarious employment and the privatization of care work. This provided lean platforms with both a large freelance supply and a demand for household-related services. The usual reactions of ICT companies were the outsourcing of costs, flexibilization of modes of employment, and wage dumping. Srnicek calls this *cross subsidization*, arguing that part of the business model of platforms is fine-tuning the balance between what is paid, what is not paid, what is subsidized, and what is not subsidized (Srnicek 2017: 46; see also Dowling as well as Ecker in this volume).

Mega platforms such as Uber, Airbnb, and Lieferando were founded in the immediate aftermath of the global financial crash (Sadowski 2020b; 2020c). Huws et al. (2019) point to an enormous growth in the global spread of online platforms, with an exponential growth between 2016 and 2019. In their research on 13 European countries, they found that the use of online platforms for obtaining and supplying services was widespread. Due to the lockdowns related to the Covid-19 pandemic, which started during the spring of 2020, the use of some service platforms received an additional boost: food delivery platforms have benefited from the lockdown of restaurants (Ecker/Strüver 2022) and childcare and private tutoring platforms have taken the pressure off parents with children in homeschooling. The new service of platform-mediated grocery delivery (e.g., Gorillas and Flink) were only established in major cities after the lockdown, competing with supermarkets to deliver groceries to customers' doorsteps within no time (see Orth in this volume). The expansion of the platform economy can therefore be understood as a consequence and accelerator of a neoliberal growth model.

Platform-mediated work

Digital labor platforms that organize and mediate short-term services, i.e., services as work on demand, are increasingly becoming part of urban socio-technical and socio-spatial everyday life and thus do not play out only in the cloud but also on the ground. As part of the 24/7 services-to-go economy, they are constitutive of the contemporary *real-time city* (Kitchin 2014), and "today's pivot towards the platform is motivated by the need to theorise contemporary platform intermediation in ways that overlap with broader theorisations of infrastructures, cities, and markets" (Barns 2019: 1; see also Huws 2020; Mörtenböck/Mooshammer 2021). This platform pivot is accompanied by the widespread use of smartphones and mobile internet, which have moved 'the internet' to people's pockets and mediate socio-economic and socio-spatial relations in new ways. However, service platforms still rely on 'old' ways of organizing societal (and individual) lives along gendered, racialized, and classed divisions of labor, especially of tasks related to care and social reproduction.

In general, platforms' profit is generated by economies of scale and that is why platforms strive for growth (*growth-before-profit logic*) to benefit from network effects in the long run. Next to mediating services, platforms compete on collecting and analyzing data. Extracting huge data sets enables platform companies to offer faster consumable services (e.g., ride-hailing, food delivery) or better matches (care services), resulting in, or so it is *assumed*, satisfied workers and customers on the one hand, and satisfied investors on the other. However, lean platforms rely on data less to exploit it as a commodity than to organize and optimize the respective service offered, i.e., data about customer demands and the spatial distribution of demand as well as the control, management, and surveillance of workers (Altenried 2021). Since platform companies are usually funded with venture capital – surplus capital seeking to make profit in times of very low interest rates – the growth-before-profit logic is one resting on network effects and monopolizing a special sector (Srnicek 2017), i.e., on competition between platform companies and their supply of services (see Ecker in this volume, also in comparison to less typical platform models).

Lean platforms providing services on demand and the conceptual frameworks of techno- and platform capitalism (Srnicek 2017; Elwood 2021) are often tied to the idea of a new era, neglecting their historical roots and developments. We will not join the major narrative of disruption by platform technologies and thus not approach platform-mediated labor as a fundamentally new form of labor. It rather seems to be an extension of neoliberal deregulation and flexibilization. In the sphere of care work, for example, platforms change not the tasks as such (cleaning, cooking, caregiving) but outsource them as single gigs: in 'lean' neoliberal societies, domestic care work is split up into micro-tasks, i.e., cooking, caring for children, and cleaning are separated from each other – and each of these tasks can be bought on platforms on demand. This changes, first and foremost, the relationships between clients and workers to formal but anonymous non-commitment as well as the competition for clients and over hourly wages and work standards (see Keller in this volume).

Most lean labor platforms for reproductive services offer a commodified response to those who can afford it (Huws 2019). These platforms take advantage not only of the digitization of society but also of the supply deficits due to the care crisis. Emma Dowling (in this volume) emphasizes that there are several

> "ways in which new care platforms offer solutions to the care crisis. First of all, they respond to the crisis of the neoliberal subject and the imperative for permanent productivity and optimization. [...] Second, new care platforms intervene in the crisis of social reproduction within the family and household, or society more generally. Especially where women are no longer available in the household as a resource for care [...]."

As such, the platforms present themselves as solutions for the care crisis and Dowling asks how they insert themselves into the political economy of care across the domains of state, market, and society in response to the ongoing care crisis.

Contexts of emerging digital labor platforms: Neoliberal capitalism and austerity urbanism

Digital platform economies result *from* capitalism's crises tendencies and are considered a social and economic 'fix' in cities. Many contributions in this volume bring crises and their fix into dialogue with urban everyday life by way of relational analyses of technocapitalist economies and their sociospatialities (Elwood 2021). This is due to the fact that platforms result *in* new urban temporalities and mobilities and thus new forms of proximity, both in spatial and temporal terms. In order to stress new urban configurations, we follow Srnicek's (2017) willful neglect of digital platforms' surveillance affordances or data mining techniques (see, e.g., Zuboff 2019) in this introductory chapter. We rather allude to the economic history of capitalism, including its basic principles such as profitability and its reliance on exploitation.

Service labor platforms target cities because of their population density of both consumers and potential workers, the latter often singled out by gender, race, and migration status, and thus need to be viewed in relation to neoliberal capitalism and austerity urbanism. Austerity programs have shifted economic crunches and hardship to local scales (to both urban and private households) and continue to turn social relations into market relations. The neoliberal deconstruction of urban social services by austerity policies and the fiscal crisis of the local state have been addressed as austerity urbanism for about a decade (Peck 2012; Theodore 2020). In the context of the platformization of daily urban life, this is an expression of "the politics of everyday austerity at the street level, where the effects of public-service cutbacks, job losses and increased exposure to socioeconomic risks are experienced in daily life, in workplaces, in households and the public sphere" (Peck 2012: 632). Yet, the combination of 'workplace' and 'household', i.e., private households as workplaces, has been neglected in research on austerity urbanism so far. This invites us to look in more detail at, for example, lean labor platforms as mediators of care tasks playing a central role in both platform and austerity urbanism as the crises related to contemporary austerity politics shift responsibility for the social and the economic to (very) local systems of support (see Dowling and Tristl/Strüver in this volume for care services in private households, and see Roelofsen/Goyette and Berfelde/Kluzik in this volume for the ways short-term rentals can become part of social reproduction). In general, and beyond the particular care services sector,

> "the reach of austerity extends beyond mere fiscal restraint and deep into neoliberal modes of governance. Take, for example, the ongoing malregulation of labor markets. In the name of greater labor market flexibility, the power of trade unions has been systematically eroded, social safety nets for the unemployed have been reduced or eliminated, and the standard

employment relationship has been substantially deregulated." (Theodore 2020: 4)

These developments therefore represent important parameters for platform-mediated labor and platformized urban life.

Modes of intermediation in urban everyday life: Entangling life, labor, and leisure

Lean labor platforms as mediators of service tasks are based on the triadic relationship between workers, clients, and platforms, although most platforms obscure the fact that they are not regular employers or employment agencies but merely brokers or intermediators for tasks as single gigs. Moreover, the algorithmic management of platform-mediated work is invisible and tied to "information asymmetries" (Pollio 2021: 51) between platform providers, workers, and clients. In sum, Huws (2020: 9) has described this type of model of work organization as "logged labor":

> "First, the component labour processes are broken down into separate 'tasks', much as a felled tree is broken down into separate logs, which (although these tasks may in practice require considerable tacit skills to deliver) are treated as standardized and interchangeable from the point of view of execution and reward. Second, the management and control processes are mediated by online platforms, with the worker or service user required to be online (or 'logged on') in order to be notified of what work is available and the progress of its delivery. Third, the very fact that every aspect of service delivery is managed online means that each interaction leaves a digital trace, generating data that can be used not only to record and track current activities but also to build ever more sophisticated algorithms to enhance the efficiency of future ones. Both workers and users are therefore subjected to close surveillance, meaning that the activities are also 'logged' in the sense that was historically used to describe the tracking of movements in ships' logs or other types of logbook."

Lean labor platforms allow for the mediation of gigs, such as food delivery or cleaning tasks, faster, anonymously, and across a larger spatial scale, e.g., within an entire city (Ecker/Rowek/Strüver 2021). This is but one example of why these types of platforms present themselves as technological fixes for societal crunches and individual time and money crises (Fraser 2016; Huws 2019;

see Dowling in this volume). Yet, platform labor is mostly unregulated labor and platforms "constitute an underworld that is not meant to be seen by platform users/customers" (Mezzadra 2021: 42). What is more, platform technologies enable an extension and intensification of what counts as work, both spatially and temporally: platforms entangle labor, life, and leisure because of the 24/7 availability via platforms' apps. Marisol Keller (in this volume) illustrates this vividly based on her auto-ethnographic research as a platform cleaner in Zurich, Switzerland. While apps seem to make it easier to find a cleaner – easier than asking friends and advertising in the neighborhood – the app-mediated (supposed) flexibility to work when, where, and for how long one wants results, however, in a kind of 24/7 standby situation for workers: their work is not limited to the cleaning job as such but also comprises constant attention for the app (new job offers, request for time changes, etc.) and having an inviting platform profile and good reviews from previous jobs. More attention thus needs to be paid to how workers incorporate and embody digital labor platforms and "how digital technologies both produce and mitigate such 'precarious' working geographies [gigs mediated via platforms] by folding in life 'beyond' work" (Richardson 2018: 246; see also Mos 2021 and Tristl/Strüver in this volume). Platform labor thus takes place in the app, on the ground, and in social media profiles (see van Doorn 2017; Ticona/Mateescu 2018). The accounts and affordances of apps, however, are experienced and embodied by workers and clients alike. For the clients, the platform is often reduced to the interface of the app – the app appears as enabler, facilitator, and as a kind of sentient access tool to flexible and convenient mobility, meals, and more. But, obviously, it is not the app that does the work or the platform that provides the service, but it is humans that do the work and provide the services that take time, take place literally, and make or change space: "Urban space becomes workplace, coordinated by 'digital platforms' that connect consumers to a service or commodity through a mobile application or website." (Richardson/Bissell 2019: 283) Spatial distance, for example, is essential for meal and grocery delivery time – and also for reaching private homes for cleaning or caregiving gigs. This means that proximity counts both in terms of urban spatiality and temporality. However, food delivery platforms, both for ready-made meals and for groceries, also change the character and materialities of local urban neighborhoods by dark/ghost/cloud kitchens and by empty or even closed-down restaurants, new grocery hubs, etc. (Ecker/Strüver 2022; see also Orth as well as Ecker in this volume).

Against disruption – against universalization

As mentioned above, we do not advance the idea that platform-mediated labor is a fundamentally new form of labor related to – and relying on – digital technologies. We rather suggest contextualizing it as part of neoliberal flexibilization on the one hand, and as extending the history of gendered and racialized informal work, especially in the sphere of domestic care services, on the other. However, going "beyond disruption" (Ticona/Mateescu/Rosenblat 2018) includes going beyond universalization as well: although the dominant *narratives* tied to the platformization of work seem to be universal and more or less the same 'everywhere', it works out differently in different social, national, and urban contexts. Kavita Dattani (2021), for example, argues against the universal framework for urban platform economies based on Uberization: "the techno-masculinist logics of on-demand domestic work platforms, which are built into the attempt to 'Uber-ise', have disregarded the socio-spatial relations of the city" (2021: 376). She illustrates this with her case study on domestic work platforms in New Delhi, which did not work out at all because female domestic workers do not always have access to smartphones, are often (digitally) illiterate and cannot engage in mobility across the city due to lack of transport and fear of unknown public spaces (for a similar argument, based on research on platform gigs in Kenya and South Africa, see Hunt et al. 2019). This is to say that, even though cities and societies in the Global North and South alike have been hit by austerity and structural inequalities by neoliberalism, resulting in even more precarious flexibility and everyday crises, context-sensitive research is urgently needed. Thus, despite this book's focus on Europe, it is always necessary to be "reflective of elsewhere" (Thieme 2018: 536) as the chapters by Krisch, Roelofsen/Goyette and Tristl/Strüver in this volume illustrate.

Lean platforms and their mediation of services are rooted in the history of informal gendered and racialized care work – and these particular platforms currently profit from the care crisis (see, e.g., Altenried/Dück/Wallis 2021; Flanagan 2019; Huws 2019; Schwiter/Steiner 2020; and see Duffy 2007 for its historical patterns). Furthermore, as we have argued earlier (Bauriedl/Strüver 2020), especially the development of gendered care work as part of the dominant division of labor is linked to a spatial division and to the invisibility and marginalization of domestic care work at home as an effect of the societal organization of work in capitalist structures (see Akteurinnen für urbanen Ungehorsam in this volume). Although the increasing commodification of care work – driven by the Covid-19 pandemic – have made it more public in terms of societal debates, it is still tied to gender norms, especially to notions of female subjectivities and their assumed caring responsibilities (see Weeks 2011; Federici 2019). Platform-mediated care work thus *challenges* the classification of such work as informal and unpaid work, but it neither resolves the problem of its invisibility nor the vulnerability as outcome of its flexibility. Moreover, digital platforms do not change the necessity of housework, i.e., the burden of the tasks as such (cleaning, cooking, caregiving), and they still rely on spatial as well as on a gendered and racialized division of labor as we summarized in a contribution on the techno-capitalist production of private and public spaces: "In a nutshell, it could be said that the invisibility of care-work and the interdependencies of gendered, racialised and classified inequality are a prerequisite for and intensified by platforms." (Bauriedl/Strüver 2020: 273)

Stressing the history of paid care services, including its interdependent spatial, gendered, and racialized dimensions, also requires considering the differences between on-demand platforms for food delivery and ride-hailing on the one hand, and marketplace platforms for cleaning and caregiving tasks on the other. Whereas work related to the former becomes more visible when turned into gigs mediated by platforms, work related to the latter remains invisible. Moreover, platform work is always based on flexibility and precarity, but it differs in terms of algorithmic management and control (applied in mobility and delivery services on demand) versus the importance of reviews, rating systems, and trust (applied in marketplace platforms for care services but also short-term rentals). And, while race, ethnicity, and nationality have always played major roles in the composition of the workforce of all these services, segregation in the sense of racialized work has intensified through platform labor (Ticona/Mateescu/Rosenblat 2018).

There is yet another approach to platform work as migrant work, that is, in the way of expanding income opportunities. Both Moritz Altenried (2021) and Niels van Doorn (2021) point out (with reference to Berlin) that, despite its precarity, platform work can be a transitory entry gate for migrants/refugees, especially newly arriving migrants without language skills: due to the platforms' quick ways of recruiting and few requirements regarding qualifications, they provide income opportunities immediately upon arrival. Of course, the general problems around these kinds of work – first and foremost, its contingency, labeled as flexibility, and lack of social security – remain, i.e., migrants are even more easily exploited because of their desperate situation during their formal recognition processes as full citizens and the 'stepping-stone' of platform work often turns into a 'dead-end' (van Doorn 2021).

Moreover, with respect to lean platforms' proposed flexibility to work when, where, and how long one wants, Hunt et al. (2019: 11) have criticized the assumption that the flexibility of platform care work improves women's social and economic positions: it might enable them to combine paid and unpaid domestic work in more efficient ways, but "it fails to recognise or challenge women's disproportionate unpaid care and domestic workload relative to that of men, and therefore accepts a situation in which the gig economy simply offers women a way to fit in still more hours of work. Yet the redistribution of unpaid care is a prerequisite for women's economic empowerment". Speaking of empowerment thus again refers to the need to avoid universalization. Platform work exacerbates social inequalities, and its analysis requires us to be sensitive to how it works out in different social and national, but mostly urban, contexts.

Platform urbanism: Spatial dimensions of platformization

While lean platforms are inherently spatial, they most often are also highly urban. They are basically an urban phenomenon. Even if the services of lean platforms are mediated digitally, physical space is crucial for the provision of the service. Economically successful lean platforms require a definable space with the largest possible number of potential platform users of their services (customers) and service providers (workers). They need and benefit from the population density and spatial proximity of customers and workers in cities. Especially food delivery platforms, such as Lieferando, Mjam, or Gorillas, depend on short distances between customers and workers, since only the delivery as such, regardless of the distance, is paid for. As mentioned above, delivery work is often equivalent to migrant/refugee work. This is an additional aspect of why lean labor platforms are expanding particularly in large cities. The number of people who are forced to accept precarious work from gig to gig – e.g., due to a temporary residence permit – is very high in most European cities (Sadowski 2020b; Altenried/Dück/Wallis 2021).

Urban development in digital times

Digitization in cities is characterized by strong dynamics in the constellation of driving actors and an increasing importance of platform companies. The early phase of digitization in cities was driven top down in public-private partnerships between city governments and IT corporations such as Cisco and IBM, which installed software and digital infrastructures for municipal management tasks (traffic control, waste disposal, etc.) and monitored them in control centers. City governments started to invest in digital tools and platforms with the task to optimize urban infrastructures and services. In particular, competition-oriented city governments guided by the ideal of an *entrepreneurial city* regard any type of digitalization and platformization as a pillar of their urban development strategy. This phase of a so-called smart urbanism (Marvin/Luque-Ayala/McFarlane 2016) differs from platform urbanism by its governmental mode and the greater influence of platform services on ordinary and everyday urban life. The goal of lean platforms is not to remedy deficits in municipal services but to diversify the range of services and thus generate additional demand (Barns 2019; Stehlin/Hodson/McMeekin 2020; Lee et al. 2020). Smart urbanism and platform urbanism can also be distinguished by their influence on everyday urban life, as Sadowski argues:

> "Smart urbanism is primarily about optimizing oversight of city systems through state procured, corporate provided 'solutions', whereas platform urbanism aims to transform and/or take over the operations of city services that tend to be more market or consumer oriented. These two models don't necessarily supersede or even compete with each other, but rather work simultaneously in different spaces." (Sadowski 2020b: 449)

However, these two models do not serve all necessary services in cities in the same way. Services that cannot be profitably commercialized by platform companies or can only be offered profitably in specific areas of the city remain the responsibility of established providers. Lee, Mackenzie, Smith, and Box therefore "note a concerning dynamic where city administration becomes 'locked in' to specific corporate products and interests, and thereby 'locked out' from alternatives" (2020: 116; on alternative practices of smart cities, see Exner/Höflehner in this volume).

Production of various urban spaces by platformization

Lean platforms are not only relevant for urban life and everyday practices as a new business model or community project but as a political-economic technology (Zuboff 2019) that produces platformized urban spaces. Lean platforms transform the supply structure in cities in various ways: (a) many goods and services are available on demand and any smartphone owner can order ready meals, groceries, or domestic care services at any time and thus compete with stationary providers; (b) short-term housing platforms displace tenants in tourist-attractive neighborhoods; and (c) platforms that mediate services with travel distances for delivery privilege inner-city neighborhoods over disadvantaged neighborhoods in the suburbs. The platformization of urban life takes place in a spatially exclusive way.

Moreover, platform economies *integrate* spaces and bodies into new relationships of use and commerce. This integration is accompanied by a *disintegration* of existing spatial patterns, i.e., the (re)production of space also affects *placemaking* as the re-inscription of spaces into new relationships. The home or spare room as a short-term rental, for example, changes perceptions and symbolic values of urban living (see Roelofsen/Goyette and Berfelde/Kluzik in this volume). Meal delivery platforms, on the other hand, may use their socio-spatial data on economic geographies to engage in property management or business development themselves (as is already obvious with so-called dark/ghost/cloud kitchens; see Richardson 2020; Ecker/Strüver 2022).

Home (as a private space) is turned into a working space for some (care workers) and public streets become working space for others (deliverers of meals and goods, bike and scooter chargers, or ride-sharing drivers). Delivery platforms visibly occupy the streets as moving advertisement columns embodied by their riders. What stays invisible, however, is the infrastructure of constantly processed information on the platform, delivering app-generated user data and behavioral profiles that are not only used to make profitable predictions of the future demand of services but mainly serve the interests of platform CEOs and shareholders (see Akteurinnen für urbanen Ungehorsam in this volume).

Capitalization of (public and private) urban space

A recurring theme in the discussion of platform urbanism is the capitalization of urban spaces (Leszczynski 2020; Sadowski 2020b; Barns 2019; Rossi 2020). Platform companies have become huge global players within only a few years and they "are increasingly acting as sites for a contemporary urban politics, through the appropriation of 'the local'" (Barns 2018). They have turned into a mode of urbanism just by the number of their users. As global companies, they promote universal expectations of an urban quality of life. Platforms invent affective notions of place and the local. A global platform such as Airbnb offers a commodity that is commercialized as an authentic experience to live and stay anywhere in the world like a local (Crampton 2009; and see Michel/Schroeder-Bergen in this volume). Platforms are more than market participants; they are market makers in the sense that they marketize 'idle resources' into maximally productive assets and unlock the value of latent space in existing places (Sadowski 2020b). Moreover, "platform companies use [both public and private] urban spaces as a profit terrain" (Pollio 2021: 48).

However, the dynamics of platform urbanism should not only be reduced to the logic of capital extraction. Following Barns (2018), we understand the city as a specific product of the historical relations of capitalism and the specific spatiality of the city as a basis for progressive political action. Instead of producing a territorial spatial pattern, platforms intervene in the production of space by reconfiguring potential uses of existing spaces and creating new spatialities (Barns 2019). Data-driven planning strategies reconfigure not only the actions of city dwellers, urban infrastructures, and services but also the socio-material reality of buildings and places (see Kropp/Braun/Boeva in this volume).

Materialities of urban platforms

Critical urban research has traced the diverse manifestations and ambivalences of digitized and platformized urban development (Söderström/Paasche/Klauser 2014; Bauriedl/Strüver 2018). Lizzie Richardson argues that "the platform is a flexible spatial arrangement that does not have a fixed territory but rather draws on other territorialized networks to actualize in urban form. The capacity for the platform to act occurs through its ability to articulate together more or less territorialized urban elements" (2020: 458). Platforms do not reorganize transport or housing through new physical infrastructures but through novel technologies of coordination of those already existing. In this sense, platforms are "simultaneously embedded and disembedded from the space-times [they] mediate" (Graham 2020: 7). For example, the case of the grocery delivery service Gorillas in Berlin shows that the company's very business model relies on a neighborhood-based network of warehouses, embedding the platform on a very local level (see Orth in this volume). At the same time, the service model is disembedded from regulations of their delivery service's business hours and does not have to provide break rooms for their riders.

Some platform services need material urban infrastructures. They occupy existing public infrastructures such as roads and parking lots, supplementing them with necessary materialities. Rabari and Storper (2015: 28) have used the term *digital skin* of cities for "the widespread implantation of sensors into urban and household environments, together with ubiquitous mobile broadband communication technologies that can transmit both deliberate communications and automated user data". This digital skin is rather invisible as a surface layer, although its effects are everywhere to be seen. Graham forcefully highlights that digital urban infrastructures become visible and a matter of concern primarily in moments of glitches, disruption, failure, and collapse (Graham 2010; see Wiechers in this volume). According to Agnieszka Leszczynski, these glitches can be productive moments for changes in social norms as soon as they make the contradictions and dissonances of digital platform practices in everyday use perceptible (Leszczynski 2020). Urban residents are not only and always passive data subjects. They can act within platform environments in order to recognize their political power within a ubiquitous techno-political environment (see Bignami/Hanakata in this volume).

Navigating between critique and creativity: Alternatives to platform capitalism

In the future, technological and digital sovereignty in the sense of data and algorithmic transparency for both cities and citizens must be a central element of urban digital transformation strategies. Cities such as Madrid and Barcelona are currently demonstrating how democratic autonomy of urban politics and economies can develop as an alternative to the neoliberal entrepreneurial city. This includes the de-privatization and municipalization of platforms for public services (e.g., energy and water supply, transport, healthcare, education) in order to coordinate them in democratic and sustainable ways. These kinds of *platform communalism* or *platform municipalism* (Piétron 2021; Thompson 2021) are complementary techno-political programs to platform cooperatives, to collaborative platforms based on and enabled by the technological sovereignty of the cities and citizens.

Platform cooperatives

Urban platform economies also comprise those that pursue not capitalist but common and cooperative concerns. Accordingly, they are based on different business models than profit-oriented platforms: cooperative-organized ownership models, for example, rely on members depositing capital rather than investment or venture capital. They aim for transparent and fair interactions rather than competition and market dominance and, often, rely on *user* ownership, e.g., workers, or even both clients and workers (Pentzien 2021). Moreover, they are not concerned with data extractivism and manipulation but with learning from the data generated as a community (crowd knowledge) and with including cooperative norms into their algorithms (Schor 2020; Scholz/Schneider 2017). Because, in addition to the principles of outsourcing as well as the high intermediation fees, the gig model of lean labor platforms entails disciplining and discrimination by data: the data produced by platform transactions are reused as knowledge resources in the sense of a data-centered and exchange-value-centered logic of exploitation – far beyond the actual function or interaction of the platform, and platform capitalism is executed by black box algorithms. To be able to counter this capitalist-exploitative variant of platforms, Trebor Scholz demands: "What we need is a new story about sharing, aggregation, openness, and cooperation; one that we can believe in." (Scholz 2016: 26)

New stories can be found in both theories and practices of collaborative commons and cooperatives, for example, on non-hierarchical peer-to-peer communities (Bauwens/Kostakis/Pazaitis 2019) whose work are now facilitated by digital technologies but in a decentralized and radical democratic way based on solidarity. Such projects aim for structural alternatives to extractive capitalism – and they replace exchange value and shareholder value by use value and thus share(able) value: "In this way, commons-centred communities backed by political (municipalities), social (intentional communities) and entrepreneurial (cooperatives) rationales can be envisioned to slowly exert increasing control over the means of production." (Gerhard 2020: 696f.; see also Sutton 2019 for a detailed reflection on civic cooperatives and cooperative cities, and see Gennburg in this volume)

Platform cooperatives operate on the basis of democratically designed ownership models and governance structures. After all, the problematic aspects of platform capitalism have their foundations neither in the idea nor in the technology of the platform but in the profit-maximizing model of techno-capitalism: "It is not technology that is the cause of injustice, rather, technology is the symptom. Treating the symptom will just result in the production of new symptoms. It is the [normative algorithmic] infrastructure itself and its imaginaries that are racist, patriarchal, homophobic, exploitative, etc." (del Casino et al. 2020: 610) Therefore, diverse, alternative, and solidarity-based economies, e.g., non-financialized sharing, digital civic commons and, of course, cooperatives, offer opportunities to use digital platforms beyond the radical marketization of basic societal and social infrastructures and the mediation of human services as dehumanized gigs (see Huws et al. 2019: 24f. for household services provided by municipal platforms; see Pentzien 2021 for the fundamental problem of funding the co-op establishment process on the 'market', i.e., the building network effects and combating limited competitiveness during the initial phase on the one hand, and for various examples of successful platform cooperatives on the other).

Platform municipalism

The idea of platform cooperatives is complemented by techno-politics on the municipal scale and refers to public infrastructures in healthcare, education, mobility, etc., and to, for example, counterbalancing trends in which Uber has replaced public transport in US cities, not *for* people but *with* people (Piétron 2021). Techno-politics is part of digital urbanism but critical of both smart and platform urbanism. It is tied to technological sovereignty as it tries to apply technological affordances in democratic ways. It refers to commons-based ownership models and a right to city citizenship (not a national one) and replaces the notion of smart urbanism understood as a neoliberal urban operating system with a digital urbanism relying on social and democratic relations. In some municipalities in Spain, first and foremost in Madrid and Barcelona, techno-politics is tied to new municipalism; for example, the platforms DECIDE (Madrid) and DECIDIM (Barcelona) have facilitated citizen participation in urban planning and budgeting on a large scale. However, these platforms "rely upon local activity taking place offline" (Smith/Prieto Martín 2021: 327). They are anchored in local communities in which technological sovereignty enables people to explore radical democratic interaction and diverse and solidarity economies beyond the capitalist hegemony, i.e., combining radical democracy with social and economic solidarity (Lynch 2020; Sutton 2019). However, because of this, the platforms are closely connected to people's everyday lives on the local scale and in the neighborhood. In this context, Franz (in this volume) points out – using various examples from Vienna, Austria – that the idea of using a platform to connect people is neither new nor bound to digital mediation but was and is rooted in ordinary urban places, which invite encounters in local neighborhoods. Against this background, she describes *analogue platform urbanism* as one relying on different intentions, characters, temporalities, and territories than technocapitalist platforms – as invitations for social interaction.

New municipalism is also based on social interaction, especially on urban solidarities in the contexts of neoliberal austerity urbanism on the one hand, and capitalist platform urbanism on the other. Municipalism is about the democratic autonomy of municipalities over political and (more social) economic structures, i.e., beyond hierarchical relations and towards transformative social change. As such, *platform* municipalism is about the establishment of digital citizen platforms, moving away from data-driven governance by democratizing and socializing the coordination of urban infrastructures and economies (Thompson 2021; see also Krisch in this volume), contrasting the neoliberal ideas of e-participation and smart citizenship (Kitchin/Cardullo/di Feliciantonio 2019). Techno-politics is a commons-based radical democratic alternative to technocracy, which only tries to steer and control citizens' lives and participation (Smith/Prieto Martín 2021).

Empowerment and the platformization of everyday urban life

As mentioned above, platform urbanism can also refer to progressive facilitation, and initiatives based on solidarity and technological sovereignty necessarily include offline participation based primarily on social relations. Against this backdrop, as editors of this book, we are concerned with pushing forward critical and feminist digital geographies and exploring "possibilities of liberatory digital politics for re-making our technologies and ourselves as digital subjects" (Elwood/Leszczynski 2018: 640). Contrary to a reading of digital subjects as being mainly focused on self-optimization and individual responsibilization, we like to stress the relevance of the caring social relations necessary to rebuild technological infrastructures in general, and platform economies in particular. In tying critical studies on platform urbanism to feminist digital geographies, we yet, and again, emphasize the role of urban everyday life as a central perspective when studying how platforms operate and interact with existing cultural, social, and political practices (Barns 2020; Elwood 2021). Feminist digital geographies are concerned with both epistemological and ontological approaches to datafied bodies, subjectivities, and space in everyday life. In our opinion, it is necessary to look beyond the platform as interface and beyond algorithms transforming workers and their labor. In the future, even more detailed research is needed that focuses on material inequalities 'in person and on the ground'. This relies on analyses of the co-constitution of digital and social structures, e.g., the relevance of care service platforms in times of care crises. The contributions to this volume provide essential examples of how digital platforms reconfigure urban space and reshape inequalities in and of urban life. They illustrate the ongoing transformation of everyday practices and power shifts brought about by the expansion of platform capitalism into all areas of urban life – and they comprise both fear and hope.

References

Altenried, Moritz (2021): Mobile workers, contingent labour: Migration, the gig economy and the multiplication of labour, in: *Environment and Planning A: Economy and Space* 0(0). doi: https://doi.org/10.1177/0308518X211054846.

Altenried, Moritz/Dück, Julia/Wallis, Mira (eds.) (2021): *Plattformkapitalismus und die Krise der sozialen Reproduktion*, Münster: Westfälisches Dampfboot.

Barns, Sarah (2018): Platform urbanism rejoinder: Why now? What now?, in: *Mediapolis. A journal of cities and culture* 3(4). https://www.mediapolisjournal.com/2018/11/platform-urbanism-why-now-what-now [27.02.2022].

Barns, Sarah (2019): Negotiating the Platform Pivot: From Participatory Digital Ecosystems to Infrastructures of Everyday Life, in: *Geography Compass* 13(9). doi: https://doi.org/10.1111/gec3.12464.

Barns, Sarah (2020): *Platform urbanism. Negotiating platform ecosystems in connected cities*, Singapore: Springer Nature.

Bauriedl, Sybille/Strüver, Anke (eds.) (2018): *Smart City. Kritische Perspektiven auf die Digitalisierung in Städten*, Bielefeld: transcript.

Bauriedl, Sybille/Strüver, Anke (2020): Platform Urbanism: Technocapitalist Production of Private and Public Spaces, in: *Urban Planning* 5(4): 267-76.

Bauwens, Michel/Kostakis, Vasilis/Pazaitis, Alex (2019): Peer to Peer. *The Commons Manifesto*, London: Westminster UP.

Crampton, Jeremy W. (2009): Cartography: maps 2.0, in: *Progress in Human Geography* 33(1): 91-100.

Dattani, Kavita (2021): Platform 'glitch as surprise'. The on-demand domestic work sector in Delhi's National Capital Region, in: *City* 25(3-4). doi: https://doi.org/10.1080/13604813.2021.1935786.

del Casino, Vincent J./House-Peters, Lily/Crampton, Jeremy W./Gerhardt, Hannes (2020): The Social Life of Robots: The Politics of Algorithms, Governance, and Sovereignty, in: *Antipode* 52(3): 605-18.

Dowling, Emma (2021): *The care crisis. What caused it and how can we end it?*, London: Verso.

Duffy, Mignon (2007): Doing the Dirty Work: Gender, Race, and Reproductive Labor in Historical Perspective, in: *Gender & Society* 21(3): 313-36.

Ecker, Yannick/Rowek, Marcella/Strüver, Anke (2021): Care on Demand: Geschlechternormierte Arbeits- und Raumstrukturen in der plattformbasierten Sorgearbeit, in: Altenried, Moritz/Dück, Julia/Wallis, Mira (eds.): *Plattformkapitalismus und die Krise der sozialen Reproduktion*, Münster: Westfälisches Dampfboot: 112-29.

Ecker, Yannick/Strüver, Anke (2022): Towards alternative platform futures in post-pandemic cities? A case study on platformization and changing socio-spatial relations in on-demand food delivery, in: *Digital Geography and Society* 3. doi: https://doi.org/10.1016/j.diggeo.2022.100032.

Elwood, Sarah (2021): Digital geographies, feminist relationality, Black and queer code studies: Thriving otherwise, in: *Progress in Human Geography* 45(2): 209-28.

Elwood, Sarah/Leszczynski, Agnieszka (2018): Feminist digital geographies, in: *Gender, Place & Culture* 25(5): 629-44.

Federici, Silvia (2019): From crisis to commons: Reproductive work, aective labor and technology, and the transformation of everyday life, in: Federici, Silvia (ed.): *Re-enchanting the world*, Oakland, CA: PM Press: 175-87.

Flanagan, Frances (2019): Theorising the Gig Economy and Home-Based Service Work, in: *Journal of Industrial Relations* 61(1): 57-78.

Fraser, Nancy (2016): Contradictions of Capital and Care, in: *New Left Review* (100): 99-117.

Gerhardt, Hannes (2020): Engaging the Non-Flat World: Anarchism and the Promise of a Post-Capitalist Collaborative Commons, in: *Antipode* 52(3): 681-701.

Graham, Stephen (ed.) (2010): *Disrupted cities. When infrastructure fails*, New York, NY: Routledge.

Graham, Mark (2020): Regulate, replicate, and resist – the conjunctural geographies of platform urbanism, in: *Urban Geography* 41(3): 453-57.

Hunt, Abigail/Samman, Emma/Tapfuma, Sherry/Mwaura, Grace/Omenya, Rhoda/Kim, Kay/Stevano, Sara/Roumer, Aida (2019): Women in the gig economy. Paid work, care and flexibility in Kenya and South Africa. https://eprints.soas.ac.uk/32330/1/Hunt%20et%20al%202019_women_in_the_gig_economy_final_digital.pdf [21.04.2022].

Huws, Ursula (2019): The hassle of housework: Digitalization and the commodification of domestic labour, in: *Feminist Review* 123(1): 8-23.

Huws, Ursula (2020): The algorithm and the city: platform labour and the urban environment, in: *Work organisation, labour & globalisation* 14(1): 7-14.

Huws, Ursula/Spencer, Neil/Coates, Matt/Holts, Kaire (2019): The Platformisation of Work in Europe: Results from Research in 13 European Countries. https://www.eurofound.europa.eu/de/data/platform-economy/records/the-platformisation-of-work-in-europe-results-from-research-in-13-european-countries [26.02.2022].

Kitchin, Rob (2014): The real-time city? Big data and smart urbanism, in: *GeoJournal* 79: 1-14.

Kitchin, Rob/Cardullo, Paolo/di Feliciantonio, Cesare (2019): Citizenship, Justice, and the Right to the Smart City, in: Cardullo, Paolo/di Feliciantonio, Cesare/Kitchin, Rob (eds.): *The Right to the Smart City*, Bingley: Emerald: 1-24.

Lee, Ashlin/Mackenzie, Adrian/Smith, Gavin J.D./Box, Paul (2020): Mapping Platform Urbanism: Charting the Nuance of the Platform Pivot, in: *Urban Planning* 5(1): 116-28.

Leszczynski, Agnieszka (2020): Glitchy Vignettes of Platform Urbanism, in: *Environment and Planning D: Society and Space* 38(2): 189-208.

Lynch, Casey R. (2020): Contesting Digital Futures: Urban Politics, Alternative Economies, and the Movement for Technological Sovereignty in Barcelona, in: *Antipode* 52(3): 660-80.

Marvin, Simon/Luque-Ayala, Andrés/McFarlane, Colin (eds.) (2016): *Smart urbanism. Utopian vision or false dawn?*, New York, NY: Routledge.

Mezzadra, Sandro (2021): Helge Mooshammer and Peter Mörtenböck in Conversation with Sandro Mezzadra, in: Mörtenböck, Peter/Mooshammer, Helge (eds.): *Platform Urbanism and Its Discontents*, Rotterdam: nai010 publishers: 41-52.

Mörtenböck, Peter/Mooshammer, Helge (eds.) (2021): *Platform Urbanism and Its Discontents*, Rotterdam: nai010 publishers.

Mos, Eva (2021): Digital care space: The particularities of a digital home care platform, in: Gabauer, Angelika/Knierbein, Sabine/Cohen, Nir/Lebuhn, Henrik/Trogal, Kim/Viderman, Tihomir/Haas, Tigran (eds.): *Care and the City*, New York/London: Routledge: 215-26.

Peck, Jamie (2012): Austerity urbanism. American cities under extreme economy, in: *City* 16(6): 626-55.

Pentzien, Jonas (2021): Vom Plattform-Kapitalismus zum Plattform-Kooperativismus?, in: Altenried, Moritz/Dück, Julia/Wallis, Mira (eds.): *Plattformkapitalismus und die Krise der sozialen Reproduktion*, Münster: Westfälisches Dampfboot: 274-92.

Piétron, Dominik (2021): Plattform-Kommunalismus – Für eine Technopolitische Infrastrukturoffensive von unten. https://www.rosalux.de/publikation/id/44476/plattform-kommunalismus?cHash=31f2aa527e3acfdaf263abbbccd24c10 [29.09.2021].

Pollio, Andrea (2021): Uber, Airports, and Labour at the Infrastructural Interfaces of Platform Urbanism, in: *Geoforum* 118: 47-55.

Rabari, Chirag/Storper, Michael (2015): The digital skin of cities: urban theory and research in the age of the sensored and metered city, ubiquitous computing and big data, in: *Cambridge Journal of Regions, Economy and Society* 8(1): 27-42.

Richardson, Lizzie (2018): Feminist geographies of digital work, in: *Progress in Human Geography* 42(2): 244-63.

Richardson, Lizzie (2020): Platforms, Markets, and Contingent Calculation: The Flexible Arrangement of the Delivered Meal, in: *Antipode* 52(3): 619-36.

Richardson, Lizzie/Bissell, David (2019): Geographies of digital skill, in: *Geoforum* 99: 278-86.

Rossi, Ugo (2020): Fake Friends: The Illusionist Revision of Western Urbanology at the Time of Platform Capitalism, in: *Urban Studies* 57(5): 1105-17.

Sadowski, Jathan (2020a): Who owns the future city? Phases of technological urbanism and shifts of sovereignty, in: *Urban Studies* 58(8): 1732-44.

Sadowski, Jathan (2020b): Cyberspace and cityscape: on the emergence of platform urbanism, in: *Urban Geography* 41(3): 448-52.

Sadowski, Jathan (2020c): The Internet of Landlords: Digital Platforms and New Mechanisms of Rentier Capitalism, in: *Antipode* 52(2): 562-80.

Scholz, Trebor (2016): *Platform Cooperativism – Challenging the Corporate Sharing Economy*, New York, NY: Rosa Luxemburg Stiftung.

Schor, Juliet (2020): *After the Gig*, Berkeley: University of California Press.

Schwiter, Karin/Steiner, Jennifer (2020): Geographies of care work: The commodification of care, digital care futures and alternative caring visions, in: *Geography Compass* 14(12). doi: https://doi.org/10.1111/gec3.12546.

Smith, Adrian/Prieto Martín, Pedro (2021): Going Beyond the Smart City? Implementing Technopolitical Platforms for Urban Democracy in Madrid and Barcelona, in: *Journal of Urban Technology* 28(1-2): 311-30.

Söderström, Ola/Paasche, Till/Klauser, Francisco (2014): Smart cities as corporate storytelling, in: *City* 18(3): 307-20.

Srnicek, Nick (2017): *Platform capitalism*, Cambridge/Malden: Polity Press.

Stehlin, John/Hodson, Michael/McMeekin, Andrew (2020): Platform mobilities and the production of urban space. Toward a typology of platformization trajectories, in: *Environment and Planning A: Economy and Space* 52(7): 1250-68.

Sutton, Stacey (2019): Cooperative cities: Municipal support for worker cooperatives in the United States, in: *Journal of Urban Affairs* 41(8): 1081-102.

Theodore, Nik (2020): Governing through austerity: (Il)logics of neoliberal urbanism after the global financial crisis, in: *Journal of Urban Affairs* 42(1): 1-17.

Thieme, Tatiana Adeline (2018): The hustle economy: Informality, uncertainty and the geographies of getting by, in: *Progress in Human Geography* 42(4): 529-48.

Thompson, Matthew (2021): What's so new about New Municipalism?, in: *Progress in Human Geography* 45(2): 317-42.

Ticona, Julia/Mateescu, Alexandra (2018): Trusted strangers: Care platforms' cultural entrepreneurship in the on-demand economy, in: *New Media & Society* 20(11): 4384-404.

Ticona, Julia/Mateescu, Alexandra/Rosenblat, Alex (2018): Beyond Disruption. How Tech Shapes Labour Across Domestic Work and Ridehailing. https://datasociety.net/wp-content/uploads/2018/06/Data_Society_Beyond_Disruption_FINAL.pdf [20.04.2022].

van Dijck, José/Poell, Thomas/de Waal, Martijn (2018): *The platform society. Public values in a connective world*, Oxford: Oxford UP.

van Doorn, Niels (2017): Platform labor: on the gendered and racialized exploitation of low-income service work in the 'on-demand' economy, in: *Information, Communication & Society* 20(6): 898-914.

van Doorn, Niels (2021): Stepping Stone or Dead End? The Ambiguities of Platform-Mediated Domestic Work under Conditions of Austerity. Comparative Landscapes of Austerity and the Gig Economy: New York and Berlin, in: Baines, Donna/Cunningham, Ian (eds.): *Working in the Context of Austerity. Challenges and Struggles*, Bristol: Bristol University Press: 49-69.

van Doorn, Niels/Badger, Adam (2020): Platform Capitalism's Hidden Abode: Producing Data Assets in the Gig Economy, in: *Antipode* 52(2): 1475-95.

Weeks, Kathi (2011): *The Problem with Work. Feminism, Marxism, Antiwork Politics, and Postwork Imaginaries*, Durham, NC: Duke University Press.

Zuboff, Shoshana (2019): *The age of surveillance capitalism: The fight for a human future at the new frontier of power*, London: Profile books.

CONDITIONS OF PLATFORMIZATION OF URBAN LIFE

Platforms Becoming Infrastructural?
Mapping Socio-Spatial Transformations

Rabea Berfelde & Vicky Kluzik

Introduction

Recent debates around *platform urbanism* point towards the complex entanglements of digital technology and urban space and consider how emerging socio-technical formations shape platform-mediated urban everyday life. In this light, platforms are often qualified as a new form of urban infrastructure and it is argued that they "have become agents not only of socio-technical transformation but also of legal and infrastructural change" (Mooshammer/Mörtenböck 2021: 12).

Our article critically reviews existing research around platform urbanism (Sadowski 2020; Bauriedl/Strüver 2020) and discusses how the infrastructural character of platforms is analyzed. We sketch out a framework to understand how an *infrastructuralization of platforms* takes place vis-à-vis ongoing socio-spatial transformations akin to *austerity urbanism* (Peck 2012).

The first part of the article reviews two different strands of infrastructure research: on the one hand, insights from Science and Technology Studies (STS) that highlight the co-constitution of technological and social structures and on the other hand, feminist political theory that theorizes *infrastructures for social reproduction*. The second part takes a closer look at literature theorizing platform urbanism and systematizes the different understandings of infrastructure guiding the analysis of platforms' operations in urban space. The third part discusses two case studies – Airbnb and care platforms that we have studied in depth elsewhere (see Berfelde 2021; Kluzik 2021). We look at these two cases to understand how platforms leverage a *crisis of care* to position their business model as a privatized infrastructure for social reproduction. What we propose is a rethinking of technopolitical theorizations with a feminist focus that understands the social-reproductive contradictions inherent to financialized capitalism as a central prism for a more nuanced analysis of the increasing infrastructuralization of platforms.

Infrastructures for a livable life? Multiple perspectives and frictions

What are we (not) talking about when analyzing infrastructure? In the past decade, one was able to witness a growing interest in the social study of infrastructure across various disciplines and fields of research. Initially rooted in Science and Technology Studies (STS), the study of infrastructure points towards the co-constitution of technological and social structures. In this first section of our article, we review different notions of infrastructure in order to work on a more general understanding of what infrastructure *is* and *does*. Furthermore, we propose a rethinking of established technopolitical theorizations vis-à-vis feminist literature to then develop a definition of infrastructures of social reproduction.

The concept of infrastructure is rooted in the Enlightenment idea of unlimited circulation of goods, people, and ideas (Mattelart 1996) and therefore inextricably linked to the idea of technological governance to secure freedom in liberal societies. In her seminal research, Susan Leigh Star (1999) most notably brought infrastructure to the forefront of the study of social relations and large technical systems. Infrastructure, in general terms, is defined by eight dimensions: through its embeddedness, transparency, reach or scope, part of membership, link with conventions of practice, embodiment of standards, it is built on an installed base and becomes visible upon breakdown (Star/Ruhleder 1996: 113).

Brian Larkin defines infrastructure as "built networks that facilitate the flow of goods, people, or ideas and allow for their exchange over space". Infrastructures "comprise the architecture for circulation, literally providing the undergirding of modern societies, and they generate the ambient environment of everyday life" (Larkin 2013: 328). The focus on the network-like character is a key feature that complements the dimensions discussed in relation to Star's work. Working on an ontological characterization of what infrastructure *is*, Larkin emphasizes how infrastructures are "things and also the relation between things", comprising different components such as "built things, knowledge things, or people things" (Larkin 2013: 329).

The types of infrastructural networks analyzed in the debates summarized above – such as transport, energy, water, telecommunications – are the "material mediators between nature and the city" and therefore form "constitutive parts of the urban" (Kaika/Swyngedouw 2000: 120). The *modern infrastructural ideal*, embodied by the Keynesian welfare state up until the 1970s, understood the provision of these basic infrastructures to be a core role of the state. At that time comprehensive infrastructural provision was also a key organizing principle for urban planning. Stephen Graham and Simon Marvin consider how these "state-backed, collectivized forms of urban infrastructure provision" (Graham/Marvin 2002: 95) fell into crisis due to changing political economies of capitalist urbanization. A fiscal and legitimacy crisis lead to a critique of supposedly inefficient state-provision and consequently to the neoliberal privatization of infrastructural provision and services. Urban infrastructural networks were *unbundled*, i.e., no longer comprehensively planned by the state but packaged into individual services provided by corporate actors. *Splintering urbanism* replaced the rationally planned urban (Graham/Marvin 2002: 33) and private investment in infrastructural projects – often orchestrated through the credit-system and debt-financed expenditures – became a means to *fix* over-accumulated capital in space (Harvey 2001; 2018: xvii).

Studies of infrastructural systems often focus on the relationality between the physical and the digital, the social and the technological, the human and the non-human. Relationality is also a core concept in feminist theory, such as early ecofeminist interventions (Shiva/Mies 2014), feminist ethico-political theory (Butler 2018) as well as feminist science studies (Haraway 1988). Judith Butler's intervention in *Notes Toward a Performative Theory of Assembly* makes a compelling case for a possible re-politicization of the livability of lives against the backdrop of neoliberal precarization. As already outlined in earlier work, Butler invites us to think mutual dependency through vulnerability and precariousness. Precariousness is understood as a generalized condition of human life – a "common human vulnerability that emerges with life itself" (Butler 2006: 31). Butler argues that "everyone is dependent on social relations and enduring infrastructures in order to maintain a livable life" (Butler 2018: 21).

By drawing on Butler's theorization, we aim to develop an understanding of infrastructure as *social infrastructure* that the reproduction of lives depends upon. In times of the neoliberal restructuring and dismantling of welfare services and increasing insecurity – a *biopolitical situation* in which diverse populations are subject to precarization – she notes how "some populations are disposable" (Butler 2018: 11). As Nikki Luke and Maria Kaika remark, an "attack on historical infrastructures of social reproduction […] is not simply a 'side effect' of gentrification, but [a] prime strategy towards urban economic restructuring". Housing privatization, the dismantling of workers' rights and welfare, the privatization of eldercare, health, educational institutions, and childcare are key to contemporary gentrifying urban politics (Luke/Kaika 2019: 579). In this way, the differential access to infrastructures for certain populations manifests whose lives and bodies are rendered disposable and whose are being cared for. Butler makes a powerful call to go beyond a neoliberal and individualizing ethics of *responsibilization* and looks for alternatives that acknowledge how lives are dependent on infrastructures.

Platform urbanism = platform infrastructuralization?

In this section we excavate how an understanding of infrastructure – as the essential background upon which everyday life unfolds and the socio-technological forces shaping, governing, and restructuring public action – structures the analysis of platform urbanism. Platforms are often considered as ubiquitous, but simultaneously urban phenomena. Jathan Sadowski, for example, in making sense of the recent urbanization of digital capitalism and the "growing presence and power of digital platform in cities", argues that platforms are centralized in cities "for many of the same reasons that capital is" (Sadowski 2020: 449-50): Platforms benefit from the population density and spatial proximity of users/workers in cities. There are more opportunities for mediating social relations and extracting economic value in large, diverse markets (Sadowski 2020: 450).

Platforms not only tap into existing urban labor markets – where precarious workers juggle multiple gigs – but they also appropriate the socially produced and collective value of urban life (Marrone/Peterlongo 2020; Rossi 2019). In the platforms' business model, the direct exploitation of human labor is combined with the exploitation of "the commonwealth of metropolitan environments (in terms of codified and socially diffused knowledge, entrepreneurial life forms, and relational abilities)" (Rossi 2019: 13).

In recent debates the concept *platform urbanism* gained traction to not only illuminate *platform capitalism* (Srnicek 2017) as an urban phenomenon, but also how platform intermediation changes urban everyday life – labor, social reproduction, interaction, consumption, and circulation. An assumed increasing infrastructuralization of platforms is often taken as the starting point to approach a conceptualization of platform urbanism (Altenried/Animento/

Bojadžijev 2021) and to think "about platforms per se as a new form of urban infrastructure" (Moore/Rodgers 2018). This part of our article takes a closer look at how critical research on platforms and the new field of platform urbanism discusses the infrastructural character of platforms. Thereby two broader strands of theorization will emerge: on the one hand the infrastructural character is associated with platforms becoming essential mediators of digitally-enabled interaction (Plantin et al. 2018; Barns 2019) and on the other hand the market-making function of platforms is interrogated by arguing that they are *digital infrastructures* connecting supply and demand for goods, services, and production (Srnicek 2017) and re-arranging existing urban operations (Richardson 2020).

Plantin et al. argue that "[d]igital technology have made possible a 'platformization' of infrastructure and an 'infrastructuralization' of platforms" (Plantin et al. 2018: 295). They come to this conclusion by looking at how Google and Facebook shaped the commercialization of the social web and argue that the two platforms have become so ubiquitous that they qualify as infrastructure. Here platforms are understood as the media environment *essential* to our daily lives. Working on the concept *platform urbanism* Sarah Barns argues that the influence of platform-mediated services "now far exceeds that of the social web" and that they increasingly influence and shape everyday socio-spatial experience (Barns 2019: 2). Barns points towards the entanglement of digital and physical infrastructure by arguing that "cities and their information infrastructure [are] now increasingly framed as dense landscapes of platform intermediation" (Barns 2019: 18). Platforms, here, are qualified as infrastructural because they are understood as the ubiquitous background upon which everyday life unfolds and the technological and social forces governing public action. As infrastructure, platforms are becoming the underlying digital condition – essential digital systems that not only make everyday life possible, but also shape and restructure public action.

In terms of materiality, the above-mentioned theorizations define infrastructure as technical systems that form the essential and underlying condition of everyday life. Agnieszka Leszczynski, for instance, argues that it is often more crucial to consider what infrastructure *does* – i.e., *infrastructural capacities* – over defining what kind of materiality infrastructure *is* (Leszczynski 2020: 192). Infrastructural capacity in Barns and also Plantin et al.'s theorization is understood to shape "mundane connectivity and interaction" (Leszczynski 2020: 190). Specifically, Barns' concept of platform urbanism considers how platforms weave themselves into and become an indispensable part of users' everyday life via their smartphones. Barns phenomenological perspective considers how platforms shape "urban experience" and how social interaction "becomes a site of platform intermediation" (Barns 2019: 8).

The second strand of theorization considers the market-making function of platforms and thereby understands them as infrastructures for economic transactions. Nick Srnicek, for example, defines platforms as "digital infrastructures that enable two or more groups to interact" matching the supply and demand for producers and consumers (Srnicek 2017: 43). Lizzie Richardson argues that "the problems and possibilities of platforms can be better understood by examining how they manifest through urban space" (Richardson 2020: 458) and thereby goes beyond an understanding of platforms as corporate and economic actors by arguing that they primarily function through reorganizing existing urban operations "such as transport, housing, and so on" "not through new physical infrastructure, but instead through novel technologies of coordination that can reterritorialize those already existing" (Richardson 2020: 460). Through the reorganization of existing urban operations, platforms produce "a new form of collective or public infrastructure" (Richardson 2020: 460).

The publicness of this infrastructure, however, is not mediated by the state, but by the market. Considering the double movement of *infrastructuralization of platforms* and *platformization of infrastructure* together with the argument that platforms create a new form of market-mediated publicness, the latter then comes to mean that the access to infrastructure is increasingly governed by private economic actors. As we have seen, Srnicek relates the infrastructural character of platforms to their market-making function and Richardson to platforms functioning as network or relation between existing urban operations that create a new economized publicness.

Platforms as infrastructures for social reproduction – considerations from housing and care-work

If we understand platforms as a new form of urban infrastructure, what is still missing after our considerations in the previous part, is how platforms' business models interact with and are embedded within the contemporary political economy of infrastructure more broadly (Shapiro 2021: 116). We will turn to this question in this section of our article by (1) analyzing Airbnb's operations in urban space and (2) how platforms, such as Care.com and Helpling, leverage care-gaps.

In December 2019 author 1 conducted interviews with Airbnb-hosts to identify their motivation to offer their private home as a service via the platform. The interviewed hosts were all personally involved in the management of their Airbnb rental and were really sharing their home with guests, meaning often renting out a single room in the flat they were living in. All hosts cited economic motives as the main motivation for renting out a part of their home through the platform. The hosts' motivations can be divided into three categories: (1) the income generated through Airbnb is a permanent and necessary source of income; (2) renting out via Airbnb serves to bridge a temporary financial hardship; (3) renting out is a sporadic source of additional income. Only one of the interviewed hosts belonged to the third group as he only sporadically used Airbnb to generate an additional income that enables a certain lifestyle.

Hosts' stories that belong to the first and second group – thus for whom the Airbnb rental is a permanent source of income or serves to bridge a temporary financial hardship – revealed that their economic motivation was often linked to precarious forms of self-employment and limited mobility on the housing market due to rising rents. The neoliberal dismantling of social infrastructures discussed above causes both insecure employment relations and rising rents due to the contemporary housing crisis. The privatization of infrastructure due to austerity politics caused a crisis of care – a crisis experienced by subjects to reproduce their lives (daily and intergenerationally) under conditions which systematically undermine their ability to do so (Fraser 2016; 2017). Airbnb positions the platform as an individualized solution for precarization processes by inciting hosts to understand their bedroom as an asset that can function as an insurance in precarious times – this is further evidenced by the company's own marketing, for example the *Economic Empowerment Agenda* announced in 2017 (Airbnb Citizen 2017).

Complementary, digital care platforms such as Helpling and Care.com offer personalized fixes for the crisis of care. These platforms serve as matchmakers to link the supply and demand for a variety of caring activities, from cleaning services to childcare and eldercare, that are offered as a paid service. As Julia Ticona and Andrea Mateescu outline for the specific case of platform-mediated domestic work in the US, the technopolitics of platforms' matchmaking and reputation systems shape the workers' experience as *cultural entrepreneurs* (Ticona/Mateescu 2018). Platforms create the infrastructure that allows for trading care as a commodity and thereby claim to contribute to the formalization of the care-sector that is historically shaped by informal labor relations.

Specifically, in the care sector, the neoliberal dismantling of infrastructures of social reproduction intervenes into broader patterns of the structural devaluation and invisibilization of care and reproductive labor which was discursively supported by its framing as unwaged and gendered labor of love (Federici 2012). Through the dismantling of state services, the provision of care and domestic labor is becoming ever more insecure. At the same time more and more women are getting into paid employment shouldering a double burden of wage labor and unwaged care labor (Dowling 2021). In addition, to fill in the *care gaps* in neoliberal welfare states, reproductive labor has been and is still externalized onto migrant women to perform the repair and maintenance of the care regimes in the Global North (see Lutz 2018). Domestic and reproductive labor is therefore not only gendered and classed, but also racialized. Platform capitalism tapped into existing care gaps by positioning diverse business models, such as Helpling and Care.com, as a techno-fix for care-burdened households providing flexible, just-in-time solutions for a historically invisibilized reproductive labor. Platforms act here as agents of social and individual insecurity by attempting to govern invisibility and informality. These infrastructures are constantly evolving, coexist and feed into the workings of other platform infrastructures. They lead to an expansion of economic practices and the commodification of ever more care-taking activities as a service. The entanglements of class, race, gender, and technocapitalism, as embodied in the platformization of care, actively shape socio-spatial relations and in doing so perpetuate and even exacerbate existing inequalities.

Conclusion

Throughout the article we have seen that the literature around platform urbanism associates an infrastructural character to platforms: they are understood as the underlying and essential digital condition that makes everyday interaction possible and as networks that facilitate the circulation of goods, people, and ideas. What remains under-examined in the literature is "urban infrastructures' role in the political economy of platform capitalism" – a research gap also identified by Aaron Shapiro (Shapiro 2021: 116).

Shapiro coins the concept *infrastructural surplus* to underline "the excess of value derived from collective resources embedded in the urbanized landscape" (Shapiro 2021: 103). The concept sheds light on platforms appropriating existing urban infrastructure and the socially produced value of urban life. Airbnb, for example, does not contribute to urban infrastructure, but merely appropriates the existing housing stock of a city where hosts are responsible for their own accommodation. The same mechanism operates for the multiplicity of services that digital care platforms provide. These platforms are, as Jathan Sadowski and Karen Gregory describe them, *biopolitical* – they "govern[s] human life by coordinating the performance of, and extracting the value from, its vital productive energy" (Gregory/Sadowski 2021: 2).

What we aimed to show in this article, is that platforms not only profit by appropriating existing urban infrastructure and the value embedded within, but also leverage the dismantling of social infrastructures akin to austerity urbanism and the care crisis to position their business model as a new privatized infrastructure for social reproduction. Social infrastructures such as housing and welfare provision are becoming ever more insecure – this forms the social-economic context into which platforms intervene.

Although households cannot be fully commodified, care platforms offer just-in-time solutions for care gaps, as small-scale reproductive activities are offered as a service via the platform. Airbnb's reproductive model incites hosts to capitalize on their unused bedroom and to understand it as an insurance in precarious times. As those platforms can be understood as a new form of privatized social infrastructure and to not reproduce corporate narratives, it will be crucial to always critically consider infrastructural access as well as dynamics of exclusion and inclusion from these reproductive models. Who is able to rent out a spare room via Airbnb to bridge a temporary financial hardship? And who can rely on commodified care-services when facing time pressure? How are these dynamics of exclusion-inclusion structured along classed, racialized, and gendered lines?

We conclude this article by giving a brief, and necessarily incomplete policy outlook. Airbnb's impact on local housing markets and gentrification processes has been widely recognized by critical research (Duso et al. 2020; Cocola-Gant/Gago 2019; Wachsmuth/Weisler 2018). Thus, for everyone who is excluded from its reproductive model, the platform's urban operations increase socio-spatial inequality and precarity. Airbnb's expansion in urban spaces therefore needs to be met by stricter regulation including (1) "enacting and enforcing bans on the misappropriation of housing" through hosts (2) for which the platform needs to be forced to provide the data on short term rental-provision in cities to ensure the enforcement of regulatory law. Furthermore, (3) platforms must be held accountable to comply with local regulations, including for example deleting non-compliant listing and the payment of tourism tax and (4) a Europe wide reform is needed in order to tax platforms where they profit – "to redistribute a portion of the exorbitant profits for the common good" (Gennburg et al. 2021: 27-29).

However, as we have shown throughout this article, platforms like Airbnb, intervene into broader crisis patterns caused by the neoliberal disinvestment in welfare state provision. Therefore, to effectively tackle corporate platforms' power, demands for stricter regulation need to go hand in hand with demands for a reinvention of welfare suitable for digital economies. Ursula Huws (2019), a prominent voice in the study of digital labor and its embeddedness within the contradictions of contemporary welfare, argues that the exploitative effects of platformization need to be met by welfare policies such as investment in public services, a minimum wage that really ensures a living and a reform of employment law (Huws 2020). Taking a closer look at the commodification of social reproductive labor through platforms, Huws concludes that new feminist strategies need to address the underlying social relations perpetuating unequal divisions of labor (Huws 2019).

Lastly, at the heart of a more just platform future is also a non-discriminatory, bottom-up design of technologies that serves the needs of households and communities rather than those of extractive platform business models. Some of these futures are already materializing in present day capitalism as the emergence of *platform cooperativism* as a movement (Scholz 2016; Sandoval 2020) shows.

References

Airbnb Citizen (2017): Introducing the Airbnb Economic Empowerment Agenda. https://web.archive.org/web/20190622102015/https://www.airbnbcitizen.com/introducing-airbnb-economic-empowerment-agenda/ [09.02.2022].

Altenried, Moritz/Animento, Stefania/Bojadžijev, Manuela (2021): Plattform-Urbanismus: Arbeit, Migration und die Transformation des urbanen Raums, in: *sub\urban. zeitschrift für kritische stadtforschung* 9(1/2): 73-91.

Barns, Sarah (2019): Negotiating the Platform Pivot: From Participatory Digital Ecosystems to Infrastructures of Everyday Life, in: *Geography Compass* 13(9): 1-13.
Bauriedl, Sybille/Strüver, Anke (2020): Platform Urbanism: Technocapitalist Production of Private and Public Spaces, in: *Urban Planning* 5(4): 267-76.
Berfelde, Rabea (2021): Das Reproduktionsmodell Airbnb: Wohnraum 'teilen' im Kontext krisenhafter sozial-reproduktiver Verhältnisse, in: Altenried, Moritz/Dück, Julia/Wallis, Mira (eds.): *Plattformkapitalismus und die Krise der sozialen Reproduktion*, Münster: Westfälisches Dampfboot: 130-46.
Butler, Judith (2006): *Precarious Life: The Powers of Mourning and Violence*, London/New York: Verso.
Butler, Judith (2018): *Notes Toward a Performative Theory of Assembly*, Cambridge, MA: Harvard University Press.
Cocola-Gant, Agustin/Gago, Ana (2019): Airbnb, Buy-to-Let Investment and Tourism-Driven Displacement: A Case Study in Lisbon, in: *Environment and Planning A: Economy and Space* 53(7): 1671-88.
Dowling, Emma (2021): *The Care Crisis. What Caused It and How Can We End It?*, London/New York: Verso.
Duso, Tomaso/Michelsen, Claus/Schäfer, Maximilian/Tran, Kevin (2020): Airbnb and Rents: Evidence from Berlin. DIW Discussion Papers 1890. https://www.diw.de/documents/publikationen/73/diw_01.c.796620.de/dp1890.pdf [09.03.2022].
Federici, Silvia (2012): *Revolution at Point Zero: Housework, Reproduction, and Feminist Struggle*, Oakland: PM Press.
Fraser, Nancy (2016): Contradictions of Capital and Care, in: *New Left Review* (100): 99-117.
Fraser, Nancy (2017): Crisis of Care? On the Social-Reproductive Contradictions of Contemporary Capitalism, in: Bhattacharya, Tithi (ed.): *Social Reproduction Theory*, London: Pluto Press: 21-36.
Gennburg, Katalin/Hertel, Jannis/Moje, Carolin/Petri, Denis (2021): *Cozy Loft with a View of Displacement. How the Rental Platform Airbnb Is Changing Berlin*, Berlin: Rosa Luxemburg Stiftung.
Graham, Stephen/Marvin Simon (2002): *Splintering Urbanism. Networked Infrastructures, Technological Mobilities and the Urban Condition*, London/New York: Routledge/Taylor & Francis Group.
Gregory, Karen/Sadowski, Jathan (2021): Biopolitical Platforms: The Perverse Virtues of Digital Labour, in: *Journal of Cultural Economy* 14(6). doi: https://doi.org/10.1080/17530350.2021.1901766.

Haraway, Donna (1988): Situated Knowledges: The Science Question in Feminism and the Privilege of Partial Perspective, in: *Feminist Studies* 14(3): 575-99.
Harvey, David (2001): Globalization and the "Spatial Fix", in: *Geographische Revue* 2: 23-30.
Harvey, David (2018): *The Limits to Capital*, London/New York: Verso.
Huws, Ursula (2019): The Hassle of Housework: Digitalisation and the Commodification of Domestic Labour, in: *Feminist Review* 123(1): 8-23.
Huws, Ursula (2020): *Reinventing the Welfare State. Digital Platforms and Public Policies*, London: Pluto Press.
Kaika, Maria/Swyngedouw, Erik (2000): Fetishizing the Modern City: The Phantasmagoria of Urban Technological Networks, in: *International Journal of Urban and Regional Research* 24(1): 120-38.
Kluzik, Vicky (2021): Zur Aktualisierung von Flexploitation: Sorge, Prekarität und digitale Plattformen, in: Altenried, Moritz/Dück, Julia/Wallis, Mira (eds.): *Plattformkapitalismus und die Krise der sozialen Reproduktion*, Münster: Westfälisches Dampfboot: 209-25.
Larkin, Brian (2013): The Politics and Poetics of Infrastructure, in: *Annual Review of Anthropology* 42(1): 327-43.
Leszczynski, Agnieszka (2020): Glitchy Vignettes of Platform Urbanism, in: *Environment and Planning D: Society and Space* 38(2): 189-208.
Luke, Nikki/Kaika, Maria (2019): Ripping the Heart out of Ancoats: Collective Action to Defend Infrastructures of Social Reproduction against Gentrification, in: *Antipode* 51(2): 579-600.
Lutz, Helma (2018): Care Migration: The Connectivity between Care Chains, Care Circulation and Transnational Social Inequality, in: *Current Sociology* 66(4): 577-89.
Marrone, Marco/Peterlongo, Gianmarco (2020): Where Platforms Meet Infrastructures: Digital Platforms, Urban Resistance and the Ambivalence of the City in the Italian Case of Bologna, in: *Work Organisation, Labour & Globalisation* 14(1): 119-35.
Mattelart, Armand (1996): *The Invention of Communication*, Minneapolis: University of Minnesota Press.
Moore, Susan/Rodgers, Scott (2018): Platform Urbanism: An Introduction, in: *Mediapolis. A Journal of Cities and Culture* 3(4). https://www.mediapolisjournal.com/2018/10/platform-urbanism-an-introduction/ [09.02.2021].

Mooshammer, Helge/Mörtenböck, Peter (2021): Platform Urbanism and Its Discontents, in: Mooshammer, Helge/Mörtenböck, Peter (eds.): *Platform Urbanism and Its Discontents*, Rotterdam: nai010 publishers: 9-40.

Peck, Jamie (2012): Austerity Urbanism: American Cities under Extreme Economy, in: *City* 16(6): 626-55.

Plantin, Jean-Christophe/Lagoze, Carl/Edwards, Paul N./Sandvig, Christian (2018): Infrastructure Studies Meet Platform Studies in the Age of Google and Facebook, in: *New Media & Society* 20(1): 293-310.

Richardson, Lizzie (2020): Coordinating the City: Platforms as Flexible Spatial Arrangements, in: *Urban Geography* 41(3): 458-61.

Rossi, Ugo (2019): The Common-Seekers: Capturing and Reclaiming Value in the Platform Metropolis, in: *Environment and Planning C: Politics and Space* 37(8): 1418-33.

Sadowski, Jathan (2020): Cyberspace and Cityscapes: On the Emergence of Platform Urbanism, in: *Urban Geography* 41(3): 448-52.

Sandoval, Marisol (2020): Entrepreneurial Activism? Platform Cooperativism Between Subversion and Co-Optation, in: *Critical Sociology* 46(6): 801-17.

Scholz, Trebor (2016): *Platform Cooperativism. Challenging the Corporate Sharing Economy*, New York, NY: Rosa Luxemburg Foundation.

Shapiro, Aaron (2021): Platform Urbanism and Infrastructural Surplus, in: Meijerink, Jeroen/Jansen, Giedo/Daskalova, Victora (eds.): *Platform Economy Puzzles. A Multidisciplinary Perspective on Gig Work*, Cheltenham: Edward Elgar Publishing: 101-22.

Shiva, Vandana/Mies, Maria (2014): *Ecofeminism*, London: Zed Books.

Srnicek, Nick (2017): *Platform Capitalism*, Cambridge: Polity Press.

Star, Susan Leigh (1999): The Ethnography of Infrastructure, in: *American Behavioral Scientist* 43(3): 377-91.

Star, Susan Leigh/Ruhleder, Karen (1996): Steps Toward an Ecology of Infrastructure: Design and Access for Large Information Spaces, in: *Information Systems Research* 7(1): 111-34.

Ticona, Julia/Mateescu, Alexandra (2018): Trusted Strangers: Carework Platforms' Cultural Entrepreneurship in the on-Demand Economy, in: *New Media & Society* 20(11): 4384-404.

Wachsmuth, David/Weisler, Alexander (2018): Airbnb and the Rent Gap: Gentrification through the Sharing Economy, in: *Environment and Planning A: Economy and Space* 50(6): 1147-70.

From Smart to Platform Urbanism to Platform Municipalism
Planning Ideas for Platforms in Toronto and Vienna

Astrid Krisch

Abstract
This chapter critically reflects on the origins and developments of recent currents in academic literature dealing with technology-led urban development and planning. It shows, how planning ideas over the last 30 years have changed the mode of institutionalizing platforms within urban politics and planning. From smart to platform urbanism to platform municipalism, this contribution unveils the values, programmatic ideas, and policies that these different planning ideas incorporate. Using Vienna and Toronto as two examples of different institutionalization processes of platforms for urban planning agendas, the chapter embeds the concept of platform municipalism as a progressive approach to platform development into wider debates on smart and platform urbanism to look beyond a techno-dystopian vision of urban futures and carve out the scope for action for urban governance in the digital age.

Introduction

Urban planning and development have gone through different ideological shifts in the last decades. From the global city of the 1990s, to the creative city of the early 2000s, to the resilient and smart cities of the 2010s, the recent currents in urban politics unveil various planning ideas, dealing with pressing urban development challenges. Underlying the smart city planning paradigm is the rhetoric of an improved future for all through technological development and progress (Karvonen 2020). Smart urbanism as a scholarly debate thus investigates, how technology increasingly governs our cities and tries to understand the various smart city initiatives (Cugurullo 2019).

Platforms as new digital infrastructures are having tremendous effects on everyday life and urban space, revolutionizing social, cultural, economic, and political structures (Karvonen 2020). Platform urbanism as a concept analyzes the spatialization of platforms and the geographies of platform capitalism (Srnicek 2017), providing a critical approach to the collection practices of urban data through platforms to manage cities in real time, overlapping with the smart city discourse (Bauriedl/Strüver 2020). Platforms interact with existing urban economies and infrastructures and transform them (Altenried/Animento/Bojadžijev 2021). Although platform urbanism is mostly concerned with the so-called lean platforms (Srnicek 2017), which try to minimize their fixed assets and benefit from outsourcing by reducing costs as much as possible (e.g., Airbnb, Uber, etc.), other types of platforms, such as advertising platforms or cloud platforms are increasingly relevant in a spatial and urban context through mergers and acquisitions in fields of urban planning (e.g., Google's Sidewalk Labs), logistics networks (e.g., Amazon Web Services), or retail (e.g., takeover of Whole Foods by Amazon) (Krisch/Plank 2018). Platform Urbanism is not yet a coherent theoretical strand, but an approach to think about new developments and urbanization and spatialization of platform capitalism (Altenried/Animento/Bojadžijev 2021).

Governance structures are increasingly challenged by these newly emerging infrastructure systems, not only by economic concerns of the size and capital accumulation of large online platforms and the subsequent challenges for public regulation, but also their power over individual consumers and citizens through AI or machine learning (Leszczynski 2016), their effects on digitizing "the urban fabric" (León/Rosen 2020: 499) and improving conditions not for the whole society or the environment, but only a selected elite (Cugurullo 2019). As platforms are very different from each other, regulators and public administrations are struggling to find nuanced measures (van Dijck/Nieborg/Poell 2019). Especially the mismatch between municipal governments and their often small-scale and bounded capabilities on the one hand and the operational capabilities and scope of technology firms on the other are tremendously challenging (Barns et al. 2016).

These concerns have given rise to progressive social movements connecting to the origins of digital technology seen as an "important incubator for social movements, digital activism and civic action" (Bannerman et al. 2019: 3). Particularly the pivot towards platforms as a focal glass for asymmetrical power structures has demonstrated the need for radical reform (Barns 2020). The concept of platform municipalism, linked to the ideas of new municipalism (Thompson 2020), is associated with these progressive values of utilizing technology for social gains and to democratize decision making within technology-led development. Thus, it provides a new current of planning ideas, that go beyond a techno-dystopian vision of urban futures and instead build an alternative future from the ground up.

To understand the evolution of planning ideas leading to the current belief of technological supremacy, this chapter traces how these different planning ideas came into being and were institutionalized through underlying values, programmatic ideas and policies, thus responding to the call to question how urban environments and communities are governed and planned in light of emerging digital infrastructures (Chiappini 2020). The current institutionalization of platforms in urban planning is analyzed for two case studies, Toronto and Vienna, to gain more in-depth knowledge on different institutional contexts and the restructuring powers of platforms in urban politics and planning. The conceptual part is guided by the theoretical concept of discursive institutionalism (Schmidt 2008) to understand the transformation of urban planning through technology and platforms more specifically. The case studies are based on field work in Toronto and Vienna, focusing on discourse analysis of the relevant strategic urban planning documents concerned with technology and platform development and interviews with experts in public administrations, think-tanks, and scholars in the field.

The chapter begins by outlining the different planning ideas since the 1990s and tracing the values, programs, and policies of smart and platform urbanism as well as platform municipalism. It then goes into detail on how these planning ideas are represented in the recent developments in two case studies, Toronto and Vienna, to analyze, which elements are pointing to a shift in ideology and which institutional factors are crucial for the transformation of digital infrastructures. The contribution ends by discussing the main points of planning ideas for digital infrastructure development and outlining reflections on future research.

Changing planning paradigms:
From smart to platform urbanism to platform municipalism

Pressing challenges for urban planning have been constantly changing, taking different approaches on how to solve urban problems according to changing planning ideas and principles. Urbanism and its multitude of different articulations – whether it be green, sustainable, smart, or any other – rely on the establishment of specific normative framings, programs, and policies to implement collective action within the planning praxis, informed by visions of how a city should look like and the self-conception of the agents of intervention (Barns 2020).

The incorporation of technology to organize urban infrastructure systems has been part of urban politics and planning for decades (Bauriedl/Strüver 2020). However, the unquestioned belief in technological progress as universally beneficial for all has prompted an incorporation of digital tools into ever more applications. Technology is supposed to provide an optimistic scenario of the future and an appropriate tool to cope with global challenges, such as climate change, economic decline, etc. In the 1990s, the notion of the global city became popular, promoting global competition between cities through specific criteria indicating their success in specific sectors, such as education, public transport, health care, etc. (Valverde/Flynn 2020). A few years later, the creative city was in fashion. Urban problems, such as the decline of inner-city commercial space, the decline of the working class and industry or environmental and cultural issues with expanding suburbanization were supposed to be solved by cities and their creative potential, although the promise of solutions through the creative class was greater than the actual evidence of proven success (ibid.).

In the 2010s, in light of increasing climate change and awareness for the negative effects on cities, amplified by concerns about inequality and global migration movements, resilience became the new slogan of urbanism. Originating from psychological studies, it promoted a rather pessimistic notion of worldwide economic decline and the hope to mitigate the damage at the local level (ibid.).

Smart cities on the rise

Today, the smart city discourse has reached a hegemonic position (Morozov/Bria 2017), following after imaginaries of green and sustainable cities as well as information and intelligent cities, activating specific political-economic paradigms that regard the city as the central mechanism of capital accumulation (Artyushina 2020; Valverde/Flynn 2020; Vanolo 2014). The first decades of technological transformations, characterized by the modern infrastructural ideal predominantly struggled with the abstract demands of modernist urban planning and keeping the urban grid up and running, whereas today, visions of smart and real-time cities with data-driven management in light of splintering infrastructure systems (Graham/Marvin 2001) and neoliberal policies of privatization and deregulation (Plantin et al. 2018) represent current challenges of the restructuring processes of our societies (Barns 2020; Janoschka/Mota 2020). Smart Cities have continuingly become an analytical concept and strategic approach of urban development worldwide since the 1990s through the institutionalization of smart growth and intelligent city projects in almost every city (Carr/Hesse 2020b; Hollands 2015; Matern 2017; Rose 2019; Söderström/Paasche/Klauser 2014).

Within the smart city logic, two things are combined: (1) the inter-city competition encouraged not just by corporate logics, but also city governments already familiar from other urbanism notions, such as the global or the creative city; and (2) the concept of innovation, in particular the unconditional belief in data-centric innovation as technological progress (Valverde/Flynn 2020). Visions from international to municipal levels are emerging, however, promoting often a mono-dimensional vision of smart cities, such as the European vision, picturing smart cities as "low-carbon and resource efficient urban environments that invest in ICT solutions for smart transport, smart buildings and smart grids" (Mora/Deakin/Reid 2019: 73).

On the municipal level, normative and pragmatic considerations promote smart city solutions, to reach widely accepted political goals through the implementation of technology, such as increased participation, individualized public services, de-bureaucratizing national and local administrations or fostering innovations to cope with austerity and increasing security and surveillance requirements. Technological innovations became the key objectives in today's data-driven world, taking over traditional urban governance goals such as democracy and financial caution (Valverde/Flynn 2020).

The emergence of platforms

Just as the smart city narrative emerged in the beginning of the 21st century, platforms as new forms of web-based intermediaries made an appearance at roughly the same time. By now, platforms have become a central part of our everyday lives, whether it be communicating with friends and work colleagues, online shopping, consuming different media, travel organization, or mobility services. These activities are predominantly offered by large online platforms, such as Google, Amazon, or Facebook. The increasing market concentration of these large online platforms shows that they position themselves as key players in their core business fields, but also increasingly in other complementary segments (Clement/Schreiber 2016). Google, for example, is the Internet platform with the most acquisitions in about the last five years. In addition to the early acquisitions of e.g., Picasa, a photo service, or Android in the early 2000s, the platform by now invests more in satellite technologies, artificial intelligence, or smart homes. Facebook invested in social media and social networking in general in the early 2000s. In recent years, however, it has increasingly invested in virtual and augmented reality. And Amazon, which was active in the online store business at the end of the 1990s, is now investing in all kinds of gaming portals, but also heavily in cloud infrastructures (Dolata/Schrape 2018; Srnicek 2017). However, not only large online platforms such as the above mentioned are relevant for digital urban infrastructures. Also large companies associated with smart city projects, such as IBM or Cisco, offer online platforms for managing urban systems. The mode of platformization of urban infrastructure systems has become a dominant organizational mode, making cities the "engines of the new data economy" (Barns 2018: 5), thus "reorganizing the geography of how value is created and who captures it and where" (Kenney/Zysman 2020: 55).

Platforms emerged from the emancipatory potential of the early 2000s, when they were still perceived as neutral spaces primarily catered to self-determined networks among different user groups. "While the wireless sensor networks and control room vendors of smart cities tend to speak primarily to municipal officials and politicians, platforms have spoken directly to city-dwellers, providing them with seducing and ergonomic digital tools that revolutionize and maximize social interaction." (Söderström/Mermet 2020: 6) However, platforms are more than just intermediaries between supply and demand side, even if they want to be seen as just technology companies providing neutral platforms for interactions. Their algorithms influence consumer interests, labor relations, and city services, making selective choices about what customers can see and obfuscating the underlying business model (Bauriedl/Wiechers 2021), resulting in increasing social polarization (Brodnig 2018). Moreover, platforms act as gatekeepers, as quasi-guardians of the Internet that cannot be bypassed, creating their own social order on the web.

In the platform age, the patterns of interaction between people are changing framed by data-driven business processes of online platforms, resulting in new negotiation processes and governance models. This outlines a new field in urban studies under the concept of platform urbanism since platforms act as "infrastructures of urban exchange" (Barns 2020: 147). The emerging platform urbanism has been shaped by planning ideas and paradigms as well as specific technological developments and business practices (Barns 2020). Whereas smart urbanism generally is concerned with the relation between IT corporations, municipalities and citizens, platform urbanism conceptualizes how platforms directly target individuals and influence urban infrastructure configurations (Leszczynski 2019; Söderström/Mermet 2020). "Unlike ordinary websites and apps, platforms operate at a meta-level because they bring together different players in which the relations between the parties becomes the service itself." (Chiappini 2020: 279) Platform urbanism is more concerned with the mediation of services, that are much more actively queried by users for their individual supply needs, and thus the information generated is fed back into the system.

Physical places for example are becoming increasingly dependent on their online representation as unequal representations online also have material consequences. Places that are invisible on digital platforms often risk disappearing completely and, in turn, places that are disproportionately represented online also suffer from touristification and gentrification effects (Heo/Blal/Choi 2019; Neuts/Kourtit/Nijkamp 2021). Moreover, this dynamic is further reinforced by all kinds of places, from restaurants to community centers, trying to improve their algorithmic ranking and adapt to the aesthetic norms disseminated by platforms to reorganize their modes of operation through platforms. This potentially reinforces tendencies towards homogenization but also towards uneven development. Digital platforms are reshaping landlord-tenant relationships, changing the structure of real estate markets on a large scale (Kadi/Plank/Seidl 2019). They are also a central concern to the labor market and its spatial repercussions, starting to create entirely new forms of precarity and exploitation (Collier/Dubal/Carter 2017; Galperin/Greppi 2017).

The role of city administrations and the associated political apparatus is shifting more and more towards facilitator and mediator of data-driven services. Thus, the effects of platforms on urban structures have become a major governance challenge through reconceptualizing how to deal with the emergence of online platforms and how to utilize urban data. "There has been a pervasive tendency to increase democratic participation together with self-determination and self-organization, which entails a further shift in planning paradigm." (Anttiroiko 2021: 37) The governance of digital infrastructures and platforms in particular is shifting from a narrow focus on technical infrastructure networks (e.g., pipes, cables, data centers, etc.) to include considerations of managing, using, accessing, and distributing data to support decision-making by city administrations (Barns et al. 2016). There are some similar ideological threads between platform urbanism and the smart city logic and the notion of smart urbanism, making urban data a central concern to manage cities in real time. Some critical scholars have pointed to the limiting effects of big data on long-term strategic planning, as the focus increasingly shifts to short-term thinking about the effective and efficient management of cities (Batty 2013). Whereas infrastructure planning in the 19th century was primarily conceived as an engineering task, today's development and management of urban infrastructure systems is more complex. There is a cleavage between surrendering to the market power of big tech, subordinating local infrastructures to their influence, and giving rise to a kind of renaissance of the expert-led planning approach, while on the other hand the understanding of infrastructure development is shifting towards a socio-political process of social co-creation in its respective local-specific and socio-political context (Barns et al. 2016; Douay 2018).

Platform municipalism as a progressive approach against "big tech"

In line with this argumentation of co-creating infrastructure systems, the notion of platform municipalism (Thompson 2020) is emerging from the social movements of new municipalism (Vollmer 2017) to develop an alternative to platform capitalist tendencies. It is a social movement that designs political and economic strategies to break down traditional boundaries between state and civil society and to rethink infrastructural configurations. *The municipal* is increasingly recognized as a strategic entry point to develop comprehensive practices and theories of transformative social change and to use new technologies in a community-building and socially progressive way (Hollands 2015; Russell 2019). The social movements of new municipalism build on two main principles: the *politics of proximity*, understood as a way to focus on forces that hold a society together, using the urban scale to achieve strategic goals, and the *feminization of politics*, which seeks to find a new way how politics is done by enforcing equality and cooperation instead of competition. Aiming at creating lasting institutional structures rooted in social wealth, platform municipalism seeks to organize new social relations with supporting forces able to maintain them by building on local actors (e.g., locally based public utilities, local anchor institutions such as universities, housing associations, hospitals, etc.) (Russell 2019). Institutions are understood as a series of social processes and social relationships, as norms (Salet 2018) to be opened up to challenge traditional politics and foster institutional innovations (e.g., neighborhood assemblies, participatory budgeting, open-source digital voting platforms, etc.) (Thompson 2020).

On the programmatic level, particularly data-harvesting and storing techniques of local governments are identified as the main problem. On the one hand, the vast amount of information and private data are in most cases not accessible for the public, and on the other hand, public data are usually inadequately processed or distributed across diverse departments, units, and operations that make up a local government and its administration (Morozov/Bria 2017). The concept of platform municipalism proposes a new possibility to move away from surveillance capitalism, building an alternative system, where data is socialized and new approaches to collaboration and co-creation are intensified to foster democratic and social innovations (ibid.). Platforms as organizational structures, inherently incorporating multi-level resource integration, can benefit a socially responsible technology-led urban politics and planning (Anttiroiko 2021).

Although platform municipalist initiatives differ geographically, ideologically, and socioculturally, Thompson (2020) differentiates between three ideal-types of platform municipalist initiatives to better understand the ideological underpinnings of these movements. The civic municipalist approach (adapted from the original term *platform municipalism* to emphasize the focus on civic mobilization) seeks to work in, against, and beyond the state through mobilizing civic organizations and establishing civic platforms (e.g., Decide Madrid, DECODE Barcelona and Amsterdam, Citizen Science Data Governance, Decidim Barcelona). Autonomist municipalist initiatives aim at a political structure outside the state through establishing cooperatives, communes, and autonomous assemblies by collective self-organization (e.g., midata.coop). The third ideal-type, the managed municipalism, wants to reclaim and regenerate local economic structures by seeking to transform the state from within. It is rooted in social wealth by building common goods, aiming at democratizing and anchoring the local economy (e.g., Preston Community Wealth Building Model).

As platform and surveillance capitalism is on the rise, governments have a responsibility to ensure that this new economy serves more than the platform-builders' profit (Morozov/Bria 2017). Thus, the concept of managed municipalist is in this context particularly interesting, to investigate governance structures for cooperative development of digital infrastructures and to understand public administrations' role as active agents of change within data-driven developments. The agency of city administrations and urban planning is highlighted in a smart city context (Exner et al. 2018; Mora/Deakin/Reid 2018; Morozov/Bria 2017). However, their agency in platform development towards a municipalist understanding of digital infrastructure development is still underrepresented in current debates. Thus, the next section tackles the institutionalization process of platforms in urban planning in Toronto and Vienna, highlighting the agency of public administrations in designing and structuring the digital transformation.

How platforms restructure the institutionalization process in urban politics and planning

As Karvonen (2020) noted, there are newly emerging trajectories, how technology is restructuring cities, including networked governance and sociotechnical imaginaries. As the previous section outlined the changing imaginaries, including values of planning paradigms and programmatic ideas as problematizations within urban politics and planning, this section focuses on the changing policies and actor constellations through the implementation of technology-led urban planning. I use examples of different cities to describe, how governance-formations shift through approaching the incorporation of the smart city discourse and the development of platforms into urban planning processes within different institutional contexts. Thus, this section outlines where and how different planning ideas, from smart to platform urbanism to platform municipalism can be found in two different planning contexts of Toronto, Canada and Vienna, Austria.

Toronto – dismissal of neoliberal platform urbanism?

In Toronto, Canada, the urban innovation start-up Sidewalk Labs, a sister company of Google, was contracted to develop the urban neighborhood Quayside at the waterfront area in Toronto through a synthesis of digital and physical infrastructure. However, as the official statement of the company says, the current global Covid-19 pandemic and the associated financial uncertainty led to the abandonment of the project in March 2020 (Flynn/Valverde 2019). The difficulties and resistance the company was facing are well researched (Barns 2020; Carr/Hesse 2020a; Flynn/Valverde 2019; Tusikov 2020). Particularly, privacy issues and the opacity of decision-making within the institutional structures were criticized, especially since Sidewalk Labs was aiming to serve as a model for cities around the world. "The Toronto project was Google's entry into the lucrative smart city industry, and it had global ambitions from the start. As Google's urban policy arm, Sidewalk Labs sought to shape data governance frameworks and standards that Google could export to smart city projects around the world." (Tusikov 2020: 71)

However questionable this neoliberal approach to urban planning by transferring responsibility to a private company already under scrutiny from international privacy courts may be, the outcome of the failed project is interesting to look at. As a response the city of Toronto is currently developing its own Digital Infrastructure Plan to counteract the negative consequences and to proactively set up a framework for the development of digital infrastructures throughout the city. They define digital infrastructure as "infrastructure that creates, exchanges or uses data or information as a part of its operation. Digital infrastructure includes physical structures, cabling and network systems, software systems, data standards and protocols" (City of Toronto 2021). Developed by the municipal division of the Connected Community/Smart City Project Team, this definition of digital infrastructure at least provides a guideline for city officials as well as companies, scholars, and community members to refer to. However, Toronto's complex governance structure, in which infrastructure development in particular is hampered by provincial power over city's agency is often an obstacle. Moreover, the tri-governmental unit Waterfront Toronto as a partnership agency between municipal, provincial, and federal agents makes the governance structure even more complex, especially in light of limited life spans and narrow mandates of public sector entities such as Waterfront Toronto, which always faces the risk of being restructured out of existence. Thus, the waterfront area is rather underdeveloped compared to other cities especially in North America (Verschuren 2021). In spite of these obstacles, the development of the digital infrastructure plan is the first step out of the often-practiced project-based developments to reach an overall strategic plan instead.

Furthermore, what is interesting about the repercussions of the failed project, is that through the massive resistance of NGOs, such as the Canadian Civic Liberties Association that filed a lawsuit against Sidewalk Labs, or the group #BlockSidewalk, the agents involved in the development process of the digital infrastructure plan are more diverse than ever, including citizens and scholars through public consultations. The City of Toronto is increasingly trying to shape technological changes to achieve public objectives in dialogue with local communities. However, a critical point remains that the city is more likely to limit their interventions to setting up a framework predominantly for the procurement process for corporations providing digital infrastructures, than actively developing a long-term vision of their own for the development and incorporation of digital technologies and platforms into urban planning agendas. An illustrative example of this dynamic is the contracting of the citywide payment system for public water supply by the transnational corporation and U.S. platform payit. This represents an outsourcing of essentially public services of general interest in the municipal sphere of responsibility. Thus, although the resistance to the Sidewalk Labs project resulted in a significant change in the strategic discourse of incorporating platforms into the urban planning agenda towards public administration providing a proactive approach to the development of digital infrastructure in conjunction with different interest groups, the actual implementation of these guidelines is still pending.

Vienna – infrastructural reform through urban platforms

In Vienna, Austria, the policy orientation towards smart city developments already began in 2014 with the publication of the first Smart City Framework Strategy. Just recently, in 2019, it was updated and changed with a stronger focus towards sustainability, shifting the orientation due to increasing criticism towards smart city developments. By now, the updated Smart City Framework, although it carries the same name, is commonly understood as *the* sustainability strategy of the city. In addition to this overarching strategy, various other sectoral strategies were developed, that are solely focused on the digital development in and of the city, such as the Digital Agenda 2014 or the Data Excellence Strategy 2019. The discourse within these documents is more catered to the notion of Digital Humanism, developing a digitization in harmony with social and democratic values. Data is increasingly seen as a 'city treasure', pointing to a shift in how public administration is expanding its responsibility to the digital realm. However, the discourse is also permeated by contradictions. Efficiency and effectiveness through technological solutions are at the same time promoted as digital equity and battling the digital divide. Moreover, digital humanism is clashing with expectations of Vienna becoming "Europe's capital of digitalisation" (Stadt Wien 2019: 65), thus promoting inter-city competition.

Particularly interesting is the shift in agency in the last few years, where an operational IT unit (MA 01 – Wien Digital) was established as a new municipal department in 2018, merging three former separate IT landscapes into one and subordinating it to the strategic IT unit, the Magistrate's Directorate. Moreover, through the elections in 2020, the operational IT department and the urban development and planning department are now under the same political leadership, raining hopes of strengthening future cooperation. Central for the development of platforms in Vienna are also the public utilities as a city subsidiary, including energy, mobility, and public service companies. However, public utilities and public administration only cooperatively develop strategic planning documents, whereas the actual implementation of platforms is organized separately.

However, the institutional context in Vienna provides the framework for a progressive approach to developing city-owned platforms, either to platformize existing infrastructure systems, platformize public services, or developing new platforms as digital infrastructure for urban planning. The strong tendency of public responsibility of public infrastructure development engrained into the planning culture in Vienna can also be observed in platform development. However, a coordinated effort for a strategic vision of incorporating urban platforms and technologies into urban planning agendas has only just begun, thus leading to a still very scattered implementation of various platforms through different actors, focusing mostly on providing individualized public services through platforms and increased participation efforts. Thus, although the strategic discourse is pointing to a shift towards platform municipalist ideas, the actual implementation of public platforms is focused predominantly on providing platforms as technological innovations as a self-serving justification rather than democratizing decision-making or focusing on financial equity and equality.

Conclusion and discussion

Since the body of literature on governance processes involved in implementing data-driven and digitally enabled innovations is still rather small (Valverde/Flynn 2020), this chapter contributes to understanding the incorporation of platforms in urban planning agendas. I looked at the different currents in academic literature to carve out the underlying planning ideas and analyzed two case studies to trace the institutionalization process within their specific planning contexts.

Although the institutional contexts of incorporating platforms into urban planning agendas in Toronto and Vienna are very different, some commonalities can be identified. Both cities have recently picked up a more progressive approach to platform development. Although the neoliberal orientation of urban planning is much stronger institutionalized in Toronto, the city is taking up a proactive approach to steer technological and platform development in urban planning issues. In both cities, the increasing criticism towards platform urbanism and smart cities and the fast pace in which technology transforms cities has spurred a discursive and institutional shift in how platforms are incorporated into urban planning agendas. Public administrations develop a more progressive take on how they can design platforms as digital infrastructures, not only in the traditionally more public service-oriented city of Vienna, but also in more neoliberal focused urban contexts such as Toronto. Platforms thus determine a new way of policy-making, not just discursively through a change in strategic planning visions, but also institutionally through changing agency and actor-constellations.

Although the official justification of Sidewalk Labs for abandoning the project in Toronto was financial uncertainty due to the global pandemic, experts in the field point to institutional challenges the company faced. Not only did the bottom-up movement of #BlockSidewalk and others resist the upcoming urban development plans, but the company itself never really got familiar with how urban planning is done in Toronto and which institutional factors have to be considered when planning a neighborhood, where a tripartite responsibility of city, province, and federal state have stakes in the decision-making process.

In Vienna the process for changing the institutionalization of technologies and platforms for urban planning agendas was far more subversive by slowly integrating strategic visions and collective actions into the urban planning practice. Not a single large-scale failed project spurred the increasing incorporation of technologies in urban planning, but a gradual shift of discursive and strategic changes due to increasing digitization over the last decades. Interestingly, inter-city competition is far more present in Vienna than in Toronto, represented by notions of Vienna wanting to become the European Digital Capital, whereas the discourse in Toronto focuses more explicitly on inclusion of different minority groups. Moreover, institutional changes in Toronto are more in line with municipalist ideas, as different non-governmental organizations challenged traditional politics and the way platforms are integrated in urban planning agendas at least for the Sidewalk Labs project. However, neoliberal policies and surveillance capitalism are more engrained into everyday politics and planning in Toronto than in Vienna. Thus, it is arguable that the failed Sidewalk Labs project and the resulting skepticism about data security and surveillance issues was publicly discussed only in this one instance, while future planning processes might tend to keep quiet about these critical issues. Whether the institutional changes brought about by the failed Sidewalk Labs project will actually have far-reaching consequences for citywide planning remains to be seen.

In both cases, platforms have been predominantly used as an aid to urban planners and decision makers rather than as a tool to challenge current institutional political structures. Thus, as Anttiroiko (2021) argues, they probably won't be able to bring about radical transformation in urban planning. With more knowledge of public officials as well as non-governmental organizations on the functioning and effects of platforms, their potential could possibly be further realized in an urban planning context. However, the challenge for politics and planning is also, not only to develop their own take on platform urbanism, but also to balance power between different actors involved in the digitization of cities to avoid the marginalization of the public sphere's role in the digital development of the city.

References

Altenried, Moritz/Animento, Stefania/Bojadžijev, Manuela (2021): Plattform-Urbanismus: Arbeit, Migration und die Transformation des urbanen Raumes, in: *Sub\urban. Zeitschrift Für Kritische Stadtforschung* 9(1/2): 73-91.

Anttiroiko, Ari-Veikko (2021): Digital Urban Planning Platforms. The Interplay of Digital and Local Embeddedness in Urban Planning, in: *International Journal of E-Planning Research* 10(3): 35-49.

Artyushina, Anna (2020): Is civic data governance the key to democratic smart cities? The role of the urban data trust in Sidewalk Toronto, in: *Telematics and Informatics* 55. doi: https://doi.org/10.1016/j.tele.2020.101456.

Bannerman, Sara/Porter, Tony/Tan, Netina/Gabel, Chelsea/Budd, Brian/Midzain-Gobin, Liam/Goodman, Nicole/Ouellette, Devin/Shoker, Sarah/Tabassum, Nowrin/Frost, Catherine/Goguen, Marcel/Detlor, Brian/Stecula, Dominik/Joseph, Ameil/Zeffiro, Andrea/Orasch, Angela (2019):

Digitization & Challenges to Democracy. Globalization Working Papers 19/2. https://globalization.mcmaster.ca/research/publications/working-papers/2019/working-paper-oct-2019.pdf [17.02.2022].

Barns, Sarah (2018): Platform Urbanism Rejoinder: Why now? What now?, in: *Mediapolis. A Journal of Cities and Culture* 3(4). https://www.mediapolisjournal.com/2018/11/platform-urbanism-why-now-what-now/ [17.02.2022].

Barns, Sarah (2020): *Platform urbanism. Negotiating platform ecosystems in connected cities*, Singapore: Palgrave Macmillan.

Barns, Sarah/Cosgrave, Ellie/Acuto, Michele/Mcneill, Donald (2016): Digital Infrastructures and Urban Governance, in: *Urban Policy and Research* 35(1): 20-31.

Batty, Michael (2013): Big data, smart cities and city planning, in: *Dialogues in Human Geography* 3(3): 274-79.

Bauriedl, Sybille/Strüver, Anke (2020): Platform Urbanism: Technocapitalist Production of Private and Public Spaces, in: *Urban Planning* 5(4): 267-76.

Bauriedl, Sybille/Wiechers, Henk (2021): Konturen eines Plattform-Urbanismus. Soziale und räumliche Ausprägungen eines digital divide am Beispiel Smart Mobility, in: *Sub\urban. Zeitschrift Für Kritische Stadtforschung* 9(1/2): 93-114.

Brodnig, Ingrid (2018): *Lügen im Netz. Wie Fake News, Populisten und unkontrollierte Technik uns manipulieren*, Wien: Brandstätter.

Carr, Constance/Hesse, Markus (2020a): Sidewalk Labs closed down – whither Google's smart city? https://regions.regionalstudies.org/ezine/article/sidewalk-labs-closed-down-whither-googles-smart-city/ [04.08.2021].

Carr, Constance/Hesse, Markus (2020b): When Alphabet Inc. Plans Toronto's Waterfront: New Post-Political Modes of Urban Governance, in: *Urban Planning* 5(1): 69-83.

Chiappini, Letizia (2020): The Urban Digital Platform: Instances from Milan and Amsterdam, in: *Urban Planning* 5(4): 277-88.

City of Toronto (2021): Digital Infrastructure Plan (DIP). https://www.toronto.ca/city-government/accountability-operations-customer-service/long-term-vision-plans-and-strategies/smart-cityto/digital-infrastructure-plan/?accordion=dip-working-principles [04.08.2021].

Clement, Reiner/Schreiber, Dirk (2016): *Internet-Ökonomie. Grundlagen und Fallbeispiele der vernetzten Wirtschaft*, Berlin/Heidelberg: Springer.

Collier, Ruth Berins/Dubal, V. B./Carter, Christopher (2017): Labor Platforms and Gig Work: The Failure to Regulate. https://doi.org/10.2139/ssrn.3039742 [17.02.2022].

Cugurullo, Federico (2019): The origin of the smart city imaginary: from the dawn of modernity to the eclipse of reason, in: Lindner, Christoph/Meissner, Miriam (eds.): *The Routledge companion to urban imaginaries*, New York: Routledge/Taylor & Francis Group: 113-24.

Dolata, Ulrich/Schrape, Jan-Felix (2018): *Collectivity and Power on the Internet. A Sociological Perspective*, Wiesbaden: Springer.

Douay, Nicolas (2018): *Urban Planning in the Digital Age*, Hoboken, NJ: John Wiley & Sons, Inc.

Exner, Andreas/Cepoiu, Livia/Weinzierl, Clara/Asara, Viviana (2018): Performing Smartness Differently – Strategic Enactments of a Global Imaginary in Three European Cities (SRE-Discussion-2018/05). http://www-sre.wu.ac.at/sre-disc/sre-disc-2018_05.pdf [17.02.2022].

Flynn, Alexandra/Valverde, Mariana (2019): Where The Sidewalk Ends: The Governance Of Waterfront Toronto's Sidewalk Labs Deal, in: *Windsor Yearbook of Access to Justice* 36: 263-83.

Galperin, Hernan/Greppi, Catrihel (2017): Geographical Discrimination in Digital Labor Platforms. Advance online publication. https://doi.org/10.2139/ssrn.2922874 [17.02.2022].

Graham, Steve/Marvin, Simon (2001): *Splintering urbanism. Networked infrastructures, technological mobilities and the urban condition*, London: Routledge.

Heo, Cindy Yoonjoung/Blal, Inès/Choi, Miju (2019): What is happening in Paris? Airbnb, hotels, and the Parisian market: A case study, in: *Tourism Management* 70(2): 78-88.

Hollands, Robert G. (2015): Critical interventions into the corporate smart city, in: *Cambridge Journal of Regions, Economy and Society* 8(1): 61-77.

Janoschka, Michael/Mota, Fabiola (2020): New municipalism in action or urban neoliberalisation reloaded? An analysis of governance change, stability and path dependence in Madrid (2015-2019), in: *Urban Studies* 11(2). doi: https://doi.org/10.1177/0042098020925345.

Kadi, Justin/Plank, Leonhard/Seidl, Roman (2019): Airbnb as a tool for inclusive tourism?, in: *Tourism Geographies*. doi: https://doi.org/10.1080/14616688.2019.1654541.

Karvonen, Andrew (2020): Urban Techno-Politics: Knowing, Governing, and Imagining the City, in: *Science as Culture* 29(3): 417-24.

Kenney, Martin/Zysman, John (2020): The platform economy: restructuring the space of capitalist accumulation, in: *Cambridge Journal of Regions, Economy and Society* 13(1): 55-76.

Krisch, Astrid/Plank, Leonhard (2018): *Internet-Plattformen als Infrastrukturen des digitalen Zeitalters*, Wien: Kammer für Arbeiter und Angestellte für Wien.

León, Luis F. Alvarez/Rosen, Jovanna (2020): Technology as Ideology in Urban Governance, in: *Annals of the American Association of Geographers* 110(2): 497-506.

Leszczynski, Agnieszka (2016): Speculative futures: Cities, data, and governance beyond smart urbanism, in: *Environment and Planning A: Economy and Space* 48(9): 1691-708.

Leszczynski, Agnieszka (2019): Glitchy vignettes of platform urbanism, in: *Environment and Planning D: Society and Space* 38(2): 189-208.

Matern, Antje (2017): Smart City-Konzepte als Impuls zur Erneuerung städtischer Infrastrukturen?, in: Engels, Jens Ivo/Janich, Nina/Monstadt, Jochen/Schott, Dieter (eds.): *Nachhaltige Stadtentwicklung: Infrastrukturen, Akteure, Diskurse*, Frankfurt: Campus Verlag: 150-73.

Mora, Luca/Deakin, Mark/Reid, Alasdair (2018): Smart-City Development Paths: Insights from the First Two Decades of Research, in: Bisello, Adriano/Vettorato, Daniele/Laconte, Pierre/Costa, Simona (eds.): *Green Energy and Technology. Smart and Sustainable Planning for Cities and Regions*, Cham: Springer International Publishing: 403-27.

Mora, Luca/Deakin, Mark/Reid, Alasdair (2019): Strategic principles for smart city development: A multiple case study analysis of European best practices, in: *Technological Forecasting and Social Change* 142: 70-97.

Morozov, Evgeny/Bria, Francesca (2017): *Die smarte Stadt neu denken*, Berlin: Rosa Luxemburg Stiftung.

Neuts, Bart/Kourtit, Karima/Nijkamp, Peter (2021): Space Invaders? The Role of Airbnb in the Touristification of Urban Neighbourhoods, in: Suzuki, Soushi/Kourtit, Karima/Nijkamp, Peter (eds.): *Tourism and regional science. New roads*, Singapore: Springer: 103-25.

Plantin, Jean-Christophe/Lagoze, Carl/Edwards, Paul N./Sandvig, Christian (2018): Infrastructure studies meet platform studies in the age of Google and Facebook, in: *New Media & Society* 20(1): 293-310.

Rose, Gillian (2019): Smart urban: imaginary, interiority, intelligence, in: Lindner, Christoph/Meissner, Miriam (eds.): *The Routledge companion to urban imaginaries*, New York: Routledge/Taylor & Francis Group: 105-12.

Russell, Bertie (2019): Beyond the Local Trap: New Municipalism and the Rise of the Fearless Cities, in: *Antipode* 51(3): 989-1010.

Salet, Willem (2018): Institutions In Action, in: Salet, Willem (ed.): *The Routledge handbook of institutions and planning in action*, New York: Routledge/Taylor & Francis Group: 3-23.

Schmidt, Vivien A. (2008): Discursive Institutionalism: The Explanatory Power of Ideas and Discourse, in: *Annual Review of Political Science* 11(1): 303-26.

Söderström, Ola/Mermet, Anne Cécile (2020): When Airbnb Sits in the Control Room: Platform Urbanism as Actually Existing Smart Urbanism in Reykjavík, in: *Frontiers in Sustainable Cities* 2(15). doi: https://doi.org/10.3389/frsc.2020.00015.

Söderström, Ola/Paasche, Till/Klauser, Francisco (2014): Smart cities as corporate storytelling, in: *City* 18(3): 307-20.

Srnicek, Nick (2017): *Platform capitalism*, Cambridge: Polity Press.

Stadt Wien (2019): Digitale Agenda Wien 2025: Wien wird Digitalisierungshauptstadt. https://digitales.wien.gv.at/digitale-agenda/ [17.02.2022].

Thompson, Matthew (2020): What's so new about New Municipalism?, in: *Progress in Human Geography* 45(2): 317-42.

Tusikov, Natasha (2020): Privatized Policymaking on Toronto's Waterfront, in: Valverde, Mariana/Flynn, Alexandra (eds.): *Smart Cities in Canada: Digital Dreams, Corporate Designs*, Toronto: James Lorimer & Company Ltd., Publishers: 68-82.

Valverde, Mariana/Flynn, Alexandra (eds.) (2020): *Smart Cities in Canada: Digital Dreams, Corporate Designs*, Toronto: James Lorimer & Company Ltd., Publishers.

van Dijck, José/Nieborg, David/Poell, Thomas (2019): Reframing platform power, in: *Internet Policy Review* 8(2). doi: https://doi.org/10.14763/2019.2.1414.

Vanolo, Alberto (2014): Smartmentality: The Smart City as Disciplinary Strategy, in: *Urban Studies* 51(5): 883-98.

Verschuren, Iris (2021): *The depth of the urban palimpsest: encountering sense(s) of place(s) in urban imaginaries from Little Jamaica to Quayside and Re-Sistering*. Master thesis. York University.

Vollmer, Lisa (2017): Keine Angst vor Alternativen. Ein neuer Munizipalismus. über den Kongress „FearlessCities", Barcelona 10./11. Juni 2017, in: *Sub\urban. Zeitschrift für Kritische Stadtforschung* 5(3): 147-56.

The Politics of Geodata in Urban Platform Capitalism

Boris Michel & Susanne Schröder-Bergen

Introduction

Much of the critical research on urban platform capitalism focuses on how digital platforms transform labor, subjectivities, and social practices in cities.[1] Be it by changing urban retail, mobility, self-care, or social interactions, platforms have been central actors in the latest round of accelerating socio-technological transformations of urban space and urban life. This paper contributes to those current debates through a close look at something that is not much discussed and that, at first glance, might seem rather technical and non-political, while it, in fact, represents a key infrastructural precondition for much of those urban platforms: the politics and the social construction of geodata and cartographic knowledge underlying these services. Furthermore, by looking at the role of geodata in general and OpenStreetMap in particular, the paper investigates the hidden inscriptions and labor that make socio-technological objects such as the apps of urban platform capitalism's apps.

This essay presents the following argument: most of those platforms critical research in urban studies focus on and that are seen as central actors in a new urban techno-capitalism are inherently spatial. That means that geodata and spatial knowledge are central to their functioning and power. Like all data, geodata is not a neutral thing that is out there only to be extracted, used, or exploited and thereby turned into useful information or knowledge. Instead, it is a social relation assembled and objectified through a myriad of interrelated political, economic, social, and technological actors (Kitchin 2014). While commercial providers of geodata are still dominant and services

---

[1] We would like to thank Finn Dammann, Yannick Ecker, Georg Glasze, and Anke Strüver for their valuable comments on an earlier version of this chapter.

such as Google Maps are paramount to many of these platforms, this paper investigates how a growing number of actors of urban platform capitalism both extract and contribute data from and to OpenStreetMap (OSM), the largest free and open geodatabase.

This example of the role of geodata for urban platform capitalism in general and that of OSM in particular is illustrative because it highlights the social production and political nature of data. Furthermore, it is an example of the complex relations and assemblages that form platforms and that go well beyond the notion of a platform as a clearly bounded entity, such as a cooperation, a business, a service, or a technological infrastructure. As such, it illustrates how platforms connect to and rely on many other platforms to act within and on the world. The example of OSM highlights the role of embedding unpaid and hidden labor and non-commodified knowledge and data into platforms and indicates the strategy of urban mobility platforms to reduce dependency on other proprietary platforms, which often exercise decisive control and power.

A word on platforms

Over the last couple of years, the term *platform* gained traction in discussions around the digital transformation of society, especially around the geographies of digital and so-called *smart urbanism*. Platforms, it is frequently argued, symbolize and represent the present state of the political and social condition. Thus, terms such as *platform society*, *platform capitalism*, or *platform power* are mobilized to describe this social mode of governing (van Dijck/Poell/de Waal 2018; Srnicek 2017; Seemann 2021). In view of this boom and the breadth of the use of the term platform, it is not surprising that the term is in danger of becoming an empty signifier and phrase, lumping together different understandings of the nature of platforms but also referring to a broad and somewhat heterogeneous set of technological, economic, and socio-technological entities and relations. As such, it might be helpful to say a few words about platforms and why a broad understanding of them is helpful within this paper. Based on a review of recent research, one might distinguish between three different conceptions of platforms and a wider variety of types of platforms.

First, there is a technical understanding: a platform is something that brings human and non-human actors together. Seemann systematizes three types of platforms. Protocol platforms, interface platforms, and service platforms refer to three types of platforms with inherently different arrangements and regimes of control and power (Seemann 2021: 33). Van Dijck et al. understand digital platforms as "a programmable digital architecture designed to organize interactions between users" (van Dijck/Poell/de Waal 2018: 4). Importantly, this bringing together of different elements and actors is not one of equals. Dunn underlines that there are "two inherent and seemingly contradictory qualities of the platform – the centralized control exerted by its core structure and its openness to modification by its participants" (Dunn 2020: 335). As Seemann argues in his work on platform power, platforms, in a very abstract and general way, are arrangements that pre-structure who interacts with whom and in what way through standardization and algorithmization (Seemann 2021).

Second, from an economic understanding, platforms are a specific business model often driven by large amounts of venture capital and a particular mode and ideology of growth and disruption. As Srnicek posits in his book *Platform Capitalism*, platforms are the logical next step in capital's drive to reduce risk and cost and are a reaction of capital to the tendency of the rate of profit to fall (Srnicek 2017). Many platforms are privatized markets or labor markets for the gig economy (Altenried/Animento/Bojadžijev 2021), and, following Staab and his portrayal of digital capitalism, one can understand platforms as strategies to establish and secure proprietary markets. Lean service platforms such as Uber, Airbnb, and Deliveroo do not sell anything but build and govern a market that they control and tax (Staab 2019). This economic mode has far-reaching consequences for the relation between labor and capital.

A third understanding regards platform as a socio-technological mode of governing – an understanding that goes "beyond the company" (Richardson 2020: 459). It is a mode of "controlling interactions between users, workers, capital, and information" (Graham 2020: 453), where platforms enter the scene as a new mode of data-driven capitalism (Beer 2018) and its uneven geographies. This socio-technological understanding is also reflexive of the ideological components of these modes of governing. While a platform such as OSM, which relies on an enthusiastic community of mapping activists, might seem antithetical to a platform such as Uber or Airbnb, there are some similarities in both the technology and the ideology, especially in its antistatist libertarianism and its techno-fix solutionism (Turner 2006; Morozov 2014).

This paper is primarily interested in the praxis of service platforms and the way they use geodata. Examples come primarily from lean mobility platforms such as Uber, Lyft, or Grab. Although this means that this paper only addresses a limited set of platforms, those platforms are the most specific for a decidedly urban mode of platform capitalism.

At the same time, this paper finds a broader and more abstract understanding of platforms helpful – one that understands platforms not only in terms of platform capitalism and a capitalist business model. Such an understanding includes all sorts of interface, protocol, and service platforms and would also include non-digital and even non-material modes of regulating connections and networks (Seemann 2021). While this runs the risk of turning everything into a platform, it helps to focus on the understanding of platforms in terms of a small number of common denominators instead of practices and processes that can be described in more traditional terms, such as precarization and flexibilization, or in terms of more general trends, such as digitalization and datafication. This rather abstract definition of platforms as socio-technological modes of regulating connections makes it essential to pay close attention to the different methods of regulation, governance, power, and control of different types of platforms. While platforms that organize and control interactions on privatized markets or that regulate communications between machines have a high degree of control over user interaction, in an open and community-based platform such as OSM, the concrete modes of interaction, the back end, the infrastructures, and the ontologies would be open for debate and negotiation, which makes a project such as OSM all the more interesting when looking at the politics and construction of platforms.

Spaces of urban platform capitalism

Most platforms associated with platform capitalism are inherently spatial. They mediate spatial interactions and help build spatial connections. While those platforms are inherently spatial, they most often are also highly urban. As Shaw puts it with regard to the platformization of real estate markets, most platforms are "prototyped *in* the city and *for* the city as a primary site of experimentation" (Shaw 2020: 1056), and they organize their services primarily in urban space, thus changing the way cities function, look like, and are experienced. By articulating a diverse set of urban and spatialized elements, they can be understood as "flexible spatial arrangements" (Richardson 2020 that express their power by both connecting (e.g., customers and companies) and disconnecting (e.g., the individualized platform workers). Furthermore, they rely on spatial knowledge and data to render the urban space a legible territory and turn cities into sites for their respective actions. While the role of connections is central to much of the critical research on urban platforms, the role of spatial knowledge and data is much less scrutinized.

In order for urban platforms to scale their businesses, their geospatial knowledge has to be simultaneously global, abstract and universal, as well as hyperlocal, real-time, and user-centric. Thus, they depend on qualities and quantities of geodata that only became available and conceivable with the rise of the very technologies these services rely upon. As Leszczynski (2019) indicates in her work on platform affects, platforms' spatiality is about abstract space and abstract geodata as cartographic data. Furthermore, platforms are closely linked to affective notions of place and the local. An example is when a global platform such as Airbnb sells a commodity marketed as the authentic experience of being and living like a local anywhere in the world. Thus, space plays a complex and multidimensional role in platforms and urban platform capitalism.

On the one hand, those platforms use existing geodata to have their services delivered. While this sounds like simply using a map to get from point A to point B, cartographic knowledge became much more complex with the rise of ubiquitous computing and new geospatial media (Crampton 2009). Routing in complex and dynamic contexts requires mobilizing a wide range of actors, such as GPS technology, geodata standards, algorithms that predict mobility patterns, local road traffic regulations, and data protection laws. Many of these actors can be understood as platforms that allow, organize, and regulate connections, exercising power over other parts of these nested networks of platforms. This growing complexity suggests varying demands and arrangements for different platforms. For example, the geodata needed by mobility platforms will differ somewhat from that needed by platforms for rating restaurants. One part of this use of existing geodata and geospatial technologies is the ongoing interest of platforms in acquiring map companies and geodata start-ups, be it Uber buying parts of Microsoft Bing in 2015, Facebook taking over Mapillary (a service that builds an alternative to Google Street View through crowdsourcing) in 2020 or WeWork acquiring a start-up that maps and surveys the spaces of in-office mobility. Geospatial technologies and technologies that extract surplus from geodata are a key commodity for those services. On the other hand, these platforms generate large amounts of dense geodata as part of their services and business. It is frequently pointed out – often somewhat hyperbolically – that the riches and real value of platforms come from the data they generate and possess. In particular, Zuboff (2019) considers behavioral surplus in user data as the foundation of future profits. Examples are the fine-grained spatial and temporal mobility patterns that can be extracted to mobilize future extractions of value. Hence, locational data becomes a commodity (Thatcher 2017).

OpenStreetMap

Despite it not being profit-oriented and even being set against state-owned and profit-oriented modes of geodata and cartography, OSM can also be seen as a platform. It is an infrastructure that allows a large number of actors to contribute geodata to one global database collectively. This database can then be turned into a map. OSM is made by a vast and diverse community of mappers with an increasingly global reach and coverage. Often seen as the most successful example of volunteered geographic information (Goodchild 2007), OSM relies on its contributors' work, labor, and care. The project is community-driven in its data and much of its basic infrastructure, it is supported by a non-profit foundation, and it is free/libre open-source software (FLOSS). Notably, the data contributed to OSM is licensed under the Open Data Commons Open Database License (ODbL)[2], allowing the free use, sharing, and adaptation of the data and database.

While these kinds of platforms are celebrated for opening and democratizing the production of geographic data and for challenging the cartographic monopolies of states and large corporations (Gartner 2009; Dodge/Perkins 2008), research has highlighted how even platforms of volunteered geographic information reproduce the digital divide and uneven geography of geographical knowledge. In all its different forms and modes, participation is highly influenced by gender, class, formal education, and access to broadband connections (Dittus/Garcia 2019; Gardner et al. 2019; Bittner/Michel/Turk 2016; Ballatore/de Sabbata 2020; Stephens 2013). Moreover, over the last couple of years, critical research and OSM activists have highlighted and problematized the increasing role of corporations, institutional actors, and organized editing in OSM (Dickinson 2021; OpenStreetMap Foundation 2018).

---

2 See https://opendatacommons.org/licenses/odbl/.

While dominated by an ethos of local attachment and ground truth and the idea of the engaged craft mapper, OSM's success made the platform attractive to institutional actors. At least three different types of institutional actors can be identified: those from the field of humanitarianism, pointing to the role of mapping and geodata for digital humanitarianism and cases of emergency (Burns 2018); the use of machine learning and artificial intelligence (AI) to produce and optimize OSM's geodata, for example through Meta's/Facebook's Map with AI project (Vargas Muñoz/Tuia/Falcão 2020; Coldewey 2019); and corporate mappers, especially lean service platforms in the field of urban mobility that use OSM as a free and open alternative or addition to services such as Google Maps (Anderson/Sarkar/Palen 2019). Although the involvement of institutional and corporate mappers in projects such as OSM is neither new nor significantly controversial, it poses challenges and questions for a project that is frequently seen as being part of non-commodified digital commons.

If one looks at the data, one can see platforms active in OSM in at least three ways, two of which are relevant to this paper's argument: the first and most obvious way is the use of existing OSM data for their services, be it by using the OSM map as a base map for apps and interfaces or by using the data for its services, for example in the form of routing or locating. The latter is much less visible to the user, and sometimes intermediate companies facilitate this interaction through tailored services.

A second way such platforms interact with OSM is by adding and maintaining data. A growing number of platforms pay employees to engage with OSM to both add and update data, as well as engage with local mapping communities and their activities. One example is Grab, a mobility platform from Singapore and Southeast Asia's start-up with the highest valuation in 2020. In South and Southeast Asia, Grab lists several hundred people in its GRABOSM data team (with different modes of employment as well as both remote and on-the-ground mapping). By adding large amounts of specialized geodata, such as addresses, building footprints, and turn restrictions, the company is responsible for a large chunk of new data in the areas it is active in. In 2018, conflicts over modes and the ethos of mapping led to a considerable upset within the Thai mapping community (Russell 2018).

Attempts to use AI and machine learning algorithms to optimize maps and extract data are, even if sometimes less focused on urban spaces, important too. In the case of Meta's/Facebook's Map with AI project, this takes place primarily through pattern recognition in satellite images but also through mobility data – for example, in a project by Lyft that uses the company's mobility and geodata, namely the routes their drivers actually took. Hence, the spatial and platial knowledge of the workers are used as feedback to optimize the company's algorithms and OSM data (Huberty/Corthell 2021; Kißling 2019). Since "AI is neither artificial nor intelligent" (Crawford 2021: 69), this often requires much manual labor and raises questions about the role of mappers as click workers for training algorithms.

A third way in which these platforms are active in OSM is their impact on the configuration of the software stack and infrastructure of OSM. One example is the editing software users use to contribute to OSM and the suggestive power of default settings and suggestions. While the default, and currently most popular, editor was introduced by Mapbox – an early institutional actor in OSM – some time ago Meta/Facebook developed the AI-supported RapiD editor, which focuses on predicting roads and buildings.

The growing role of institutional – especially corporate – mapping in OSM reflects an increasing demand for free-to-use and easy-to-modify geodata. However, while one could argue that little harm is caused by more data and that those companies contribute to an open and free digital common, there are conflicts and challenges. Those conflicts range from questions around the politics of representation to conflicts around a disregard for community standards and neglect of the ethos of OSM, which highlights attachment to places, the local and ground truth.

Discussion

Geodata is deeply embedded as an infrastructure in urban platform capitalism. As frequently pointed out in the geographies of infrastructure and the infrastructural turn, infrastructures are hardly visible and noticeable in the everyday. This is also true for the infrastructures that facilitate the "technological everyday" (Amin 2007: 109) of the digital present. As Graham forcefully highlights, urban infrastructures become visible and a matter of concern primarily in moments of glitches, disruption, failure, and collapse (Graham 2010). Thus, there is good reason for paying closer attention to the working of infrastructures and how they shape the technological everyday of the platformized city.

All infrastructure and all geodata are social and political. The same applies to geodata as cartographic data and as maps. While much of the literature on critical cartography and geodata highlights the politics of the data, its erasures and its silences, the politics of geodata in OSM are more far-reaching. Hence, they are an excellent example of negotiations and conflicts that otherwise often remain hidden within institutions. Beyond the general fear of data extractivism and the appropriation of a crowd-based data project by private operations, there are also conflicts around ethics and commitments.

This paper calls for looking at the back end and the underbelly of urban platforms. By looking at work that is often hidden or not seen as work at all – such as reviewing other mappers' edits in a neighborhood one cares about in one's free time – this paper followed the call for placing labor more centrally in the discussions about platform urbanism. Furthermore, it wanted to add a focus on the labor that takes place behind or under the platform. In addition to looking at the working conditions and labor in the gig economy of food delivery, transportation, and holiday flats, there are work and politics of the socio-technological arrangements that underly this gig economy.

It is nothing new that tech companies use open and free data and software to make a profit. The integration of open source and open data has been a vital part of the internet since its very beginning both ideologically and technically. Hence, a clear distinction between platform capitalism and a world of collaborative and free platforms and software is often hard to make. The rise of corporate engagement with OSM "is not simply a case of capitalist appropriation of an open data project, but rather the latest stage in an evolving project comprised of a wide array of stakeholders, each coming from a different value system" (Anderson/Sarkar/Palen 2019: 4). Nonetheless, data extractivism, the externalization of costs and risks to projects such as OSM, outsourcing to crowdsourcing (Ettlinger 2016) and an "open-source washing" as a strategy (Daum 2020: 59), all highlight the politics of geodata and of all the stuff that, in most apps, appears as nothing more than a map.

References

Altenried, Moritz/Animento, Stefania/Bojadžijev, Manuela (2021): Plattform-Urbanismus. Arbeit, Migration und die Transformation des urbanen Raums, in: *sub\urban. zeitschrift für kritische stadtforschung* 9(1/2): 73-92.
Amin, Ash (2007): Re-thinking the urban social, in: *City* 11(1): 100-14.
Anderson, Jennings/Sarkar, Dipto/Palen, Leysia (2019): Corporate Editors in the Evolving Landscape of OpenStreetMap, in: *ISPRS International Journal of Geo-Information* 8(5): 232.

Ballatore, Andrea/de Sabbata, Stefano (2020): Los Angeles as a digital place: The geographies of user-generated content, in: *Transactions in GIS* 24(4): 880-902.

Beer, David (2018): *The data gaze. Capitalism, power and perception*, Los Angeles/London/New Delhi/Singapore/Washington DC/Melbourne: SAGE.

Bittner, Christian/Michel, Boris/Turk, Cate (2016): Turning the spotlight on the crowd: examining participatory ethics and practices of crisis mapping, in: *ACME: An International E-Journal for Critical Geographies* 15(1): 207-29.

Burns, Ryan (2018): Synergizing Geoweb and Digital Humanitarianism Research, in: Thatcher, Jim/Eckert, Josef/Shears, Andy (eds.): *Thinking big data in geography. New regimes, new research*, Lincoln, NE: University of Nebraska Press: 214-28.

Coldewey, Devin (2019): *Facebook empowers OpenStreetMap community with AI-enhanced tools*, in: TechCrunch, 24.07.2019. https://techcrunch.com/2019/07/23/facebook-and-openstreetmaps-empower-the-mapping-community-with-ai-enhanced-tools/ [14.08.2021].

Crampton, Jeremy W. (2009): Cartography: maps 2.0, in: *Progress in Human Geography* 33(1): 91-100.

Crawford, Kate (2021): *Atlas of AI. Power, politics, and the planetary costs of artificial intelligence*, New Haven: Yale University Press.

Daum, Timo (2020): *Agiler Kapitalismus. Das Leben als Projekt. Nautilus Flugschrift*, Hamburg: Edition Nautilus.

Dickinson, Cory (2021): *Inside the 'Wikipedia of Maps', Tensions Grow over Corporate Influence*, in: Bloomberg City Lab, 19.02.2021. https://www.bloomberg.com/news/articles/2021-02-19/openstreetmap-charts-a-controversial-new-direction [15.02.2022].

Dittus, Martin/Garcia, David (2019): Caretography – Mapping Difficult Issues with OpenStreetMap during Difficult Times. https://2019.stateofthemap.org/sessions/F9D8QG/ [28.11.2020].

Dodge, Martin/Perkins, Chris (2008): Reclaiming the Map, in: *Environment and Planning A* 40(6): 1271-76.

Dunn, Peter T. (2020): Participatory Infrastructures: The Politics of Mobility Platforms, in: *Urban Planning* 5(4): 335-46.

Ettlinger, Nancy (2016): The governance of crowdsourcing: Rationalities of the new exploitation, in: *Environment and Planning A: Economy and Space* 48(11): 2162-80.

Gardner, Z./Mooney, P./de Sabbata, S./Dowthwaite, L. (2019): Quantifying gendered participation in OpenStreetMap: responding to theories of female (under) representation in crowdsourced mapping, in: *Geojournal* 85(6): 1603-20.

Gartner, Georg (2009): Web mapping 2.0, in: Dodge, Martin/Kitchin, Rob/Perkins, Chris (eds.): *Rethinking Maps. New Frontiers in Cartographic Theory*, London: Routledge: 68-82.

Goodchild, Michael F. (2007): Citizens as sensors: the world of volunteered geography, in: *Geojournal* 69(4): 211-21.

Graham, Mark (2020): Regulate, replicate, and resist – the conjunctural geographies of platform urbanism, in: *Urban Geography* 41(6): 453-57.

Graham, Stephen (ed.) (2010): *Disrupted cities. When infrastructure fails*, New York, NY: Routledge.

Huberty, Mark/Corthell, Clara (2021): How Lyft discovered OpenStreetMap is the Freshest Map for Rideshare. https://eng.lyft.com/how-lyft-discovered-openstreetmap-is-the-freshest-map-for-rideshare-a7a41bf92ec [18.04.2021].

Kißling, Kristian (2019): *Kartendaten: Lyft verbessert Openstreetmap im Vorbeifahren – Golem.de*, in: Golem.de, 10.09.2019. https://www.golem.de/news/kartendaten-lyft-verbessert-openstreetmap-im-vorbeifahren-1909-143759.html [18.04.2021].

Kitchin, Rob (2014): *The data revolution. Big data, open data, data infrastructures & their consequences*, Los Angeles/London/New Delhi: SAGE.

Leszczynski, Agnieszka (2019): Platform affects of geolocation, in: *Geoforum* 107: 207-15.

Morozov, Evgeny (2014): *To save everything, click here. The folly of technological solutionism*, London: PublicAffairs.

OpenStreetMap Foundation (2018): Organised Editing Guidelines. https://wiki.osmfoundation.org/w/images/6/62/Organised_Editing_Guidelines.pdf [10.06.2020].

Richardson, Lizzie (2020): Coordinating the city: platforms as flexible spatial arrangements, in: *Urban Geography* 41(3): 458-61.

Russell, Jon (2018): *Grab is messing up the world's largest mapping community's data in Southeast Asia*, in: Techcrunch, 20.12.2018. https://techcrunch.com/2018/12/19/grab-maps-osm-thailand-southeast-asia [15.02.2022].

Seemann, Michael (2021): *Die Macht der Plattformen. Politik in Zeiten der Internetgiganten*, Berlin: Ch. Links.

Shaw, Joe (2020): Platform real estate: Theory and practice of new urban real estate markets, in: *Urban Geography* 41(8): 1037-64.

Srnicek, Nick (2017): *Platform capitalism*, Cambridge: polity.

Staab, Philipp (2019): *Digitaler Kapitalismus – Markt und Herrschaft in der Ökonomie der Unknappheit*, Berlin: Suhrkamp.

Stephens, Monica (2013): Gender and the GeoWeb: Division in the production of user-generated cartographic information, in: *Geojournal* 78(6): 981-96.

Thatcher, Jim (2017): You are where you go, the commodification of daily life through 'location', in: *Environment and Planning A: Economy and Space* 49(12): 2702-17.

Turner, Fred (2006): *From Counterculture to Cyberculture*, Chicago/London: University of Chicago Press.

van Dijck, José/Poell, Thomas/de Waal, Martijn (2018): *The platform society. Public values in a connective world*, New York: Oxford University Press.

Vargas Muñoz, John E./Tuia, Devis/Falcão, Alexandre X. (2020): Deploying machine learning to assist digital humanitarians: making image annotation in OpenStreetMap more efficient, in: *International journal of geographical information science IJGIS* 35(9): 1725-45.

Zuboff, Shoshana (2019): *The age of surveillance capitalism. The fight for a human future at the new frontier of power*, New York: PublicAffairs.

Looking for Glitches in Mobility Platforms

Henk Wiechers

> "[...] the glitch trains the eye on those space-times where platforms don't seem right"
> Leszczynski 2020: 201

Introduction

This article and the narrative it presents originated from an Uber trip in Hamburg (Germany) from the city's central train station to the Elbphilharmonie concert hall in June 2021. I had arranged the trip in order to experience mobility platforms in an everyday setting, to identify their potential to open up emancipatory practices, and to explore a specific theoretical approach. In the pages below, I combine a selective reading of platform urbanism, which focuses on everyday contradictions and Legacy Russell's concept of *glitch feminism* (2020), with a sectoral focus on mobility platforms.

The concept of platform urbanism describes the production of urban space, that is influenced by platforms and a corresponding platform logic. The term platformization refers to platforms' growing societal influence and their permeation into almost all aspects of (urban) life. My reading of platform urbanism derives from and is largely influenced by Legacy Russell's (2020) concept of glitch feminism and its application in feminist geography by Agnieszka Leszczynski (2020). Leszczynski uses the concept of the *glitch* to offer an alternative theorization of the platform-mediated production of urban space. She highlights the dynamic and incomplete nature of platform urbanism, which opens up opportunities for "everyday digital praxes that remake, unmake, and make differently platform/city interfaces" (Leszczynski 2020: 202). Following Russell and Leszczynski, I look for glitches that can expose underlying contradictions in urban platforms, searching for ways to envision more hopeful platform futures than the dystopian, totalizing scenarios depicted by platform capitalism (Leszczynski 2020). In doing so, I view platform urbanism mainly as a phenomenon of the urban everyday, and platforms as "ecosystems of mundane connectivity and interaction" (Leszczynski 2020: 190).

I combine this reading of platform urbanism with a critical analysis of mobility platform infrastructure and the consequences of the mobility sector's ongoing platformization. Describing these processes, I focus on platform-mediated mobility infrastructures as systemized by Stehlin, Hodson, and McMeekin (2020). Because of their inherently material characteristics and the unavoidable friction that arises when platform companies try to implement their services across a range of different urban spaces, mobility platforms are a central focal point through which we can detect contradictions in platform urbanism as a whole. Thus, looking for glitches in mobility platforms can be a fruitful way to identify the emancipatory potentials in platform urbanism and the processes of platformization. To apply this approach, I used a qualitative and explorative research approach centered on autoethnographic observations during an Uber ride. From these observations, I deduced three scenes and then wrote a narrative for each scene, situating it within the context of platform urbanism and adding background information when necessary.

The text is structured as follows. In the following section I contextualize my argument by surveying the scholarly literature on my chosen theoretical and methodological approach. In section two, I illustrate my reading of platform urbanism and outline the concept of glitch feminism. In section three, I discuss how mobility platforms work in the context of platform urbanism and the fact that mobility platforms are inherently material and error-prone, making them vulnerable to technological or material malfunction, contradictions, and unintended usage – and thus to glitches. In section four, I present three scenes from my Uber trip and offer a short interpretation of each, identifying three different kinds of glitches that represent moments with emancipatory or critical potential when investigating mobility platforms. To conclude, I summarize the points made in sections two, three, and four and suggest topics for further investigation that may yield theorizations that highlight emancipatory potential in platform-mediated urban infrastructures.

Glitches in the everyday workings of platform urbanism

The starting point of my analysis is a specific focus on contradictions and glitches in the everyday roll-out of platform technologies in the context of platform urbanism. The implementation of platform infrastructures is often framed as a smooth, seamless process, ignoring the many frictions that accompany this process. But in the words of Leszczynski (2020: 200) "platform urbanism is not only a project of imperfect ambition [...], but one which is also incomplete". This implies that there is a divergence between claim and reality. The goal here is not only to point out and criticize social inequalities and discrimination, but also to frame the corresponding disruptions and contradictions that enable individual actors to appropriate these glitchy conditions for their own benefit.

To find these disruptions, Leszczynski and others propose to focus on everyday (urban) experiences. The basic premise here is that the incompleteness of the platform urbanism project can be found in many everyday aspects of urban life, which is messy and unpredictable. Following that idea, both Leszczynski and Barns assign a specific kind of agency to people's everyday interactions with platform surfaces. This focus on individual agency runs counter to the idea of the above mentioned dystopian, totalizing scenarios of platform capitalism that tend to predominate in academic discussions of the topic (Leszczynski 2020: 208). In the face of such universalistic platform visions, individual action is still deemed important and influential within the datafied co-creation of the city (Barns 2020: 13; Leszczynski 2020: 200). It allows us to envision a more hopeful platform future, one built around everyday action (Leszczynski 2020: 189).

Following up on these studies, I refer to the concept of glitch feminism developed by Legacy Russell (2020) to conceptualize the incompleteness of the platform urbanism project. Glitch feminism offers "a way to work, understand and interact with digital material to make sense of the often-contradictory nature of a digitalized world" (Russell 2020: 135) – including the world of platform urbanism. Russell's manifesto defines the glitch as an analytical concept that can help researchers navigate the contemporary dynamics of digitization, the interaction between and close connections between the online/offline worlds. Derived from the linguistic origins of the Yiddish *gletshn* (to slide, glide, slip) and the German *glitschen* (to slip), the concept refers to a sense of movement – or slipping – beyond and between binary categories (Russell 2020: 28). This focus on movement shifts our focus beyond the standard definition of the word *glitch* as "a technological error", viewing it instead as a positive starting point from which to begin questioning existing social and technological routines and conventions. The concept of the glitch has already been applied in feminist geography by Agnieszka Leszczynski (2020) and Sarah Elwood (2020; Elwood/Leszczynski 2018). In the pages below, I draw on this broader definition of the glitch and its existing applications in feminist geography. My analysis starts from a classic reading of glitches as technological malfunctions and continues to societal and interpersonal irritations that indicate when platform infrastructures "don't seem right" (Leszczynski 2020: 201). In the words of Russell (2020: 29): "a glitch is something that extends beyond the most literal technological mechanics: it helps us to celebrate failure as a generative force, a new way to take on the world."

Mobility platforms in the context of platform urbanism

For several reasons, I chose mobility platforms as my research object. Glitches might occur in any other type of platform infrastructure, but I deem the mobility sector as a fitting test case for the purposes of this study because of its relevance to everyday urban interactions, the strong influence of global platform companies such as Uber, and the sector's inherently material characteristics, which make the occurrence of glitches more likely. In this section, I want to point out some of the consequences of the ongoing digitization of the mobility sector.

Stehlin, Hodson, and McMeekin (2020) point out several characteristics of the mobility sector that support this connection between the mobility sector and research on platforms. First and foremost, they highlight the specific materiality of mobility platforms in urban contexts which gives concrete form to the manifold material and social connections between the platform and the city (Stehlin/Hodson/McMeekin 2020: 1255). They also join other authors in framing mobility as a constituting factor of social life (Cresswell 2010; Sheller/Urry 2006) and as a key dimension of socio-spatial and transport-related inequality and exclusion (Lucas 2012). Mobility can be seen as a societally relevant phenomenon since it is interwoven with almost every aspect of everyday urban life. Mobility is a key signifier for living standards and social (in)equality inside a city.

Like all other sectors of the urban infrastructure, the mobility sector is currently undergoing processes of platformization. Although in many ways the influence of platform companies exacerbates already-existing tendencies, it also poses new questions. Looking at the platformization of mobility, Stehlin, Hodson, and McMeekin (2020) identify a range of different strategies and developmental trends, from ride-hailing companies like Uber, which exploit mobility gaps by building on existing informal mobility practices, to state-wide mobility infrastructure programs that focus the large-scale implementation of new mobility platform technologies. This article focuses on ride-hailing services like Uber. Ride-hailing in its original meaning encompasses "the activity of asking for a car and driver to come immediately and take you somewhere, or a service that lets you do this" (Cambridge Dictionary 2021). This form of mobility takes different forms in different regulatory and institutional contexts, which leads to varying degrees of friction during the service's implementation in each context – and thereby to possible glitches.

This relationship between new mobility platforms and existent mobility infrastructure, as one finds in many ride-hailing companies, can also be described through the interplay between two contradictory processes inherent to the workings of platform urbanism: the infrastructuralization of platforms and the platformization of infrastructures. The former describing a process in which platforms provide indispensable infrastructural societal services, the latter referring to the colonization and/or transformation of extant infrastructures by platforms (Leszczynski 2020: 192). As Stehlin, Hodson, and McMeekin point out, companies like Uber use and exploit existing services (such as taxis or personal cars) by incorporating them into the platform. This setup enables the platform company to frame itself not as the owner, but only as a mediator between independent drivers and their customers (Stehlin/Hodson/McMeekin 2020: 1257).

Illustrating this relationship, Pollio (2021) is exploring the interdependencies between Uber and international airports on the basis of two ethnographic field studies in Cape Town and Mumbai. In contrast to the narrative of being merely a mediator platform, Uber is extending its services into physical space by logistically organizing the matching-up of ride-hailing customers and their designated Uber cars. This process relies on the existing airport infrastructure and is enabled by small material adaptions. These adaptations include, for example, easily visible signs (installed by Uber) that point passengers towards a specific pick-up area, which itself is also referenced in the app.

Another consequence of platformization and ongoing digitization in the mobility sector is the exacerbation of mobility-related social exclusion. As Sören Groth (2019) has shown, smart mobility trends are aggravating mobility-related social exclusion tendencies. Analyzing processes of digitization specifically within the context of transportation, Groth frames this technology-driven intensification of social inequalities as multimodal divide – that is, a social rift in which the already-existing tendency towards a digital divide is intensified by the multiple modal options that transportation users face, all of which work together to reproduce mobility-related social exclusion. Thus, people with few transport mode options sometimes also lack the technological requirements to take part in platform-mediated mobility infrastructures. In this regard, the need to possess a functioning smartphone and a connected credit card for flexible payment potentially prevent them from participating in new mobility services. Even as smartphone possession becomes more and more ubiquitous, mobility apps and platform services in general still require an updated and technologically full-functioning device. Maintaining and updating such devices, moreover, is often expensive and requires technological expertise.

Finally, all of these processes related to the digitization of mobility find material expression in urban spaces. Because mobility infrastructures are inherently material, mobility platforms are omnipresent in public space. Thus, one would expect a certain amount of friction and malfunction to arise when such platforms are deployed and implemented in differing urban contexts. If so, the digital *quick fix* that companies engaged in the platform-mediated mobility infrastructure often tout as a cure-all for urban mobility infrastructural problems seems utopian, and without consideration for the different regulatory and material conditions of different urban spaces. This notion of the *fix* opposes the concept of the glitch, with the fix being the solution to a sometimes rather imaginary problem, and the glitch being the crack in a seemingly perfect system and the angle on which to base possible emancipatory practices.

Finding glitches in mobility platforms

Following the concepts summarized in sections two and three, I set out to look for glitches in the workings of mobility platforms. To do so, I focused on everyday interactions between the platform, urban space, and myself in an explorative observation. The focus on ride-hailing platforms like Uber offered the advantage of being able to build on an existing rich corpus of discussion in the field of critical urban studies and to investigate this specific type of service within a local context.

The following scenes emerge from a single auto-ethnographic observation. They each show one dimension of a very short quotidian event: a person leaving a train station books a ride on her/his phone, and then exits the station. Every short scene is followed by associations and contextualizations about the things I felt and observed during my trip. To further contextualize the scenes, I add relevant theoretical and empirical information geared towards the key issues concerning the rolling-out of mobility platforms in practice.

Immersions in my phone

When I took out my phone in front of the train station, I tried to act normal – as though this were something I did every day. I had downloaded the FreeNow[1] application to experience platform urbanism firsthand. I was excited and a little nervous. When I opened the app and tried to book a ride, an error message immediately popped to inform me that the service wasn't operating in this area. Under normal circumstances I would have immediately switched to another mode of transportation, but since my plan was to use the service of a platform-mediated ride-hailing service my trip took another direction.

So, I downloaded the Uber app. As I knew from my previous research, the company has been operating in Germany for some years. They always faced heavy legal and societal pushback, but managed to expand service to several German cities. As a (or rather *the*) ride-hailing platform, Uber met the criteria I set out to investigate.

To gain access to the platform, I had to download the application to my phone and re-establish the connection to my account, which I had created years ago. I also had to reconnect the payment option and update my personal data. All of this was done on-the-fly, while standing in front of the train station as many taxis, cars, and travelers went by. My behavior in this instance was the complete opposite of what one would expect of train station

---

[1] FreeNow (formerly known as mytaxi) was founded in 2019 and is part of the ridehailing joint venture by the BMW Group and Daimler AG (FreeNow n.d.).

behavior. While everyone else was busy catching their train or getting on a taxi, I was temporarily stuck inside my own – or my phone's – limitations.

After several minutes, I was set to book the ride. I remembered Uber experiences from other countries and had a similar feeling. The communication with the app and the driver were like how it worked in the US. After booking the ride, I could see the available cars as small symbols on my screen and watch to see whether they would choose to pick me up or not. After I was matched, I could see the symbol on the screen coming towards me.

By now I was completely detached from my surroundings, fully immersed in the app and the task at hand. I sent further information on my location to the driver, and a few moments later I got a call.

This first scene starts with a glitch – an irritation in the smooth interface of the app. The platform app I had planned to use did not work, and I had to find another way. The app's malfunction causes a change of plans, which already speaks to the fact that users should be able to navigate the digital and physical mobility landscape, should be aware of the different modes of travel available to them, and should know about the technological requirements for their use. Since my investigation of platform-mediated mobility service required that I use a ride-hailing service, I looked for an alternative that would fulfill the conditions of my research design. Of course, I could have used a service of the Hamburg public transport system, but I wanted to stick to my plan. So, after downloading and re-connecting with the Uber app, everything concerning my ride until the arrival of my car took place inside my smartphone. The malfunction of one app and the process of immersion into another app exemplify the user's dependency on a working smartphone while navigating the platform-mediated mobility landscape.

Here, I refer to the different dynamics of mobility-related social exclusion and the multimodal divide (Groth 2019; Lucas 2012) that are increased by the individual's growing dependency on platforms and digital interfaces while using the mobility infrastructure. Raising the bar of access to mobility infrastructures means that some people can be excluded. Technological malfunctions that require spontaneous reactions, such as those I experienced in this scene, are only the most obvious modes of exclusion from new platform-mediated mobility services. The most important and most relevant requirement in this first scene would be the possession of a smartphone and the required connection to an online payment system or possession of a credit card. This shows that ride-hailing services like Uber intensify social exclusion on a most basic level, which is not surprising because apps like these implicitly don't target people who are already marginalized and disadvantaged regarding the provision and usage of mobility options relative to other user groups. Given these platforms' own claim that their services positively intervene in society and enrich the mobility mix, it should be taken into consideration. In this sense, finding and tracing the glitch uncovers inequality in the provision and possible usage of the platform infrastructure.

Optical illusions

> When I arrived at the train station where my trip was supposed to start, I randomly chose one of the exits and found myself standing next to a taxi parking spot. I stood beside a long line of waiting taxis. The drivers were either waiting in their cars, cleaning the windows of their taxis, or talking to each other. Under normal circumstances I wouldn't have recognized anything special about this situation. But in this context, in which I had specifically planned not to use a traditional taxi service but rather a platform-mediated service, I felt some sense of guilt. This feeling intensified as I watched the Uber car, I had ordered drive past the line of waiting taxis. Normally, as a rule the first taxi in line would get the next customer. The Uber minibus looked exactly like other taxis and there was no way to distinguish it from other taxis except for the way that it drove past the queue, and a sticker (Uber cars have such stickers on the windshield or on the side of the car) indicating that it was driving for Uber.
>
> Not only did it feel awkward to see my Uber car drive past the waiting taxis, but I also realized that I had accidentally booked a minibus for myself, which was supposed to carry up to four passengers in the back. Even if it didn't bother anyone, I felt the gazes of the waiting taxi drivers while I got into the minibus and sat in the back seat of my own private platform-mediated mobility option.
>
> During this encounter I was struck by the spatial proximity of two opposing business models, which are only distinguishable by the behavior of their drivers and the position of their cars at a train station – one waits, the other

drives by. In this scenario, two cars look visually the same, but are embedded in two opposing institutional contexts.

The most apparent glitch in this scenario is the visual overlap between the different (yet similar) kinds of mobility services and their contrasting kinds of institutional embeddedness, an embeddedness that materializes in the form of urban spaces and in the working conditions of the drivers. The seemingly clear distinction between the categories of *taxi* and *non-taxi* are visually blurred through the almost identical appearances of the cars. This overlap serves as entry point for examining the specific characteristics of Uber Germany that underlie and give rise to this glitch or disruption. For this we will need a brief overview of the strategies deployed by Uber in Germany.

The Uber company has battled a wide range of different institutional actors, at both the local and national levels, concerning the legality of its business model and the working conditions and required skills of its drivers (Stehlin/Hodson/McMeekin 2020: 1257). Unsurprisingly, the same goes for Uber Germany. First, Uber Germany claims not to offer any mobility service and does not see itself as responsible for the ride itself. Rather, it frames itself as a mediator between customers and independent and licensed *Mietwagenunternehmern* (rental car entrepreneurs) (Uber Deutschland 2020). A German federal court ruled in 2019 that Uber would need a legible rental car concession because the company – although they seemingly only connect customer with independent drivers – seems to the customer like the provider of the service. Also, it pre-selects the specific driver and states the price of each ride. Since then, Uber has been operating through one general entrepreneur, under whom every driver in Germany works as sub-contractor. Taxi driver unions see this as an insufficient solution and still frame Uber's activity as illegal (Handelsblatt 2021). Many Uber drivers, they claim, still find ways to get around the changes made in the jurisdiction (Taxi Deutschland 2021).

Uber Germany (2020) has countered these accusations and what they imply about the company's relationship towards the existing taxi infrastructure in Germany. Apart from assuring critics that all Uber drivers are properly insured, secured, and skilled, the company also claims that the direct mediation of the app and the resultant high level of sufficiency enables it to offer rides that are cheaper than taxi rides. The company also notes its positive impact on broader societal and urban issues related to the connection between city centers and urban peripheries, and its contribution to climate protection. These observations suggest that Uber sees itself as offering material and systemic fixes to existing problems, like car congestion and peripheralization, that go beyond the role of a simple mediator. In its projected self-image, Uber portrays itself as filling some sort of gap by adding a valuable feature to the mobility mix in Germany.

This notion of filling a gap or fixing a relevant problem is typical of the narrative framings that companies like Uber promote about their platforms (see previous chapter: "Mobility platforms in the context of platform urbanism"; Stehlin/Hodson/McMeekin 2020). To put this in a broader context, Lizzie Richardson asks: "What is the question to which the concept of platform urbanism claims to be an answer?" Referring specifically to Uber, she states that the only new element that the company offers is the corresponding app (Richardson 2018). It becomes clear that platforms – and especially mobility platforms – "are dependent upon a host of other arrangements that are outside of their control" (Richardson 2018). In the case of mobility platforms, these "other arrangements" beyond the platform's control might include elements of the existing transport infrastructure (like taxi companies or road networks) that are necessary to the proper functioning of ride-hailing app services. On the surface, therefore, the working of Uber Germany effectively illustrates how the platformization of infrastructure can arise through a process of colonizing and transforming existing services and resources – in this case, the existing German taxi infrastructure.

The situation of Uber in Germany and the conflict between this platform company and the taxi industry serves as an example of a multi-facetted and long-lasting process of adaption, conflict, and (re-)negotiation between a platform company, other businesses, and local and national political institutions. In witnessing the material process of negotiation in situ as the Uber car I had ordered drove by the other taxis, I felt like the conflict had manifested itself before my own eyes. Such small situations are embedded in this larger process of platformization, and they (re-)produce new situations while also potentially disrupting the flow of urban life. The gray areas that are explored in these spaces that lie between taxi companies and Uber may shed some light on new modes of cooperation and overlap that might diverge from the drastic positions of each side.

(Not) being one's own boss

> When I entered the car, I sat down at the right back end where I could see the driver's face through the rear-view mirror. Between my area and the driver's

seat there was a transparent plastic sheet and a COVID information sheet. I noticed the taxi meter under the rear-view mirror and thought about the function of the Uber app, which fixes the price of the ride in advance. Right next to the driver there were two phones attached to the car dashboard. I could see that there were two different apps running on the phones. One of them was the Uber app. Inspired by this observation, I started a conversation. I asked the driver if he was only driving for Uber. He answered that he was self-employed. He is driving for Uber as well as for FreeNow. I said: "The app wasn't working earlier so I switched to Uber." He answered that the app indeed was working earlier the same day and that these temporary malfunctions sometimes happen. He added that he had already given some rides for FreeNow that same day.

After hearing from him that he was self-employed, I asked him if he owned the car we were riding in – since it looked a lot like a normal taxi. He said: more or less. After two years it will be his, he explained, and then he will get something out of it. I assumed that he must be in a leasing contract with a rental car company or taxi agency. He pointed out that he is satisfied with his current mode of employment. In contrast to working for a taxi company, he said that he is his own boss and can decide when to take which ride. By using both apps at the same time, he can decide spontaneously whether to use one or the other app and make more profit.

All in all, he seemed confident and positive in the way he told me his story. He seemed determined in what he was doing. He also seemed open to talk about his working conditions and share his experience.

In this scene, the glitch manifests in the contradiction between Uber's proclaimed image of independent, skilled, and financially and socially secured drivers and the more differentiated and complex reality represented in the scene. The driver was working for different platforms at the same time while being "his own boss" and while still being dependent on good ratings on the app and obliged to pay off his car debt. The challenge here is to move beyond this binary of entrepreneurialism and exploitation and look for contradictions and dissonances (see Mazumdar 2021), as well as the potential for resistant and emancipatory behavior and signs of agency in the driver who sit between both binary poles.

The information gathered on the first two scenes now connects in the person of the driver. He situates himself in the context of platform capitalism in a way that can neither be classified as (self-)exploitation nor as a pure success story of entrepreneurialism. These two alternatives create binary categories that can be overcome by zooming in and closely examining the different forms of embeddedness. In the case of a technological glitch (such as when one app does not work properly), the driver can use the other one and still make money. He manages to find a strategy that enables him to bypass technological glitches to some extent, simply by using an alternative. Moreover, he uses the flexible business model by Uber and FreeNow to his own advantage: as the driver indicates, he is satisfied with the freedom and profit surplus that these two apps offer him in comparison to taxi apps. As I have shown, it is worthwhile to move beyond these binaries and focus on grey areas.

Conclusion

The descriptions and reflections on the three scenes presented in this text show the multi-layered nature of mobility platforms and the complex and sometimes contradictory everyday entanglements of individual actors in platform urbanism narratives. By observing and analyzing three kinds of glitches in the platform interface, experienced in the context of a single everyday interaction within an urban platform infrastructure, I was able to show the rich potential that a close observation of intra-urban entanglements that are mitigated through mobility platforms can uncover. Unjust mobility provision certainly is one part of dystopian platform futures, but it is important to focus exactly on ways through which these can be understood, anticipated, and prevented.

In this process, the mobility sector has proven to be an excellent example of the material, discursive, political, and social entanglements of platform infrastructures. The claim of the fix and the reality of the glitch, as well as the processes of infrastructuralization of platforms and platformization of infrastructures, can perfectly be exemplified by rapidly emerging mobility platforms. Mobility platforms like Uber frame themselves as being part of the solution that will lead us towards a more sustainable mobility, but they don't consider the friction that automatically ensues when the service is implemented within existing regulatory and political contexts. Rather, they offer a fix that automatically gives rise to a multitude of glitches. These can serve as evidence for existing social inequalities, on the one hand, while they serve as point of appropriation and unintended usage of their service, on the other.

Although I was able to present an approach to the study of platform-city relationships from a small-scale, exploratory perspective that focused on mobility platforms, it remains for other studies to apply this approach to different topics that go beyond the rather material approach I chose in this text. Scene three has shown the research potential of studying how actors can (spontaneously) appropriate platform infrastructures to fulfil their own goals and agendas. This might encompass actors using technological glitches for their own benefit or undermining the platform companies' algorithmic control by different forms of social organization. In exploring these and other topics, upcoming research should apply an intersectional lens – for example, by zooming in on gender and race inequality in the provision and usage of ride-hailing services.

Lastly, in addition to these diagnoses of glitches in moments where mobility platforms 'don't seem right', more work must be done on platform futures in which individual agency continues to matter (Leszczynski 2020). The story of the driver in scene three has shown the potential insights to be gleaned from exploring the gray areas between exploitation and entrepreneurialism and suggests that platform logics haven't fully replaced the everyday strategies of the individual actors navigating these urban infrastructures. Prioritizing their strategies and looking beyond simple binaries might be one way to identify new ways of reinterpretation, (re-)appropriation, and resistance of platform infrastructures in the mobility sector and in general.

References

Barns, Sarah (2020): *Platform Urbanism: Negotiating Platform Ecosystems in Connected Cities*, Singapore: Springer Singapore.
Cambridge Dictionary (2021): Ride-hailing. https://dictionary.cambridge.org/de/worterbuch/englisch/ride-hailing [10.11.2021].
Cresswell, Tim (2010): Towards a Politics of Mobility, in: *Environment and Planning D: Society and Space* 28(1): 17-31.
Elwood, Sarah (2020): Digital geographies, feminist relationality, Black and queer code studies: Thriving otherwise, in: *Progress in Human Geography* 45(2): 209-28.

Elwood, Sarah/Leszczynski, Agnieszka (2018): Feminist digital geographies, in: *Gender, Place & Culture* 25(5): 629-44.

FreeNow (n.d.): Eine Geschichte, die zur Revolution wurde. https://free-now.com/de/ueber-free-now/ [14.03.2022].

Groth, Sören (2019): Multimodal divide: Reproduction of transport poverty in smart mobility trends, in: *Transportation Research Part A: Policy and Practice* 125: 56-71.

Handelsblatt (2021): https://www.handelsblatt.com/unternehmen/dienstleister/fahrdienst-vermittler-uber-verliert-frankfurter-berufungsverfahren-in-taxi-streit/27212172.html?ticket=ST-11510888-a9hL97TdwACSjNf3E2etap5 [22.08.2021].

Leszczynski, Agnieszka (2020): Glitchy vignettes of platform urbanism, in: *Environment and Planning D: Society and Space* 38(2): 189-208.

Lucas, Karen (2012): Transport and social exclusion: Where are we now?, in: *Transport Policy* 20: 105-13.

Mazumdar, Anurag (2021): Between Algorithms and the Streets: The Everyday Politics of Ride-Hailing Taxis in India, in: Hodson, Mike/Kasmire, Julia/McMeekin, Andrew/Stehlin, John G./Ward, Kevin (eds.): *Urban platforms and the future city: transformations in infrastructure, governance, knowledge and everyday life*, London: Routledge/Taylor & Francis Group: 235-47.

Pollio, Andrea (2021): Uber, airports, and labour at the infrastructural interfaces of platform urbanism, in: *Geoforum* 118: 47-55.

Richardson, Lizzie (2018): Platforms as urban technology?, in: *Mediapolis: A journal of Cities and Culture* 3(4). https://www.mediapolisjournal.com/2018/11/platforms-as-urban-technology/ [22.08.2021].

Russell, Legacy (2020): *Glitch feminism: a manifesto*, London/New York: Verso.

Sheller, Mimi/Urry, John (2006): The New Mobilities Paradigm, in: *Environment and Planning A: Economy and Space* 38(2): 207-26.

Stehlin, John/Hodson, Michael/McMeekin, Andrew (2020): Platform mobilities and the production of urban space: Toward a typology of platformization trajectories, in: *Environment and Planning A: Economy and Space* 52(7): 1250-68.

Taxi Deutschland (2021): https://blog.taxi-deutschland.net/2021/05/25/taxi-deutschland-gegen-uber-verbot-von-uber-in-deutschland-erneut-bestaetigt [22.08.2021].

Uber Deutschland (2020): Fakten zu Uber in Deutschland. https://www.uber.com/de/newsroom/fakten-uber-deutschland-sachlage [22.08.2021].

PLATFORM-MEDIATED CARE-WORK IN CITIES

Platform Care as Care Fix

Emma Dowling

It has almost become a truism in the social sciences to state that technology does not develop in a vacuum. It matters who makes those decisions, who deploys technology, and to what end; it matters who the programmers and engineers are and what assumptions they hold (Wajcman 2006; Pettinger 2019: 136ff.). Moreover, technology never merely replaces a task. Instead, the nature and even the meaning of tasks are transformed, while new tasks are also created in the process. As Larry Lohmann (2019: 46) puts it, "there is no 'thing' that stays constant through the process of 'being mechanized' any more than there are discrete objects called 'technologies' that, when sprinkled onto humanity, help it attain its desires but otherwise leaves it just as it is". It also matters what investment decisions, forms of ownership, and business models inform the development and use of technology. Consequently, the digital platforms relating to *care* and the business models they are premised on reshape the everyday social relations of care, the relationship between public provision, while they are also linked to the privatization and financialization of social infrastructures. Thus, platformization is not only a techno-social process, it is also a political-economic one.

In this contribution I discuss the political economy of the contemporary platformization of care that ranges from self-care health apps to online agencies for care services. The examples I refer to all stem from the UK context and I draw on the research I carried out for the book *The Care Crisis* and the arguments and analysis presented there (Dowling 2021). I discuss the ways in which the current platformization of care is part of a *care fix*, entailing a process whereby digital platforms insert themselves into a mounting care crisis, offering to plug the care gaps that are experienced by individuals and households in an everyday context and in the wake of the neoliberal restructuring of the British welfare state and its correspondent care regime.

Care crisis

Feminist scholarship has sought to draw attention to a growing care crisis (Rosen 2007; Rai/Hoskyns/Thomas 2013; Elias et al. 2016; Fraser 2016), which has been both exacerbated and made more visible by the coronavirus pandemic (de Henau/Himmelweit 2020; Barry/Jennings 2021: 36ff.). In its most general terms, a crisis of care means that more and more people are unable to access adequate care, while those who provide care to others are unable to do so satisfactorily and under dignified conditions. This care crisis is premised on changes to the material conditions for the provision of care – whether within households and families, in communities, by public or social services, or through the market, private corporations, and agencies – and pertains to the growing gap between care needs and the resources made available to meet them (Dowling 2021: 6). Key dynamics include the demographic changes of *ageing* societies, with the associated increase in care needs; the neoliberal dismantling and restructuring of public services; the attempted commodification of services; dual-earner models in the context of stagnating real wages, i.e., the requirement of households to spend a high proportion of time in gainful employment. These developments are occurring against the backdrop of a heightened personal responsibility for care along with the reliance on the compassion and sense of responsibility of those who care to continue to do so under adverse conditions, precisely because they care. All of this perpetuates and even deepens existing traditional relations of care and *social reproduction* together with intersectional inequalities, reinforcing the devaluation of care and worsening conditions under which care is provided, both paid and unpaid.

Care fix

A care fix entails efforts at crisis management that do not resolve one and for all, but merely displace the crisis, thereby perpetuating the structural feature of capitalist economies to off-load the cost of care and social reproduction to unpaid realms of society. This is because the dynamic of capitalism is to seek a care fix in ways that will allow for the continued pursuit of profitability. Care fixes lie at the heart of the current reorganization of the relations of production, social reproduction, and care. In the face of limits or impasses, capitalist economies reorganize to overcome crises. David Harvey (1975; 1982) and Beverly Silver (2012) have respectively termed such forms of reorganization a *fix*, analyzing the ways in which capitalist production undergoes spatial, technological, organizational, or financial fixes to solve the pressures of maintaining profitability. This can very well mean is that the underlying problems that led to the crisis in the first place are not actually addressed, instead being merely displaced. The analogy of the fix can be applied to the social relations of care to understand how particular care fixes (Dowling 2018: 334-35; 2021: 14-15) reorganize care in the face of both an economic and a care crisis.

Each regime of accumulation (the way that goods are produced and consumed) has a corresponding care regime, understood as the arrangements through which care is provided and labor power is produced, e.g., within the household and kinship arrangements, through a welfare state, in neighborhoods and communities, or via the market in commodified form (Brown et al. 2012: 80). As Nancy Fraser (2016) has elaborated, historical periods have specific configurations characterized by different institutional forms, as well as norms that govern the provision of care across state, market, and society on the basis of a gendered and racialized social division of reproductive labor in ways that (re)draw the boundaries between production and reproduction.

The way that the economy and politics are governed is one realm, another is the terrain of the everyday, where social life is organized. Care fixes can be analyzed with regard to three dynamics. First, a care fix repairs, seeking to re-establish favorable conditions for the pursuit of profitability in the face of crisis. Second, a care fix displaces, postponing the underlying causes of crisis and their symptoms into future, or off-loading them elsewhere. Third, a care fix pins down certain configurations of care for a given historical period (Dowling 2018: 334). These configurations are either political-economic, socio-cultural and technological, or affective-ideological. Political-economic configurations pertain to the way the economy is governed, i.e., the relationship between states, markets, and commons. For example, questions of the public provision of care, legal regulations with regard to access to care, or the extent of commodification. By socio-cultural and technological configurations of care I mean the social relations of care, e.g., the provision of care in households or families, or the role of civil society organizations along with the extent of mechanization, automation, and digitalization. The affective-ideological configurations of care include the feelings and meanings attached to ideas about care and caring; norms, values, and responsibilities; gender, race, and class dynamics as well as relationships to the body. Of central importance here are the affective mediations through which a sense of self is gained and subjectivities are shaped. Of importance also are the narratives, or more rather the *ideologies of caring* (Dowling 2021: 38) that justify, legitimize, and normalize unequal or exploitative care arrangements in a given society.

A brief clarification is necessary at this point regarding the terms care and social reproduction. Analytically it is useful to distinguish between the two. Social reproduction refers to the activities and spheres of society in which unpaid or underpaid work takes place to ensure the maintenance of labor power and life in a capitalist economy. These are activities that form the backbone of any society, yet they are routinely rendered invisible and devalued, not least precisely because they constitute a cost to society and to capital (Weeks 2011; Federici 2012). Care encompasses qualitative dimensions pertaining to the *modus operandi* of an activity, the correspondent affective dispositions (such as empathy, concern, or attention) as well as the correspondent ethical relations (such as interdependence) (Finch/Groves 1983: 15; Care Collective 2020). Care encompasses endeavors to meet the needs of others and assist them to live well (Himmelweit 2007: 581). Caring affects are not merely optional or a simple add-on: tending to someone with care may very well enhance their wellbeing and impact on their quality of life. Moreover, it is precisely the cathexis of caring that serves as a basis for its exploitation, by relying on the fact that someone *wants* to care or feels a sense of responsibility. Indeed, caring can be instrumentalized in the pursuit of profitability or to maintain social cohesion for capital accumulation to continue (Dowling 2018: 344; 2021: 20).

Consequently, we can examine the causes and manifestations of the growing care crisis and the emerging solutions to it and investigate the kinds of care fixes currently taking shape. What becomes apparent is that care inequalities are rising, while the responsibility for caring is systematically handed down a societal care chain of paid, underpaid, and unpaid caring labor based on a core structural feature of capitalist economies. This feature is the systemic imperative to expand markets in the pursuit of profitability, which goes hand in hand with a devaluation of the work of care and social reproduction, either by making this work invisible or by offloading its cost.

The platformization of care as a care fix

Current care technologies can be divided into two categories: information and communication technologies (ICT) and assistive technologies (Dowling 2021: 122). It is with regard to ICT that digital platforms are particularly relevant.

ICTs can enable a variety of functions and interactions such as remote diagnosis, consultation, and therapy. They can also facilitate information-sharing among care workers and can better integrate the wishes and needs of care recipients, saving time and enabling communication when someone cannot travel. People in need of care can stay in touch with friends and family, while digital platforms and social networks allow care and support to be provided locally, by connecting those in need of care with formal and informal carers, including volunteers, community organizations, and local services on- and offline. Such digital infrastructures do not simply enable more or better communication; they also have a political economy.

Platforms are digital intermediaries to enable two or more groups to interact, providing the digital infrastructure that enables communication and exchange, rendering user data collected in the process productive in order to develop and marketize services. They rely heavily on the so-called *network effect*, which is why they tend towards monopolization, thus exercising control over the "rules of the game" (Srnicek 2016: 46). In other words, they shape the protocols that govern interactions. Moreover, the price structures, that is to whom they charge how much for what, vary between different providers, and indeed can also vary over time within the same platform. Srnicek refers to this as "cross subsidization" (ibid.) arguing that part of the business model of platforms is "fine-tuning the balance between what is paid, what is not paid, what is subsidized, and what is not subsidized" (ibid.). The platformization of care entails the provision of paid and unpaid care services by digital intermediaries that enable the communication and exchange between multiple users. These platformized care services with their concomitant business models insert themselves into the existing political economy, offering solutions to social as well as economic problems.

Digital self-care

In the wake of the coronavirus pandemic, there has been a considerable surge in the use of all kinds of digital apps, as people have been confined to their homes and face to face meetings have not been possible under conditions of lockdown, including health and self-care (Inkster et al. 2020). Care-apps range from online therapy, i.e., a virtual meeting with an actual therapist, to apps that help track moods and offer advice on how to manage these through a combination of self-care ranging from mindfulness activities and apps that measure and monitor physical performances. There are also apps that helps to manage depressive episodes or keep anxiety in check (Ratcliffe 2017). Often, these draw on cognitive behavioral therapy, which focuses mostly on changing existing patters of thinking and acting where they prove to be inadequate (Burns 2020). Apps for online counselling are also part of these developments.

With regard to therapeutic models in particular, there is the question of the role of embodied human connection in therapy. Where the therapeutic relationship is reduced to the virtual, it could be that the quality of the connection between therapist and client becomes more superficial without the full range of embodied communication and the qualities of co-presence. This is an aspect that requires more research and is not only pertinent to the therapeutic context but pertains more broadly to the benefits of in-person presence in a whole variety of contexts, from personal relationships to educational settings and workplaces. In this broad dimension this is an issue that has come to the fore very acutely in the wake of the pandemic where lockdowns and remote communications have heightened awareness not only of the benefits, but also the potential drawbacks of digital communications popularized as *zoom fatigue* (Bailenson 2021). If key aspects of the therapeutic process are automated, e.g., advice for particular feelings or thoughts, this raises the questions of whether computers really can deliver on the key components of the therapeutic relationship if these include not simply becoming aware of or verbalizing problems and seeking solutions but experiencing the compassion and understanding of and connection with another human being (Burns 2020). Moreover, the political question of the collection and interpretation of data from bodies and behavior and the commercial (or other) uses that this is put to is acutely relevant, as is the imposition of measure. When we count up what we do and what we achieve in ratings and measurable outcomes that can in turn be routed through financial markets for the purposes of extracting surplus value.

All in all, the promotion of this kind of sense of self puts personal responsibility center-stage and is a kind of care fix that privatizes the responsibility for care and turns self-care into a coping mechanism in the face of an inadequate and ailing care infrastructure. The question for a political economy analysis then is twofold. First, what needs are care platforms responding to and how are they shaped by or in turn shape existing and emerging ideologies of caring (such as self-care)? Second, what are the business models of these platforms and how do these in turn insert themselves into the political economy of care across the domains of state, market, and society in response to the ongoing care crisis? In what follows I discuss some examples of new care platforms and their business models in order to ascertain the particular care fix they offer.

Online healthcare services

In recent years the National Health Service (NHS) in England has been exploring the use of a digital healthcare app in parts of London and Birmingham under the name *Babylon GP at Hand*. The private company contracted to provide the service is Babylon Health, a venture capital-backed digital health start-up with *unicorn status*.[1] It provides users with data-driven tools for the self-management of conditions that include health, mood, and activity monitoring as well as symptom checking and using artificial intelligence and machine learning to refine the interpretation of symptom descriptions by users and improve diagnostics.[2] Aside from these tools, users are able to consult a General Practitioner (GP) online 24/7. If a user needs to see a medical doctor in person, they visit a Babylon Health clinic. The aim is to increase user self-management of healthcare needs and decrease the need for interaction with medical professionals (Babylon Health 2017). Users who sign up privately pay a subscription fee, the version available via the NHS is free for users. Users who register with the Babylon GP at Hand service through the NHS are automatically de-registered from their existing GP practice and must use a Babylon clinic.

Here, the self-care fix intertwines with a fiscal fix (Dowling 2021: 180). Babylon Health offers purported cost-savings to the public sector. First, because patients can avoid long waiting lists and waiting times and have a video consultation with a doctor within two hours. Second, because the app promises to save the NHS money, by increasing the occasions when users can self-manage their health without needing to be seen by a doctor. However, critics have argued that the company takes away resources GP practices need by taking away younger and healthier patients who are more likely to use the app (Crouch 2018; Downey 2019). In the British healthcare system, GP practices are currently funded through weighted payments for each patient that consider the healthcare needs of the particular population a practice serves,

---

1 This means the privately held start-up is valued over $1 billion.
2 See babylonhealth.com/ai.

including factors such as age or socio-economic situation. Risk is pooled, because those who are younger and fitter require less attention and therefore fewer resources. The basic principle of risk-pooling is that a population's health needs vary over the course of a lifetime. Babylon's business model actively undermines both the principle and the material base of the collective solidarity and risk-pooling that are fundamental to a public healthcare system. Emphasizing individual freedom and the right to choice, this is a tech-driven mode of accumulation fueled by the privatization of public cost savings. More and better self-care aided by digital technology (at a fee to the public purse) is supposed to save Britain's public health service money and mitigate the crisis of public healthcare funding through reduced visits to the doctor. However, a first evaluation of the service revealed that the use of the symptom checker reduced over time, as patients – especially those above the age of 30 – preferred to speak to someone in person (Ipsos Mori 2019: 31). Moreover, at least in the present model continuity of care is not given because usually there is no longer-term link between particular doctor and the patient (Ipsos Mori 2019: 51). Overall, digital divides are deepened where older persons and persons with more complex needs are less likely to use such apps and find them accessible. Finally, Babylon Health draws on a medical workforce of younger, part-time, and locum (temporarily employed) doctors working from home (ibid.: iii), which follows the trend towards precarious work.

Helping people with disabilities

Yet, platform care is not just about self-care, but also about caring for others. Be My Eyes is a platform that enables volunteers to assist visually impaired people over the internet. The platform is free to users and volunteers, but charges corporations to access its ecosystem and offer support to visually impaired users as a way of optimizing its products and services.[3] In the longer term, the company envisages using the data collected from each interaction between user and volunteer to help with machine learning for the development artificial intelligence (AI) products (Singularity University 2018). This means that the interactions between users (those who provide and receive help) are a learning ground to which corporations pay to gain access in order

---

3   See bemyeyes.com.

to optimize their services to visually impaired users. But also, these interactions serve in the long-run as raw data to optimize machine learning for AI products that the developers of the platform seek to monetize in the long-run. The point here is certainly not to criticize assistive technologies nor the people who offer their time to help visually impaired persons. The concern here is to reflect on the business model of the platform and understand its political economy. We can identify here how there is an affective-ideological dimension at play in enlisting the online (micro-)volunteer labor of individuals wishing to help. This fits with analysis of platforms as spaces where unpaid labor is performed to produce products that are sold by those who control the platforms (Altenried 2020).

Online care agencies

The broader need for care within the household has also facilitated the development of new platforms. One of the most well-known platforms so far is Care.com, a transnationally operating platform that charges private households a subscription fee to connect with care workers offering childcare or eldercare services on an hourly basis. Hired as independent contractors, the workers offering their services are part of a growing precarious workforce in the gig economy. As Ursula Huws (2019: 21) argues, here it is particularly the combination of public service retrenchment and time pressures that push people towards platform services in the area of care. Sybille Bauriedl and Anke Strüver (2020: 274) emphasize that this does little to reshape existing intersectional inequalities with regard to care and social reproduction. Functioning similarly to a temp agency, the platform charges those seeking care services (i.e., the buyers), it does not charge those offering care services (i.e., the sellers), although it offers help with writing a resumé and promoting one's services.[4] The business model relies on the network effect.[5] While one path of analysis is to *follow the money* and understand how care platforms generate profitability, another line of analysis is the affective-ideological dimension. In her survey of a number of different care work platforms, Miranda Hall (2020)

---

4 See care.com.
5 See https://digital.hbs.edu/platform-digit/submission/care-com-a-two-sided-marketplace-for-all-your-care-needs/.

poignantly observes that "these childcare platforms explicitly promote themselves as a silver bullet for the crisis of social reproduction". Hall highlights how the platform also markets its services to companies who have employees with caring responsibilities and explains that "the pitch to these companies is that unexpected caring responsibilities damage productivity and therefore damage profit" (ibid.). In offering a quick and effective crisis management in the face of a lack of time for care as other calls beckon, this kind of empowerment follows what Sara Farris (2017: 131) has termed a "productivist ethics", rendering female empowerment synonymous with labor market participation and freedom from subordination through the chores of care and domestic work. All the while the tab is picked up by precarious gig economy workers brought in to plug the care gaps in a labor market that continues to be stratified by the intersections of gender, race, and class.

Electronic monitoring in homecare services

In Britain, zero hours contracts, which do not guarantee hours for work and often circumvent holiday and sick pay, have come to complement the expansion of the gig economy, because they function on the principle of limiting what is considered to be the time that workers are productive, and hence paid. In the homecare sector, zero hours contracts are particularly prevalent (Bessa et al. 2013: 21) and syncs all too conveniently with electronic monitoring. Electronic monitoring can mean that homecare workers sign in and out by phone of a monitoring system when they arrive at and leave someone's home, scan a tag on the person's file with their smartphone or are tracked via smartphone using Global Positioning System (GPS) technology. Sian Moore and legal scholar Lydia Hayes have researched the introduction of electronic monitoring by local authorities in the UK (Hayes/Moore 2016; Moore/Hayes 2017). They have shown how electronic monitoring facilitates a distinction between time spent working and time not spent working during a shift through the precise monitoring of *contact time* – the duration of a visit in someone's home. In the context of what is known as *time-and-task commissioning*, contact time becomes the metric for commissioning homecare services, as opposed to a set price for a visit. For local authorities on extremely tight budgets due to austerity (Local Government Association 2018: 3), this can be a way to make money go further, with several councils publicly stating the benefits of electronic monitoring for saving money. The consequences for homecare workers are a reduction in wages and a deterioration of working conditions, while service users also suffer the repercussions of care workers being pushed for time. When under severe time pressure, homecare workers routinely have to cut out anything that is not absolutely necessary to getting the job done. This routinely includes the emotional and affective dimensions of caring. Yet, the research that Moore and Hayes conducted showed that care workers may very well log out of the electronic monitoring system to stay beyond the allotted time if something unexpected happens, to offer company to someone who might otherwise be alone or help someone with a task they needed, precisely because they cared (Moore/Hayes 2017: 111). The fact that they would not be paid for this is an example of the ways in which unpaid work motivated by compassion and sense of responsibility is enlisted to prop up an underfunded system.

Care in the community

Paid care workers doing overtime is one aspect of a care fix, another is the reliance on volunteering. Casserole Club is a UK platform currently used by a small number of local authorities in England in the Southeast, North, and Midlands. It involves tools to allow neighbors to coordinate to bring round a meal for someone who might in the past have been eligible for *meals on wheels*. These members of the local community step in voluntarily where local councils have cut such services due to austerity, with the added benefit of conversation and social interaction as a way of combatting social isolation among elderly residents. Local councils pay an annual fee to use the platform (FutureGov n.d.). This is an example of the shift away from local authorities providing inhouse services or commissioning them to renting software for such services to be provided by the community, where the unpaid work of volunteers is enlisted, while digital companies charge local councils high sums on a rolling basis in order to provide the digital infrastructure.

The limits of platform care

There are three ways in which new care platforms offer solutions to the care crisis. First of all, they respond to the crisis of the neoliberal subject and the imperative for permanent productivity and optimization. Self-care apps offer solutions for time-management, but also for managing stress, burnout, and the psychological and physical pressures of managing a healthy work-life balance. This individualizes the problem, offering solutions that are a mix of self-help and self-governance that in turn feeds quantified data about mind and body to the private corporations developing such apps. Second, new care platforms intervene in the crisis of social reproduction within the family and household, or society more generally. Especially where women are no longer available in the household as a resource for care, other, for the most part highly precarious, workers step in to take care of children and pets, or care for elderly relatives. This is even construed as conducive to female empowerment within the confines of financialized capitalism, while externalizing the responsibility for and cost of care and social reproduction further to the individual household. Concurrently, inequality between those who can afford such services and those who cannot increases, not to mention to the precarious employment conditions that prevail in the gig economy, as has been well-documented (Woodcock 2021). Third, in the face of a crisis of public services and the welfare state, digital technologies used to help councils cut costs for staff and services, as well as promising to help curtail health and social care costs. This risks not only acting as a conduit for new kinds of public-private partnerships that facilitate the privatization of public funds, but again, the work and the costs of care and social reproduction are offloaded to individuals and households, as well as to communities and volunteers. In sum, the dominant mode of platform care at present is one of privatization in two senses of the term, namely personal responsibility and marketisation.

In Europe the personal and household services sector is the second-fastest growing sector behind ICT (Decker/Lebrun 2018: 13) and in fact with the platformization of care these two sectors are becoming more intertwined. Critical questions pertain to the extent that these platforms exacerbate the further casualization of labor and pose new challenges with regard to the privatization of public funds, the extraction of profits and the commercial use of data. Further questions pertain to the working conditions are of the digital workers employed as data analysts, software developers, blog and website managers, and so forth and what their relationship is with those gig workers or volunteers providing services, along with the political decisions are automated through algorithms in the provision of care. Moreover, the problem is not always necessarily the technology itself, but the particular ways that technologies are orientated towards or premised upon capitalist valorization and accumulation. And while critical research on the societal (and ecological) consequences of new technologies is crucial (e.g., the dramatic expansion of virtual communication in the wake of coronavirus), making sense of the current platformization of care requires a consideration of the broader political economy of care under conditions of financialized capitalism.

References

Altenried, Moritz (2020): The Platform as Factory: Crowdwork and the Hidden Labor Behind Artificial Intelligence, in: *Capital & Class* 44(2): 145-58.

Babylon Health (2017): NHS 111 Powered by Babylon – Outcomes Evaluation. assets.babylonhealth.com [01.02.2022].

Bailenson, Jeremy (2021): Nonverbal Overload – A Theoretical Argument for the Causes of Zoom Fatigue, in: *Technology, Mind, and Behavior* 2(1). doi: https://doi.org/10.1037/tmb0000030.

Bauriedl, Sybille/Strüver, Anke (2020): Platform Urbanism: Technocapitalist Production of Private and Public Spaces, in: *Urban Planning* 5(4): 267-76.

Barry, Ursula/Jennings, Ciara (2021): Gender Equality: Economic Value of Care from the Perspective of the Applicable EU Funds – An Exploration of an EU Strategy Towards Valuing the Care Economy. https://www.europarl.europa.eu/RegData/etudes/STUD/2021/694784/IPOL_STU(2021)694784_EN.pdf [23.01.2022].

Bessa, Ioulia/Forde, Chris/Moore, Sian/Stuart, Mark (2013): *The National Minimum Wage, Earnings and Hours in the Domiciliary Care Sector*, Leeds: University of Leeds.

Brown, Gareth/Dowling, Emma/Harvie, David/Milburn, Keir (2012): Careless Talk: Social Reproduction and Fault Lines of the Crisis in the United Kingdom, in: *Social Justice* 39(1): 78-98.

Burns, Matthew Seiji (2020): When You Say One Thing but Mean Your Motherboard, in: *Logic Magazine* (11). https://logicmag.io/care/when-you-say-one-thing-but-mean-your-motherboard/ [23.01.2022].

Care Collective (2020): *The Care Manifesto – The Politics of Interdependence*, London/New York: Verso.

Crouch, Hannah (2018): *Doctor's Union Chairman Calls for GP at Hand to Be Scrapped Immediately*, in: Digital Health News, 21.06.2018. https://www.digitalhealth.net/2018/06/doctors-union-chairman-gp-at-hand-scrapped/ [23.01.2021].

Decker, Aurelie/Lebrun, Jean-Francois (2018): PHS Industry Monitor – Statistical Overview of the Personal and Household Services Sector in the EU. http://www.efsi-europe.eu/fileadmin/MEDIA/publications/2018/PHS_Industry_monitor_April_2018.pdf [13.03.2022].

de Henau, Jerome/Himmelweit, Susan (2020): A Care-Led Recovery from Coronavirus. https://wbg.org.uk/wp-content/uploads/2020/06/Care-led-recovery-final.pdf [23.01.22].

Dowling, Emma (2018): Confronting Capital's Care Fix – Care Through the Lens of Democracy, in: *Equality, Diversity and Inclusion: An International Journal* 37(4): 332-46.

Dowling, Emma (2021): *The Care Crisis – What Caused It and How Can We End It?*, London/New York: Verso.

Downey, Andrea (2019): *Babylon's GP at Hand Model Risks 'Destabilising' Care, Professor Warns*, in: Digital Health News, 07.08.2019. https://tinyurl.com/ym3ykup8 [23.01.22].

Elias, Juanita/Pearson, Ruth/Phipps, Belinda/Rai, Shirin M./Smethers, Samantha/Tepe-Belfrage, Daniela (2016): Towards a New Deal for Care and Carers. Report of the PSA Commission on Care, 2016. http://www.commissiononcare.org/wp-content/uploads/2016/10/Web-Care-Comission-Towards-a-new-deal-for-care-and-carers-v1.0.pdf [23.01.2022].

Farris, Sara (2017): *In the Name of Women's Rights – The Rise of Femonationalism*, Durham, NC: Duke University Press.

Federici, Silvia (2012): *Revolution at Point Zero – Housework, Reproduction and Feminist Struggle*, Oakland, CA: Common Notions/PM Press.

Feher, Michel (2009): Self-Appreciation, or the Aspirations of Human Capital, in: *Public Culture* 21(1): 21-41.

Finch, Janet/Groves, Dulcie (1983): *A Labour of Love: Women, Work and Caring*, London: Routledge/Kegan Paul Books.

Fraser, Nancy (2016): Contradictions of Capital and Care, in: *New Left Review* (100): 99-117.

FutureGov (n.d.): Casserole Club – Software as a Service Pricing Document. digitalmarketplace.service.gov.uk [17.01.2020].

Hall, Miranda (2020): *The Crisis of Care.com*, in: Open Democracy, 11.02.2020. https://www.opendemocracy.net/en/oureconomy/crisis-carecom/ [23.01.2022].

Hayes, Lydia J.B./Moore, Sian (2016): Care in a Time of Austerity: The Electronic Monitoring of Homecare Workers' Time, in: *Gender, Work and Organization* 24(4): 329-44.

Harvey, David (1975): The Geography of Capitalist Accumulation: A Reconstruction of the Marxian Theory, in: *Antipode Journal of Radical Geography* 7(2): 9-21.

Harvey, David (1982): *The Limits to Capital*, Oxford: Oxford University Press.

Himmelweit, Susan (2007): The Prospects for Caring: Economic Theory and Policy Analysis, in: *Cambridge Journal of Economics* 31(4): 581-99.

Huws, Ursula (2019): The Hassle of Housework: Digitalization and the Commodification of Domestic Labour, in: *Feminist Review* 123(1): 8-23.

Inkster, Becky/O'Brien, Ross/Selby, Emma/Joshi, Smriti/Subramanian, Vinod/Kadaba, Madhura/Schroeder, Knut/Godson, Suzi/Comley, Kerstyn/Vollmer, Sebastian J./Mateen, Bilal A. (2020): Digital Health Management During and Beyond the COVID-19 Pandemic: Opportunities, Barriers, and Recommendations, in: *JMIR Mental Health* 7(7). doi: https://doi.org/10.2196/19246.

Ipsos Mori/York Health Economics Consortium/Salisbury, Chris for NHS Hammersmith and Fulham CCG and NHS England (2019): Evaluation of Babylon GP at Hand – Final Evaluation Report. https://www.hammersmithfulhamccg.nhs.uk/media/156123/Evaluation-of-Babylon-GP-at-Hand-Final-Report.pdf [13.03.2022].

Local Government Association (2018): Local Government Funding: Moving the Conversation On. https://www.local.gov.uk/sites/default/files/documents/5.40_01_Finance%20publication_WEB_0.pdf [13.03.2022].

Lohmann, Larry (2019): Labour, Justice and the Mechanization of Interpretation, in: *Development* 62(1): 43-52.

Moore, Sian/Hayes, Lydia J.B. (2017): Taking Worker Productivity to a New Level? Electronic Monitoring in Homecare: The (Re)production of Unpaid Labour, in: *New Technology, Work and Employment* 32(2): 101-14.

Pettinger, Lynn (2019): *What's Wrong with Work?*, Bristol: Policy Press.

Rai, Shirin/Hoskyns, Catherine/Thomas, Dania (2013): Depletion – the Cost of Social Reproduction, in: *International Feminist Journal of Politics* 16(1): 86-105.

Ratcliffe, Rebecca (2017): *Thousands Go Online for Therapy. But Does It Work?*, in: The Guardian, 12.02.2017. https://www.theguardian.com/society/2017/feb/12/online-therapy-thousands-but-does-it-work [01.02.2022].

Rosen, Ruth (2007): *The Care Crisis*, in: The Nation, 27.02.2007. https://www.thenation.com/article/archive/care-crisis/ [23.01.2022].

Silver, Beverly (2012): *Forces of Labor: Workers' Movements and Globalization Since 1870*, Cambridge: Cambridge University Press.

Singularity University (2018): Be My Eyes Case Study – Startup Customer Stories. https://tinyurl.com/2fecbk6r [17.01.2020].

Srnicek, Nick (2017): *Platform Capitalism*, Cambridge/Malden: Polity.

Wajcman, Judy (2006): New Connections: Social Studies of Science and Technology and Studies of Work, in: *Work, Employment and Society* 20(4): 773-86.

Weeks, Kathi (2011): *The Problem with Work. Feminism, Marxism, Antiwork Politics, and Postwork Imaginaries*, Durham, NC: Duke University Press.

Woodcock, Jamie (2021): *The Fight Against Platform Capitalism: An Inquiry into the Global Struggles of the Gig Economy*, London: University of Westminster Press.

Second Shift 2.0
Intensifying Housework in Platform Urbanism

Maartje Roelofsen & Kiley Goyette

Introduction

Digital platforms which allow people to earn extra income, sometimes glossed as the *gig economy*, have given rise to forms of commodified labor which may not be new in terms of the tasks undertaken but have entered spaces that may not have been previously accessible and enrolled workers who were not necessarily previously involved in these tasks. Spaces of work and of leisure in the city are transformed through these platforms, including the home as a workplace, such as in the case of short-term rental platforms like Airbnb. These transformations are modulated by race, class, age, and gender, not only of the positionality of individuals participating in platform-mediated labor, but also through the attitudes and ideologies that inform the ways the work itself is imagined.

With this chapter we wish to contribute to the burgeoning literature on the politics and practices of labor in platform urbanism (Barns 2020; Chen 2017; Ravenelle 2019; Richardson 2016; van Doorn 2017; 2020) and on short-term rental platforms in particular (e.g., Borm 2017; Bosma 2019; 2022; Goyette 2021; Knaus 2020; Roelofsen 2018; Roelofsen/Minca 2018; Saturino/Sousa 2019). Platform urbanism suggests that digital platforms are increasingly central to dynamic socio-spatial processes of urban transformation (Barns 2020). Aside from providing spaces of connection and socialization, platforms have become embedded in and central to urban governance, urban infrastructures, and urban economies (van Doorn 2020). By monetizing domestic space and forms of work that were previously considered *unproductive* (Sadowski 2020), platforms like Airbnb play an important role in further blurring the boundaries between spheres of production and reproduction in cities (Knaus/Margies/Schilling 2021). Yet, digital platforms tend to reproduce rather than eliminate existing socio-spatial inequalities, both in terms of the economic benefits that are produced through urban platform work (Schor 2020) and the way different types of work and workers are valued socially (van Doorn 2017). Leszczynski (2020: 190) notes that a significant share of platform urbanism scholarship has been dominated by "dystopian critiques of the universal capitalist and/or neoliberal essence of platforms and the platform-mediated city". And indeed, within the Airbnb-centric literature, there tends to prevail a theoretical and empirical tendency to foreground how the platform shapes cities merely by capitalist interest. Instead, in this chapter we focus on everyday interactions and attend to how platform-mediated spaces and places, like the Airbnb-ed home, are always already socially produced (ibid.). We explore how Airbnb hosts approach the labor of operating short-term rental accommodations, a means of earning extra income which has grown rapidly around the world since the platform first launched in 2008. We examine how hosts manage the demands of hosting while balancing this labor with the other duties in their lives such as housework, childcare, and paid employment. Airbnb is unique among gig economy platforms in that not only do hosts "work from home" (Doling/Arundel 2020), but they also welcome other people *into* this major site of social reproduction for their household. By social reproduction labor we refer to "various kinds of work – mental, manual, and emotional – aimed at providing the historically and socially, as well as biologically, defined care necessary to maintain existing life and to reproduce the next generation" (Laslett/Brenner 1989: 383). We will argue that, for those households that turn to hosting to supplement their regular income sources, strategies to accommodate the added social reproduction labor that is required when taking in guests result in divisions of labor which often mirror historical divisions in terms of location, gender, race, and other social categories.

In this study, we draw on over four years of ethnographic work, which was carried out by Maartje Roelofsen over different periods of time between March 2015 and December 2020. In-depth semi-structured interviews were carried out with 33 Airbnb hosts living and working in Bulgaria, Denmark, Ghana, and the Netherlands. The interviews with hosts in Bulgaria were carried out face-to-face, whereas the interviews with the hosts living in other countries were mostly conducted through video-conferencing software. These episodes of data collection relied on *snowball sampling*, meaning that the participants helped us connect with other potential research participants. The participants consist of 16 men and 17 women representing 29 households. Of these 33 hosts,

25 hosts were engaged in full-time paid employment (including self-employment), three hosts were students, two hosts were homemakers, and three hosts were pensioners. All participants in this study were white except for the participants Sally, who identified as a Black woman, and Mahjoub, who identified as a Moroccan-Belgian migrant man. Fourteen households rented out a room within their homes and stayed with their guests on the premises. Out of these households, seven were single-person households of hosts who either identified as widowers, singles, or in a relationship with someone they did not co-habit with. The other seven households who rented out rooms, consisted of hosts who co-habited with their partners, friends, or family members. 14 households rented out their entire primary or secondary homes temporarily (nine) or permanently (five) and did not stay with their guests. Out of these households, eleven lived in a heterosexual co-habiting couple form and three households were made up of single hosts. Three couples were interviewed together, while the other interviews were carried out with an individual household member.

In this chapter, we examine the complexities of power, privilege, and representation that shape Airbnb work by considering how the dynamics between gender and other social categories are reflected in who is assigned the various types of labor involved in taking guests. We highlight how this labor is distributed within different household compositions, including couples, singles, families, and cohabiting friends, when accommodating the extra social reproduction labor that hosting Airbnb guests demands.

Intensifying housework in short-term rental platforms

Airbnb and other short-term rental platforms transform the home-as-workspace by creating a monetary incentive to bring guests into the home, adding their social reproduction needs and the emotional labor of hosting on to the existing household reproduction. Home sharing, as Airbnb calls its service, therefore intensifies the social reproduction labor of the household. Since guests pay for these services, it could be tempting to read this as an incarnation of the feminist campaign of the 1970s, *Wages for Housework* (Dalla Costa/James 1975): rather than housework being an unpaid *labor of love* expected of a housewife (the architype at the center of the critique), they are instead materially compensated with money. But the goal of Wages for Housework was not to provide houseworkers with a wage (Federici 1975);

housework had already been paid in many instances, but these workers, often racialized women, remained in exploitative and subordinate positions despite earning a wage (Glenn 1991; 1992; Collins 1990). The Wages for Housework campaign attacked the ways in which housework – and by extension all female-coded labor – was *ideologically* devalued despite being integral to male-coded *productive* labor (Federici 1975; Weeks 2011). That housework is not *really* work, despite its obvious necessity, is a notion that persists in short-term rentals. Housework is often still seen as incidental or even absent in media representations, where Airbnb stays tend to be romanticized as mere 'experiences' of local life and space. Similarly, some hosts in this study brushed off Airbnb housework as merely part of their regular household activities. Yet the interviews also suggest that the additional labor of hosting is enough to require specific social and economic (re-)arrangements to address this added work.

An intensification of social reproduction labor in short-term rentals is created through the extra labor created by the guest(s), as in the physical and emotional labor that their presence demands, but also through increased standards of cleanliness related to hosting. On the most basic level, rooms must be prepared for use by the guest, and rounds of communication assure their needs are met. Additionally, some strenuous and/or undesirable tasks that were usually only done occasionally in the household must now be done for each guest. Some hosts viewed this in a positive light, as illustrated by Maggie, a 29-year-old self-employed social worker in Sofia, Bulgaria who rented out a room in her apartment on Airbnb for additional income: "I'm not crazy about cleaning, but I don't mind it, like, I clean my flat anyways. So, yeah, I just make sure it's like even cleaner when there's someone else. Which is quite nice, to have the house, like spotless, cause when it's just me it's like 'ok I'm not going to do the dusting right now'." The gratification that Maggie felt from doing the household tasks that she usually found undesirable was echoed by other hosts such as Rose, a 75-year-old pensioner in Aarhus, Denmark, who rented out a room in her rental apartment: "What I really do like with having the guests is, when you become a pensioner, you can get quite lazy and you can have stuff lying about the kitchen and haven't washed the dishes. But when they are here, I am happy about the fact that I actually get the dishes washed. So, it really has some benefits." Although these women interpret having a clean house as a benefit of being pushed to do this work, it is nonetheless an investment of their time that they might not otherwise make to attain a standard of cleanliness higher than what they find acceptable in their everyday.

This higher standard of cleanliness when taking in guests is reinforced in Airbnb's platform through the listing's cleanliness rating. Joanna, a 30-year-old self-employed tour guide in Sofia, Bulgaria who would sleep in her living room when she rented out her room on Airbnb, noted the difference between hosting through a free home sharing platform and Airbnb: "For me, [non-paying] Couchsurfers can say about my place that it is dirty and I don't care about it. But if Airbnb guests rate my place as dirty then I'm going to lose opportunities. I mean if my rating drops down then... it's a business after all. I'm doing it for money." Unlike the Couchsurfing platform, on Airbnb the cleanliness rating is an important factor determining the listing's position in Airbnb's search results and influences whether they are selected (or passed over!) by guests (Minca/Roelofsen 2021). Success on the platform is tied to the cleanliness expectations of the guests who rate them, whether the hosts get satisfaction from having a clean home or not. The added work that hosts face to prepare for and sustain an Airbnb stay, between two to four hours per turnover according to our participants, must be addressed without an increase in hours in the day. What are the strategies hosts use to address them? And who does the housework in short-term rentals?

Arlie Russell Hochschild considers similar questions in her book *The Second Shift* (1989), which charts how two-career heterosexual couples with young children in the United States went about the division of social reproductive labor, including housework, childcare, and other aspects of daily life that take place after the paying work was done. Hochschild asked who does the housework when it becomes concentrated in fewer hours – at least in comparison with households where a housewife assumed these responsibilities, a model which had come to be considered the norm in middle-class America until the 1960s when women started to enter the paid workforce in higher numbers. Hochschild called these unpaid tasks at home (which amounted to an extra month of work) the *second shift*, with the *first* shift being renumerated work for an employer. In the cases examined in Hochschild's study, the difference between the first and second shift was clear. The tasks were distinct, either in their location outside the home, or, in the case of those who worked from home, their nature. With short-term rental hosting, however, the nature of the tasks can be identical to those necessary for the household's own social reproduction (e.g., cleaning a toilet, making breakfast). Therefore, the distinction between income-generating social reproduction labor for the Airbnb guest and the necessary reproduction labor for the household is not always clear. For this reason, we call the added housework that results from hosting on the Airbnb platform the *second shift 2.0*.

Although hosting requires quantitatively more housework, hosts' attitudes toward this labor do not seem to be transformed qualitatively, perhaps because of this blurred distinction. Many participants still consider Airbnb housework as taken-for-granted activities or as a 'natural attribute' of the home, and it is often not seen as *real* work despite being added as part of the income-generating activity of hosting. "You also clean for yourself anyway, so it's not like you do it especially for them. I did not see Airbnb-related work as work. I just made my home available", says Laurens, a 37-year-old former Airbnb host who rented out a room in his apartment in Rotterdam, the Netherlands. Another participant noted that because the money generated from hosting goes directly into supporting the social reproduction of their household, it was unnecessary to make a distinction between housework for Airbnb or for their own needs: "I see cleaning for our Airbnb guests as something that we do for ourselves because in the end we use the money that we earn to go on holidays or to save money, we use that money to treat ourselves. In that sense, I view it as part of our private lives, not as work. I don't experience it as work. It's an extension of how we live and want to live." (Tina, a 39-year-old host who rented out her entire home occasionally with her partner Mahjoub) As these hosts' statements suggest, housework for the household's own needs and housework for guests was generally seen a single category of work regardless of whether it was income-generating or not.

Divisions of Airbnb labor and the role of household members

One important contribution of Hochschild's study was highlighting the role of gender ideologies in the division of labor at home. Even though both partners in the couples studied were working in paid employment, the study concluded that women largely continued to take on more or all responsibility for the unpaid work at home compared to their partners and spouses. It demonstrates that the gendered division of labor in the home is as much social as structural, and that how this work is negotiated between parties is shaped by the ideologies held by the individuals involved. Housework is clearly gendered, but not all women's work is valued equally, and the heaviest, dirtiest work is often pushed off onto racialized women. Critiques of Hochschild's work point to the way it failed to provide a critical comparative historical analysis of reproductive labor in the United States (Brailey/Slatton 2019). Marginalized groups of working women have throughout history engaged in unpaid, underpaid, involuntary, devalued labor, often doing work in the homes of other women. Mignon Duffy (2007) similarly argued that research which focused on women's entrance in the labor market in the 1970s was important, yet also "obscured the empirical reality that Black women, immigrant women, and poor women had been engaged in paid market work in large numbers for many decades" (ibid.: 314). Dorothy Roberts (1997) conceptualized the racial division of labor in housework as a dichotomy. *Spiritual housework* encompassed such tasks which aligned with white bourgeois femininity, such as educating children, decorating the home, or managing servants. By contrast, *menial housework*, or what Duffy simply refers to as *the dirty work*, was the physically demanding and thankless drudgery like cleaning, cooking, laundry, and daily childcare that women with means chose to delegate. Within the hospitality and tourism sector, cleaning is oftentimes referred to as *back-of-house* work (Zampoukos 2021). Back-of-house work is not only rigidly gender-segregated and oftentimes carried out by racial or ethnic minorities, but it is also spatially segregated: it is work that usually takes place out of the sight of guests, whereas *front-of-house* work signifies work that requires presence and social interaction with guests, such as reception work and hostessing. In the hospitality and tourism industry, most women still occupy lower-level jobs that are typically coded as female and associated with housework, such as cleaning, caring, and maintaining a pleasant ambience (Cole 2018). In the context of platform urbanism, such histories and conceptualizations of labor are likely to persist. Niels van Doorn (2017) astutely outlined ways labor platforms perpetuate historical race and gender inequalities in low-end service work. Specific to short-term rentals, Kiley Goyette (2021) has traced how gender ideologies framed the importance of taking lodgers and boarders for women's supplemental income strategies in early industrial cities and pointed to continuities with platform-mediated short-term rentals in the twenty-first century. Attention to historical practices and attitudes toward this work is crucial to any analysis of how the social reproduction labor for short-term rentals is negotiated. Accounts from the research participants demonstrate a division of labor among household members and outsourcing of labor which sometimes reflect gendered, classed, and racialized conceptions of housework, especially cleaning as women's work and dirty work, which the following sections outline.

Divisions of labor among ethno-racially mixed couples

This study's participants included two ethno-racially mixed couples: Sally, a Black woman and full-time housewife in a relationship with Joost, a white man who has a paid full-time job; and Mahjoub, a Moroccan-Belgian man full-time who has a paid full-time job and is in a relationship with Tina, a white woman, who also has a paid full-time job. Sally and Joost have class privileges which are evident in the way housework was organized in their primary home as well as their second home which they rented on Airbnb on a full-time basis. In their primary home they maintained what might be considered a 'traditional' gendered division of housework. Sally took on tasks associated with women's work such as cooking, educating the children, and bringing them to school, while Joost predominantly worked his paid full-time job, doing almost no housework other than helping to get the children ready for school. But Sally and Joost also hired a woman to carry out the more physically demanding, menial housework like cleaning. In their Airbnb Sally maintained both front- and back-of-house work but was also supported by another woman hired for back-of-house tasks. Concierge work was also outsourced to the guards who were always on site and ready to assist their Airbnb guests during their stay. Joost, on the other hand, took care of the administration and finances in relation to their Airbnb-ed home, and was in charge of the online, written communication with guests and how their home was visually and textually represented on the platform. Sally took on the majority of the second shift at home and part of the back-of-house work of the second shift 2.0 of their Airbnb, which is consistent with the gendered and racialized ideologies of housework. As a relatively affluent woman, however, she did so with the assistance of hired help, reflecting her class position, and allowed her to take on front-of-house work in the Airbnb.

In a contrasting example, Tina and Mahjoub – the other ethno-racially mixed couple in our study who both worked full-time paid jobs – considered their division of housework at home and Airbnb work to be "egalitarian". They aimed to spend the same amount of time preparing their home for the Airbnb guests' stay as well as for their regular housework. The division of cleaning tasks was arranged based on their individual preferences. However, Mahjoub's work is intentionally obscured from the guest's view. As he explained:

"We do everything in Tina's name. The listing is in Tina's name, it shows her head, a blond woman. I do communicate with the guests, but I always undersign with her name. But if for some reason I have to do the check-in by myself, I will send the last message to our guests in Tina's name and tell them Tina can't be there but Tina's partner Mahjoub will be there."

He explained that although there were certain administrative reasons to keep Tina's profile as the host at first, they also felt guests might find a white woman's profile more trustworthy compared to Mahjoub's with his foreign-sounding name and racialized appearance. Although Mahjoub engaged in typically male front-of-house work by communicating with the guests, he remained hidden as if he were in the back-of-house, out of sight as a racialized worker, through the virtual interface and Tina's avatar.

Divisions of labor and household relations

The Airbnb households interviewed in this study represent a diversity of household structures beyond the normative nuclear family that were the focus of Hochschild's study. Some hosts lived in co-habiting couples, but some were also singles, friends, adult children, or intergenerational households. Even in non-couple households, starkly gendered divisions of labor can be seen. Coco, a 33-year-old clinical psychology student in Sofia, Bulgaria, worked as a freelance journalist and rented out the apartment she shared with her male housemate. Although they split the income from Airbnb, Coco estimated that she did 90 % of the work related to hosting. In part, this was due to her work as a freelancer being more flexible, so she was able to be available when guests arrived and to do the turnover between. But Coco was clear that her housemate did not like cleaning and when he did, it was not well done: "I share the Airbnb money with the roommate. But he does not put in as much effort as I do. So, we have fights about this sometimes. But he's a man. Sometimes he will say 'ok, I will clean this time' and then I check and the cleaning is not so…" Gender ideologies related to cleaning work appear to be clearly expressed here. Coco explained that she is fine with doing the work although she doesn't love cleaning, but she felt "pissed off" because she did it alone. Their apartment was large and in poor condition, which made cleaning more difficult. But the standards of cleanliness imposed by the platform also meant she could not rely on her housemate's poor-quality work if she hoped to make a reliable income through taking guests.

While Coco took on the second shift 2.0 largely by herself, a common strategy among hosts dealing with the intensification of housework was to seek help from family members or to hire help. Although the focus of Hochschild's study was the division of labor of couples, she observed that her participants sought help from (usually female) relatives and outside help, especially to meet the demands of childcare. Among the Airbnb hosts interviewed, many relied on their parents for help, or occasionally siblings or older children. Vera, a 26-year-old IT specialist, relied on her mother to clean their Airbnb, as did Niko, a 27-year-old marketing executive, both hosting in Sofia. These young people, fluent in English and tech savvy, retained most of the front-of-house work, while they described their mothers as being suited to the cleaning work, either "enjoying" it or at least being "used to it". They also saw preparing for guests as a way for their mothers to pass their time, earn a little money, and interact with people from around the world.

It was not only the hosts' mothers who helped with the second shift 2.0, such as in the case of Jeny, a 25-year-old student who rented out her sister's old room in her family home in Sofia. Both her mother and father helped her prepare for and take care of the guests, but rather than a division of labor by gender, what work each person contributed depended mainly on their work schedule. As Jeny's mother was often out of town for work, it was her father who helped the most with the cleaning and welcoming guests. The flexibility of a family member's schedule was a common reason for the division of labor, particularly for those who rented out their homes full time, as the cleaning between check-out of one guest and check-in of the next usually needed to take place in the middle of the day. Bruna, a teacher, was only able to help her husband Bobo with hosting duties in their Sofia apartment if there was an extra day between bookings or if the checkout was on the weekends. Some hosting households dealt with pressures related to the second shift 2.0 by intentionally keeping time between bookings. Jamilla, a 28-year-old social worker, decided to spread out the time between guests and limit the number of stays per month in order to keep the workload "fair" for her mother, who cleaned her Airbnb in Copenhagen, Denmark, while she was abroad. Other hosts reported a similar strategy when faced with the more strenuous cleaning requirements of the COVID-19 pandemic. Peter, a 58-year-old student counsellor who hosted in Aarhus with his partner, explained: "It is a pleasure to welcome the guest. Cleaning has been challenging though [...]. That is why we have often made sure to block one day in the calendar, so it will not become stressful for us to take care of cleaning." Allowing more time for cleaning clearly reduced the stress of this work and may also help accommodate those with less flexible work schedules.

Outsourcing Airbnb labor to waged workers

Some hosts hired outside help to address the cleaning for their Airbnb. The majority of the hosts who rented out entire homes outsourced the cleaning and other back-of-house labor to independent cleaners, agencies, or family members, unlike hosts who only rented out rooms who mostly took care of the cleaning work themselves (see also Bosma 2022). Of the hosts in our study, the ones who hired cleaners for their Airbnb already employed a cleaner for their own home. Hiring a "cleaning lady" (as all the interviewees called their cleaners) was an investment of money that some hosts felt was too great a cost, but it ensured a quality cleaning. "The one time that I did not get a five-star review was when I had cleaned the apartment myself. So, I will never do that again", laughed Iannos, a 33-year-old man who rented his secondary apartment in Sofia, Bulgaria. Flexibility was sometimes an issue with hired cleaners as well, as some would not be available for last minute bookings, which is how Iannos and other hosts who hired cleaners would on occasion find themselves doing the cleaning.

Significantly, the front-of-house work that ensures Airbnb encounters are amiable or emotionally satisfying was usually still carried out by the hosts who outsourced the cleaning work. There were various motivations for retaining these tasks. Hosts used the moment of welcome to vet their guests and to nudge them towards responsible behavior in their homes. According to Tim, a 42-year-old project manager who occasionally rented out his entire home in Amsterdam, the Netherlands, which was already cleaned by a woman he hired, but now was also cleaned by her before and after an Airbnb stay, commented:

"I only asked the cleaning lady once to do the check-in as well as my brother and mother but did it myself usually. I found it more reassuring. [...] Usually, I would communicate with [the guests], see how they responded when I would say 'please be nice to my neighbors'. I would have some time to have a brief chat with them. Usually things were OK."

Other reasons for retaining the front-of-house work were related to hosts' technology and language skills, which they perceived to be superior to those who carry out the cleaning work, as in the case of the mothers of Vera and Niko mentioned above. This was not always the case, however, as Bobo took care of the majority of guest interactions despite having weak English, meanwhile his wife Bruna was an English teacher whose schedule largely prevented her from assuming this work.

Concluding remarks

In this chapter, we set out to make visible the work involved in hosting on Airbnb in platform urbanism. We also questioned how gender ideologies and attitudes towards housework shaped the spaces and divisions of Airbnb work, particularly vis-à-vis other forms of paid and unpaid work already carried out in these households. The examples highlighted above illustrate some ways that households address the intensification of housework related to the additional needs of guests and raised standards of cleanliness required for hosting, which we refer to in this chapter as the second shift 2.0. Divisions of Airbnb labor often reflect and manifest existing gender ideologies within the households that consist of both men and women, such as the cohabiting couples, and in the households of men living alone who relied on the help of hired cleaning ladies. In these households, women mostly do the dirty work and men maintain the managerial front-of-house work. Although there were only two non-white, racialized hosts in our study, they both carried out back-of-house work to some extent. Both also took part in front-of-house work in ways that reflect the intersection of gender and class. When communicating with their guests through the Airbnb platform about their future stay, one of these hosts engaged in typically male front-of-house work, but remained *virtually* invisible behind the image of his white partner until guests literally arrived at their doorstep. Likewise, the other racialized host was responsible for tasks typical to her gender, but her class position allowed her to delegate the dirty work to hired help, freeing her to engage in front-of-house work such as welcoming guests.

While some hosts dealt with the second shift 2.0 by hiring cleaning workers, others sought help from family members. Mothers were often assigned responsibility for cleaning Airbnbs, with the work depicted as something that was natural or enjoyable for them. Which family members contributed also depended on whether their work schedule could accommodate the timing of guest departure and arrival. Interestingly, and perhaps unsurprisingly, a generational division of labor appeared in which the front-of-house work was assumed by young adult children with strong language and technology skills, while the back-of-house tasks were taken on by fathers as well as mothers. This division of labor may have also been related to the schedules of the presumably retired parents, as the hosts saw Airbnb work as a valuable way for their parents to occupy their time. Finally, place and mobility may be a factor in this generational division of labor as well. Parents who helped with the second shift 2.0 often lived in or near the property, which was often the former room or residence of the host who had moved to another neighborhood or was living abroad. Through the platform, many front-of-house tasks can be done remotely, but the dirty work remains fixed in place and relies on workers who are physically present in conjunction with the timing and scheduling demands for busy properties.

These findings reflect ways that the work required for short-term rental platforms like Airbnb intensifies the social reproduction demands on hosting households, whose strategies to accommodate this second shift 2.0 at times reflect and reproduce historical ideologies around housework and at other times organize this labor in different ways. Platform urbanism literature on Airbnb has understandably focused on how such platforms are shaping access to housing and issues of urban governance (van Doorn 2020; Wachsmuth/ Weisler 2018). This chapter contributes to platform urbanism scholarship by attending to the mundane reconfigurations of labor relations within the home that are brought about by users' engagement with Airbnb. In so doing, we reaffirm the social reproduction of housework as fundamental to urban life and to platform urbanism, whether done as a labor of love or commodified, for immediate family or complete strangers. For those households that take in guests by hosting through short-term rental platforms like Airbnb, housework is shaped by the conditions that the platforms introduce. Yet, at the same time, platform enterprises depend on the (inter)actions of hosts, hired workers, family members, and co-habitants. The way these households organize this work in response is informed by ideologies around the work and its workers as much as the technologies, but neither is it over-determined by them.

We suggest that future research in platform urbanism could further explore the blurring and intensification of social reproduction labor resulting from participation in short-term rental platforms like Airbnb in different contexts, attentive to both how they reproduce and deviate from historical patterns of labor. Scholarship should continue to investigate how platform companies benefit from undervalued forms work already taking place within households, and how availing of these platforms shape and reshape social relations and ideologies modulated by gender, race, age, and class.

Acknowledgements

Maartje Roelofsen's visit to Bulgaria and related fieldwork was supported by the University of Graz Doctoral Stipend and the 2015 Rudi Roth Grant. Maartje Roelofsen wishes to acknowledge Simon Lind Fischer at Erhvervsakademi Dania for collaborating on their research project *Accommodating Guests During Pandemic Times* and for being able to draw on the related data that underpins this study. Maartje Roelofsen's research was supported by the Universitat Oberta de Catalunya postdoctoral stay. Kiley Goyette is supported in part by funding from the Social Sciences and Human Research Council of Canada.

References

Barns, Sarah (2020): *Platform Urbanism: Negotiating Platform Ecosystems in Connected Cities*, Singapore: Palgrave Macmillan.

Borm, Brigitte (2017): Welcome Home. An Ethnography on the Experiences of Airbnb Hosts in Commodifying Their Homes, in: Frömming, Urte Undine/Köhn, Steffen/Fox, Samantha/Terry, Mike (eds.): *Digital Environments. Ethnographic Perspectives across Global Online and Offline Spaces*, Bielefeld: transcript: 39-52.

Bosma, Jelke R. (2019): *Labor and Property on Airbnb*, in: Platform Labor, 16.06.2019. https://platformlabor.net/blog/labor-and-property-on-airbnb [10.02.2022].

Bosma, Jelke R. (2022): Platformed Professionalization: Labor, Assets, and Earning a Livelihood through Airbnb, in: *Environment and Planning A: Economy and Space* 54(4): 595-610.

Brailey, Carla D./Slatton, Brittany C. (2019): Women, Work, and Inequality in the U.S.: Revising the Second Shift, in: *Journal of Sociology and Social Work* 7(1): 29-35.

Chen, Julie Yujie (2017): Thrown under the Bus and Outrunning It! The Logic of Didi and Taxi Drivers' Labour and Activism in the on-Demand Economy, in: *New Media & Society* 20(8): 2691-711.

Cole, Stroma (ed.) (2018): *Gender Equality and Tourism. Beyond Empowerment*, Wallingford, UK/Boston, MA: CABI.

Collins, Patricia Hill (1990): *Black Feminist Thought: Knowledge, Consciousness, and the Politics of Empowerment*, New York: Routledge.

Dalla Costa, Mariarosa/James, Selma (1975): *The Power of Women and the Subversion of the Community*, Bristol: Falling Wall Press.

Doling, John/Arundel, Rowan (2020): The Home as Workplace: A Challenge for Housing Research, in: *Housing, Theory and Society* 39(1): 1-20.

Duffy, Mignon (2007): Doing the Dirty Work: Gender, Race, and Reproductive Labor in Historical Perspective, in: *Gender & Society* 21(3): 313-36.

Federici, Silvia (1975): *Wages against Housework*, Bristol, UK: Falling Wall Press.

Glenn, Evelyn Nakano (1991): Cleaning up/Kept down: A Historical Perspective on Racial Inequality in Women's Work, in: *Stanford Law Review* 43(6): 1333-56.

Glenn, Evelyn Nakano (1992): From Servitude to Service Work: Historical Continuities in the Racial Division of Paid Reproductive Labor, in: *Signs* 18(1): 1-43.

Goyette, Kiley (2021): 'Making Ends Meet' by Renting Homes to Strangers: Historicizing Airbnb through Women's Supplemental Income, in: *City* 25(3-4): 332-54.

Hochschild, Arlie Russell (1989): *The Second Shift*, New York, NY: Avon Books.

Knaus, Katharina (2020): At Home with Guests – Discussing Hosting on Airbnb through the Lens of Labour, in: *Applied Mobilities* 5(1): 68-85.

Knaus, Katharina/Margies, Nina/Schilling, Hannah (2021): Thinking the City through Work: Blurring Boundaries of Production and Reproduction in the Age of Digital Capitalism, in: *City* 25(3-4): 303-14.

Laslett, Barbara/Brenner, Johanna (1989): Gender and Social Reproduction: Historical Perspectives, in: *Annual Review of Sociology* 15: 381-404.

Leszczynski, Agnieszka (2020): Glitchy Vignettes of Platform Urbanism, in: *Environment and Planning D: Society and Space* 38(2): 189-208.

Minca, Claudio/Roelofsen, Maartje (2021): Becoming AirbnBeings: On Datafication and the Quantified Self in Tourism, in: *Tourism Geographies* 23(4): 743-64.

Ravenelle, Alexandrea J. (2019): *Hustle and Gig: Struggling and Surviving in the Sharing Economy*, Oakland, CA: University of California Press.

Richardson, Lizzie (2016): Feminist Geographies of Digital Work, in: *Progress in Human Geography* 42(2): 244-63.

Roberts, Dorothy E. (1997): Spiritual and Menial Housework, in: *Yale Journal of Law & Feminism* 9(1): 51-80.

Roelofsen, Maartje (2018): Performing "Home" in the Sharing Economies of Tourism: The Airbnb Experience in Sofia, Bulgaria, in: *Fennia* 196(1): 24-42.

Roelofsen, Maartje/Claudio Minca (2018): The Superhost. Biopolitics, Home and Community in the Airbnb Dream-World of Global Hospitality, in: *Geoforum* 91 (May): 170-81.

Sadowski, Jathan (2020): Cyberspace and Cityscapes: On the Emergence of Platform Urbanism, in: *Urban Geography* 41(3): 448-52.

Saturino, Rodrigo/Sousa, Helena (2019): Hosting as a Lifestyle: The Case of Airbnb Digital Platform and Lisbon Hosts, in: *Partecipazione e Conflitto* 12(3): 794-818.

Schor, Juliet (2020): *After the Gig: How the Sharing Economy Got Hijacked and How to Win It Back*, Oakland, CA: University of California Press.

van Doorn, Niels (2017): Platform Labor: On the Gendered and Racialized Exploitation of Low-Income Service Work in the 'on-Demand' Economy, in: *Information, Communication & Society* 20(6): 898-914.

van Doorn, Niels (2020): A New Institution on the Block: On Platform Urbanism and Airbnb Citizenship, in: *New Media & Society* 22(10): 1808-26.

Wachsmuth, David/Weisler, Alexander (2018): Airbnb and the Rent Gap: Gentrification through the Sharing Economy, in: *Environment and Planning A: Economy and Space* 50(6): 1147-70.

Weeks, Kathi (2011): *The Problem with Work: Feminism, Marxism, Antiwork Politics, and Postwork Imaginaries*, Durham: Duke University Press.

Zampoukos, Kristina (2021): The Hospitable Body at Work – A Research Agenda, in: *Gender, Work & Organization* 28(5): 1726-40.

"When Clean Angels Calls, I Run"
Working Conditions of a Gigified Care-Worker

Marisol Keller

>I am standing in the middle of a store when I receive my first call from Clean Angels. I am rather unprepared at first. I've had some annoying calls from call centers in the last few days. That's why I am a little bit unfriendly to the employee of Clean Angels at first, because I assume that it is a call center call again. Also, I am not expecting a call from Clean Angels at all – and definitely not at this time of day. Even so, the woman is very friendly and asks for references from my previous cleaning jobs. She adds that it is important for me to send a reference, because Clean Angels sees itself as an intermediary and therefore has to guarantee a certain quality. She emphasizes that I will not be employed through the platform, but directly with their customers.
>
>I tell her that I will try to organize a reference. She says that without one, unfortunately they will not be able to consider my application. I immediately start to think about how I can organize the reference. I do not have any contact with my former employers and I feel a little bit embarrassed to ask them for a reference. Then I remember that I am standing in a store and continue shopping (Fieldnotes 08.10.2020).

The incident described above was my first personal contact with Clean Angels, a digital platform that matches gigs in the domestic house cleaning sector. In the context of my research project, I conducted autoethnographic fieldwork on the platform. In this chapter, I hope to provide a differentiated view of the consequences of platform labor architecture for workers' everyday lives. While ride hailing platforms or courier service platforms have been the subject of intense attention (cf. Berg et al. 2018; Ivanova et al. 2018) less is known about the experiences in the care-sector.

In what follows, I shine a light on the kind of domestic house cleaning that is mediated via digital platforms. In line with feminist geographers, I identify platform workers not simply as laborers but as individuals living within complex social relations. In addition, the concept of platform urbanisms helps me to understand the subjective experiences of a worker within the urban space.

While a growing body of literature discusses the logics and realities of digital care platforms (e.g., Ivanova et al. 2018; Shapiro 2018; van Doorn 2021), lately calls for more knowledge about subjective perceptions, positions, and realities within the gig economy have gained momentum (Altenried/Dück/Wallis 2021; Bauriedl/Strüver 2020; Elwood/Leszczynski 2018). A subjective perspective puts forth important insights on the workers' socio-spatial experiences, especially in the gig economy, in which workers become the platform's good (Kluzik 2021: 220). Against this background I ask: how do care platform workers experience socio-spatial practices that are created by the platform?

I used this episode from my fieldwork to start this chapter because it specifically illustrates aspects of how the working relationships between the platforms and the workers are shaped and shows how this affects the workers' subjectivity. It raises key questions about dependencies, power relations, availabilities, and hierarchies. My autoethnographic research findings will facilitate understanding of the ways in which working as a gigified care-worker in the urban context affects workers' lived realities. Through this research, I will demonstrate how the anticipation of constant availability encroaches on workers' lives. The daily life as platform worker, shaped by the socio-technic relationship to the platform, is highly complex and pervaded by contradictions. At times, workers might relish the freedom to accept or decline the offered cleaning gigs and thus decide when, where, and how long they do paid work. At many other times, however, they will vividly feel their ultimate dependence on the platform. Furthermore, I will show that platform workers must repeatedly negotiate unclear role assignments that have been deliberately created by the platforms. These perpetual negotiations take place within a socio-spatial context comprising multiple players and interests and reinforce existing hierarchies.

Digital platforms in the city

One example of how digital transformations affect cities are intermediation platforms. Platforms emerged in line with the idea of a smart city. According to Leszczynski (2020: 193) platforms present a "diversification, and intensification" of smart cities' "constituent practices, processes, and technologies". In practice, intermediation platforms scale smart city processes from the city administration onto personal networks and devices of citizens. Therefore, platforms create opportunities to use codes and algorithms for exchange of information, goods, and services for urban citizens. In this way, digital technologies affect various spheres of public and private life in the city. The labor market is involved in this development as well. One manifestation of this development is a growing number of digital platforms for labor intermediation that offer their services in the urban space (Lee et al. 2020: 116). Digital labor platforms have thus been evolving into "critical infrastructures of urban societies" (Barns 2019: 1). This is also the case in the sector of domestic house cleaning. Booking a cleaning person through a platform has become standard for many households. This encourages the platforms to depict themselves as important players who combat the high prevalence of informal working arrangements.

As critical infrastructures, digital platforms for labor intermediation shape urban life and, especially, urban work realities (Bauriedl/Strüver 2020: 270; Ecker/Rowek/Strüver 2021: 119). The emerging practices sound promising as framed by the platforms: an algorithm matches workers to customers within seconds. The result is that work is placed at shorter notice, for shorter periods of time, and more anonymously. In order to guarantee a match in any case, a huge workforce is available for the customer of the platforms. For workers, flexible working hours and the promised freedom to accept or decline gigs are pitched as positive aspects.

However, because of deliberate decisions in the design and architecture of the platforms, the new working arrangements define socio-spatial experiences in the urban space (Barns 2019: 1). Workers' daily life is characterized by fragmented working hours, a lot of (unpaid) travel time and major ambiguity about the quantity of assigned jobs. Platforms remain in the powerful position of transforming how, when, and where work is done, while workers have to adapt to the conditions. Therefore, several scholars emphasize the potential of platforms to shift and shape existing power relations in a daily urban life (Bauriedl/Strüver 2020: 270).

The controversy surrounding digital platforms has inspired thorough and continuous research on some sectors of the gig economy in recent years. Platforms for ride hailing, courier services, or food delivery especially have attracted increased attention (cf. Ivanova et al. 2018; Richardson 2020; Shapiro 2018; van Doorn 2017; Zwick 2018). Strikingly, these sectors are particularly dominated by male workers and mediate the type of work that is visible in the public urban life.

In contrast, the platformization of paid care work that is performed in the private space of the home (child and senior care, tutoring, cleaning, etc.) receives less public and academic attention. Care.com, Helpling, or Mamiexpress.ch are examples of such emerging platforms that have both embraced features of the on-demand economy and function within this logic (Ticona/Mateescu 2018: 4386). Digitalization allows new scales and facilitates network effects that would not previously have been possible in the care sector (Altenried 2021: 57). For example, in the cleaning sector, which is the focus of this contribution, the hiring process changes fundamentally. In the past, cleaners were either hired directly by the customer or they were employed by an intermediary company. Therefore, it remained clear who was the formal employer (with the associated responsibilities) and who would actually show up for the cleaning. This changed with the use of digital apps. The customer of the platform becomes unintentionally an employer of an unknown person. In some cases, the customer and the worker never even meet.

This new development in the sector needs increased attention in research, as it has a heavy impact on urban labor. Independently of digitalization, a care crisis, namely an externalization and commodification of care work can be observed. House cleaning for example is externalized because of a lack of capacity in the household, whether from more intensive burdens in gainful employment or because it has become something affordable (cf. Altenried/Dück/Wallis 2021; Huws 2019). Following the logic of commodification, social reproduction and care of households and people has become something that needs to be efficient (Altenried/Dück/Wallis 2021: 10). Digital platforms are an example of how efficiency and flexibility can be maximized: cleaners can be ordered exactly when they are necessary and with just one click on an app, the hiring is done in no time. Therefore, digital intermediation platforms present themselves, and are discussed, as part of the solution for the above-mentioned care crisis (Huws 2019).

In contrast to this affirmative rhetoric, I shift my perspective of analysis from the customer to the worker. In this paper, I aim to shed more light on how platform workers themselves experience the everyday socio-spatial interactions with a care platform. In this, I strive to better understand how digital platforms (re)produce and reinforce socio-spatial differences and inequalities. To provide a focus on such subjective experiences I work with the method of autoethnography.

Doing autoethnographic research

The method of autoethnography allows me to link my own lived experiences as platform worker to broader socio-cultural experiences (cf. Ritchie 2019: 71) and vice versa. Or in Reed-Danahay's (1997) terms, I understand "autoethnography as a form of self-narrative that places the self in social contexts". The method therefore presents a suitable match for my research interest in experiencing the subjective socio-spatial practices of a platform worker.

This paper draws on autoethnographic fieldwork I conducted on three different platforms in 2020-2021. I registered on all three platforms and created a profile with my interests, my documents, and my experiences. In this paper, I explicitly discuss material that I collected during fourteen weeks working in the cleaning sector between October 2020 and January 2021. And while the Covid-19 pandemic did affect public life during the aforementioned period, Switzerland was not under a strict lock-down at the time. This meant that there was a steady demand for cleaners for private households to conduct fieldwork. In effect, my access to domestic household cleaning gigs turned out to be easier than anticipated as I received several job offers in a short period of time. In Switzerland, platform labor in the care sector has been a growing market in recent years. International companies and Swiss specific platforms have been on the rise, spending noteworthy resources in marketing and advertising strategies. A variety of business models and employment conditions have been developing, configuring specific characteristics in each different platform. Whilst some platforms provide online market places without any support in the hiring processes, others assign jobs and provide working contracts. Recently, innovative forms of online platforms, Platform based cleaning cooperatives, emerged. Examples such as that of Plattformkooperative Autonomía in Zürich, ought to be monitored in the coming years. Especially considering the constant conversion of the market and its under researched socio-economic repercussions, online labor intermediation platforms in Switzerland deserve more academic attention.

The platform I worked on – dubbed Clean Angels here – is one of the major online domestic household cleaning platforms in Switzerland. Within the hiring and working process on this platform I experienced life as care platform worker, bearing many of the risks of the business model myself. Recording my own experiences as a platform worker constitutes the data material used for this paper. While I talked to workers in other contexts, I did not get to meet a single other Clean Angel during these fourteen weeks. In contrast to delivery riders, care workers are invisible in the city, therefore, I could not identify in public space and contact them. The platform also does not provide networking opportunities, there were no organized meetings nor public groups on social networks.

Clean Angels connects workers to customers in need of cleaning assistance, for short-term and flexible gigs or long-term regular arrangements. In line with care-work platform logic, everything is organized through an app and all the necessary documents and transactions are provided by the platform (Ticona/Mateescu 2018: 4387). With this, the platform conforms to what Altenried (2021: 57) describes as one of the main strategic goals of online labor intermediation platforms, namely becoming an indispensable infrastructure of our daily live. This also corresponds to the feedback I got from my customers. They highly value the uncomplicated hiring process and assure to me that booking a cleaning person via an app is a service they wouldn't want to miss.

My living circumstances and positionality are strongly intertwined with my research outcomes, especially when doing autoethnography. Although this approach offers detailed insights into a field (Butz/Besio 2009) it remains tied to the lived reality of one individual. On the one hand, my Swiss identity and my job as researcher are not the usual profile of a platform worker (cf. van Doorn 2021). On the other hand, identifying as a woman and my previous work experiences in household cleaning as a student gave me legitimacy with the platform and with my customers. I will reflect on further aspects of my positionality in the chapter below. In the following sections, I will first show how my autoethnographic research allowed me to experience and reflect on socio-spatial practices in domestic household cleaning intermediated via a digital platform.

Learning from subjectivities: Living a platform worker's life

My autoethnographic data gives me an in-depth insight into the omnipresent negotiations of platform workers. By following the typical day of a platform worker, I will show how spatiotemporal work patterns and hierarchies are constantly (re)negotiated. The quotes are all extracted from my fieldnotes. I have arranged them to portray the usual day of a platform worker.

Starting the day – dealing with time and space

Organizing starts in the morning. I get a call from Clean Angels:

> Clean Angels offers me a cleaning gig for this afternoon. As I do not want to reject the offer (I am afraid that I will get fewer offers), I accept, even though I know that it will be a stressful day (Fieldnotes 26.11.2020).

The spontaneous and flexible arrangement of the gigs hides a lot of background work. While the platform itself is reimbursed for the time they invest to assign their gigs (otherwise their business models would make no sense), as a platform worker I do not get any financial compensation for all the organization. Very soon into my new job as gig worker, I realize that the platform does not only interact with me via its app, but platform employees also call me at any time that is convenient to them. Often, this happens when I am not prepared to receive calls. In the example at the very beginning of this chapter, Clean Angels called me at a very inconvenient time. The platform does not really care about office working hours and expects their workers to be ready at any time. Both examples demonstrate the unpaid (administrative/organizing) work required to make the gig care economy work (Bor 2021: 158). Nevertheless, planning the gigs and scheduling the day is one of the main tasks as platform worker. Interestingly, digital tools on the platform are provided as a solution for this planning problem. Within the app I receive all the job offers and should theoretically be able to manage all the scheduling whenever I want to do it. However, the platform keeps on calling me to force me to immediately answer all the requests they have already sent me via their app. It is clear, therefore, that the platform overlooks, or does not care, that workers exist in a social and spatial context outside of paid work that influences working availabilities in every decision of whether to take a gig or not.

Fortunately, not every decision has to be made on the spot. Some customers are on a fixed or regular arrangement and facilitate the planning:

> Today I have my 'routine cleaning'. The apartment of the couple who are never home needs to be cleaned. I know I will have a very tight lunch break as I have another cleaning job immediately afterwards in the afternoon. In general, the day is stressful because I then have to go to a meeting right after cleaning. I know that my schedule will only work out if everything goes well and I can save some time in the morning. Since the people are not at home anyway, I decide to go to the apartment a little earlier so that I can then also go into my mini lunch break a little earlier. However, I don't dare to go more than ten minutes early because I'm afraid the couple might still be home. Of course, that's not the case and I regret not coming even earlier (Fieldnotes 26.11.2020).

There is a lot to think about every day. The success of planning depends not only on organizing but also on other circumstances (e.g., if customers are at home or not). The quote above illustrates a typical working day of a platform worker. Thinking about time, places, (social) conditions at the different homes, commuting time and other obligations becomes normal and constant. Nevertheless, it is exhausting and neither the platform operators nor the customers take this into consideration. Platform workers are left alone with the scheduling and arranging. That went so far that I had to ride my bike through piles of snow on another day, because it would not have been possible to get from one house to the next on time with public transport.

As in many other instances, the time pressure on this day is produced by my feeling of having to accept every job the platform offers me. I work with the constant feeling of being under surveillance: I know that the platform keeps track of how often I decline. I have no idea where I stand in comparison to other workers, and I fear that they will no longer offer me gigs if I turn them down too many times. This latent fear is central in many of my decisions of accepting jobs even though they do not fit well into my schedule. The platform clearly profits from my dependency on their job offers.

Working through the day – negotiating (assigned) positions

Back to the day in question, the level of stress did not abate even though I got there in plenty of time. It goes so far, that I have to skip my lunch. This was not the only situation in which I put my own social reproduction on hold. Not having enough time to eat or having too short breaks in between two customers for taking a shower to appear fresh again to the next customer was no exception on fully packed days.

> In the end, however, I finish after exactly two hours, which means that I have nearly lost the time I had gained. I quickly drive home so I can eat something small. Just knowing that everything is a bit tight today stresses me out. However, I can eat something and drink a coffee. Then I'm already off again, to a new customer. When I get there, it takes a long time for the customer to open the door for me. She's still in her pajamas, even though it's already 1:30 p.m. and she booked me. She tells me she completely forgot that she had ordered me (Fieldnotes 26.11.2020).

Apart from the time stress, this quote shows how I was forced to negotiate positions in social encounters that seemed to be regulated by the platform but in the end had to be negotiated repeatedly between me as worker and the corresponding customer. The encounter with the person in her pajamas is a first glimpse into the power relations that are shown to workers again and again. The customer not remembering having ordered a Clean Angel generated a feeling of being unimportant as a cleaning person. This forgetting might be a result of the easy ordering process via a mere click on a digital platform.

While the hierarchies were negotiated in subtle way in this setting, my next customer made it quite clear. After I had waited for her for more than fifteen minutes, she opened the door and without offering any greeting or apology, she asked me: "You know what you have to do, or do you have any questions?" When I responded that it was my first time in this flat and that she would need to show me around she was very surprised. She told me she supposed that Clean Angels would have informed me about the tasks and the circumstances in the flat. She was convinced that booking a cleaning person via a platform would also liberate her from her duties of providing the tools and detailing how the work has to be done. This understanding is at odds with the platform's emphasis that not Clean Angels, but the customer is in the role of employer.

My last customer on this stressful day was not the only one that had a completely different understanding of the roles of the platform, the worker, and the customer/employer (who often believes that the platforms would take care of everything for them). Bor (2021), who also conducts research on domestic housework platforms, also refers to this problem. She states that it is the platforms' intention to blur the responsibilities. The platform deliberately creates vague roles of customer, employer, and worker and profits from withdrawing from responsibility.

Call it a platform day – keep on reflecting

I finish all my gigs for the day and I make it to my meeting on time. On the way, I reflect on the day. Looking back, all the time stress seemed unnecessary. Nevertheless, it was an omnipresent feeling today. I realize that the platform plays a central role in producing my temporal and therefore also spatial patterns. In this moment, I take out my phone again and see:

> Clean Angels has called me again, but I didn't see the call, because I was riding my bike to my meeting. I do not have time to call back. When I arrive at the meeting, I check my profile on the app. Three new cleaning requests have come in. I can't deal with them right now though, as I would have to check my agenda. I also intentionally don't look at my mails, which, among other things, would tell me to confirm the requests (Fieldnotes 27.11.2020).

As this example illustrates, the repeated calls of the platform force me to deal with their requests whenever it is convenient to them. The longer I work for them, the more I resent the feeling of the platform dominating my life this way. More often, I take the liberty to ignore calls or requests. I am aware that this is an advantage that surely not every platform worker has. As I am not dependent on the financial income of the platform, I do have the privilege of saying I "don't feel like" dealing with demands at a specific moment. Making my living is not conditional on the number of gigs I get. This surely affects my behavior towards the platform and the customers. Even though I am responsible and polite, I am not willing to answer calls 24/7 and I am less tolerant towards rude behavior of my customers.

This example points to the specialties of the autoethnographic method: I am able to dive deep into a platform worker's daily life and the experiences workers make in the gig economy. At the same time, my findings are closely related to my positionality which is clearly visible in the analysis. For example, I cannot imagine what it would mean to be financially dependent on the number of gigs I can get. Furthermore, I realize how much I am used to great time flexibility in my job as a researcher. This might exacerbate my feelings of stress when I am forced to work tightly scheduled cleaning gigs in other peoples' places at specific prescheduled times. As a researcher, I am used to manage my own work schedule with considerable freedom of when to work on what. Even though that is exactly one of the promises of platform labor, I experience much more time constraints in my work as platform worker. Platforms seems to measure with another scale in this regard. The platform's idea of flexibility did not fit at all with mine.

Conclusion

What are the consequences when platforms start shaping domestic cleaning labor in the cities? By presenting a typical day in the life of myself as a platform worker I shone a light on two central aspects of domestic platform workers' daily routines.

First, working on a platform demands constant availability from the workers. This means that workers need to react immediately whenever a gig offer arrives. Furthermore, workers feel the pressure to be available for any possible gig. The platform performs constant but subtle control through repeated phone calls, app requests, and surveillance mechanisms that monitor not only performance at work but also the speed of responses to gig offers and the numbers of accepted and declined gigs. Connecting these findings to the idea of platform urbanism it becomes clear that platforms wield enormous power to shape the daily lives of an increasing number of workers in today's cities.

Second, short-term domestic housework being mediated via platforms creates situations in which customers/employers as well as workers have to (re)negotiate power relations. These negotiations are shaped by and at the same time (re)shape inequalities based on categories such as gender, residency status, or race. As a Swiss passport holder, I was privileged in comparison to an overwhelming multitude of migrants who work in this sector. As we know from research on offline cleaning, workers without residency or a work permit will find themselves in much weaker negotiating positions (cf. Knoll/Schilliger/Schwager 2012). As these situations take place in the invisible space of the private home, it is of essential importance to unveil the dynamics platform workers face in these interactions. As platform workers they face the additional hurdle that platforms seem to deliberately create vague role assignments and profit from not serving as formal employers. Even though they shape gigs in key aspects, they then leave it up to the workers to negotiate the specifics of their deals.

In conclusion, the digital 'solution' for the care crisis for customers produces new crises for workers (Altenried/Dück/Wallis 2021). The presented findings make it clear how the responsibilities are allocated: workers are forced to navigate our urban spaces in rhythms demanded by the platforms. Understanding *navigate* in a spatial and temporal sense, workers are obliged to follow the specifications of the platform. Even though a certain flexibility is promoted, the discussed empirical case shows how the platform remains in a dictating position by pushing workers to accept offered gigs. Understanding *navigating* the urban space in a social sense, workers need to shift between the blurry roles assigned by the platforms whenever they negotiate with customers that need to be processed (unpaid) by the workers. In these encounters the customers remain in the more powerful positions.

While workers do the care work for others their own social reproduction is put on hold. I had the privilege of not being dependent on this work, many care platform workers do rely on this income. They often do their work silently and remain invisible in public space. Therefore, I consider it of major importance to continue research on how working arrangements are shaped by labor intermediation platforms.

References

Altenried, Moritz (2021): Was ist eine Plattform? Politische Ökonomie und Arbeit im Plattformkapitalismus, in: Altenried, Moritz/Dück, Julia/Wallis, Mira (eds.): *Plattformkapitalismus und die Krise der sozialen Reproduktion*, Münster: Westfälisches Dampfboot: 50-69.

Altenried, Moritz/Dück, Julia/Wallis, Mira (2021): Zum Zusammenhang digitaler Plattformen und der Krise der sozialen Reproduktion: Einleitung, in: Altenried, Moritz/Dück, Julia/Wallis, Mira (eds.): *Plattformkapitalismus und die Krise der sozialen Reproduktion*, Münster: Westfälisches Dampfboot: 7-26.

Barns, Sarah (2019): Negotiating the platform pivot: From participatory digital ecosystems to infrastructures of everyday life, in: *Geography Compass* 13(9). doi: https://doi.org/10.1111/gec3.12464.

Bauriedl, Sybille/Strüver, Anke (2020): Platform urbanism: Technocapitalist production of private and public spaces, in: *Urban Planning* 5(4): 267-76.

Berg, Janine/Furrer, Marianne/Harmon, Ellie/Rani, Uma/Silberman, Michael Six (2018): *Digital labor platforms and the future of work. Towards decent work in the online world*, Geneva: ILO International Labor Organization.

Bor, Lisa (2021): Helpling hilft nicht – zur Auslagerung von Hausarbeit über digitale Plattformen, in: Altenried, Moritz/Dück, Julia/Wallis, Mira (eds.): *Plattformkapitalismus und die Krise der sozialen Reproduktion*, Münster: Westfälisches Dampfboot: 148-67.

Butz, David/Besio, Kathryn (2009): Autoethnography, in: *Geography Compass* 3(5): 1660-74.

Ecker, Yannick/Rowek, Marcella/Strüver, Anke (2021): Care on Demand: Geschlechternormierte Arbeits- und Raumstrukturen in der plattformbasierten Sorgearbeit, in: Altenried, Moritz/Dück, Julia/Wallis, Mira (eds.): *Plattformkapitalismus und die Krise der sozialen Reproduktion*, Münster: Westfälisches Dampfboot: 113-29.

Elwood, Sarah/Leszczynski, Agnieszka (2018): Feminist digital geographies, in: *Gender, Place & Culture* 25(5): 629-44.

Huws, Ursula (2019): The Hassle of Housework: Digitalisation and the Commodification of Domestic Labour, in: *Feminist Review* 123(1): 8-23.

Ivanova, Mirela/Bronowicka, Joanna/Kocher, Eva/Degner, Anne (2018): Foodora and Deliveroo: The App as a Boss? Control and Autonomy in Application-Based Management – The Case of Food Delivery Riders. Working Paper Forschungsförderung. Number 107. https://www.econstor.eu/bitstream/10419/216032/1/hbs-fofoe-wp-107-2018.pdf [09.03.2022].

Kluzik, Vicky (2021): Zur Aktualisierung von Flexploitation: Sorge, Prekarität und digitale Plattformen, in: Altenried, Moritz/Dück, Julia/Wallis, Mira (eds.): *Plattformkapitalismus und die Krise der sozialen Reproduktion*, Münster: Westfälisches Dampfboot: 209-25.

Knoll, Alex/Schilliger, Sarah/Schwager, Bea (2012): *Wisch und Weg! Sans-Papiers-Hausarbeiterinnen zwischen Prekarität und Selbstbestimmung*, Zürich: Seismo Verlag.

Lee, Ashlin/Mackenzie, Adrian/Smith, Gavin J.D./Box, Paul (2020): Mapping Platform Urbanism: Charting the Nuance of the Platform Pivot, in: *Urban Planning* 5(1): 116-28.

Leszczynski, Agnieszka (2020): Glitchy vignettes of platform urbanism, in: *Environment and Planning D: Society and Space* 38(2): 189-208.

Reed-Danahay, Deborah E. (1997): *Auto/Ethnography: Rewriting the Self and the Social*, Oxford/New York: Berg.

Richardson, Lizzie (2020): Coordinating office space: Digital technologies and the platformization of work, in: *Environment and Planning D: Society and Space* 39(2): 347-65.

Ritchie, Michelle (2019): An Autoethnography on the Geography of PTSD, in: *Journal of Loss and Trauma* 24(1): 69-83.

Shapiro, Aaron (2018): Between autonomy and control: Strategies of arbitrage in the "on-demand" economy, in: *New Media & Society* 20(8): 2954-71.

Ticona, Julia/Mateescu, Alexandra (2018): Trusted strangers: Carework platforms' cultural entrepreneurship in the on-demand economy, in: *New Media & Society* 20(11): 4384-404.

van Doorn, Niels (2017): Platform labor: On the Gendered and Racialized Exploitation of Low-Income Service Work in the 'on-demand' Economy, in: *Information, Communication & Society* 20(6): 898-914.

van Doorn, Niels (2021): Stepping Stone or Dead End? The Ambiguities of Platform-Mediated Domestic Work Under Conditions of Austerity. Comparative Landscapes of Austerity and the Gig Economy: New York and Berlin, in: Baines, Donna/Cunningham, Ian (eds.): *Working in the Context of Austerity. Challenges and Struggles*, Bristol: Bristol University Press: 49-69.

Zwick, Austin (2018): Welcome to the Gig Economy: neoliberal industrial relations and the case of Uber, in: *GeoJournal* 83(4): 679-91.

Platforms for Basic Needs
Rethinking their Infrastructuralization as Reflective of Elsewhere

Christiane Tristl & Anke Strüver

Introduction

The platformization of everyday life is part of an evolving *platform society* (van Dijck/Poell/de Waal 2018) in which daily life is organized by digital platforms mediating information, goods, and services. In this paper, we will look at digital service platforms as critical infrastructures of daily life and at their role in securing basic needs, i.e., 'providing' essential goods and services. Out of many basic needs, we will focus on care work as a service to be mediated by digital platforms in cities of the Global North, and water as a good to be accessed through payment platforms in rural Kenya. We will concentrate on the question in which ways the flexibility narrative tied to the platform economy will increase the commodification and intensify the commodified and privatized infrastructuralization of meeting basic needs. Although our two examples are very different – and stem from very different spatial contexts – they share the flexibility narrative of convenience and on-demand availability shaped by both international platform companies and public discourse.

Digital platforms mediating goods and services change how people live, work, interact, and consume. Although the *gig economy* is known for its precarious working conditions, the dominant narrative stresses the flexibility of the workforce – to work when, where, what, and for as long as you want (Anwar/Graham 2021; Heiland 2021). Care work platforms, for example, are prototypical of so-called lean platforms of platform capitalism's gig economy (Srnicek 2017): similar to Uber and Airbnb, as the most well-known types of service platforms, care platforms such as Care.com offer domestic care services on demand and match care workers and households. At the same time, *fintech* (financial technology), which describes an emerging field of digital retail monetary and financial services, is discussed in the context of platform capitalism (Langley/Leyshon 2021). In the Global North and South, fintech, such as payment platforms, is increasingly utilized for (municipal) water provision (for an example for the Global North, see Krisch, this volume). Regarding fintech on the African continent, Bateman et al. (2019b) argue that the mobile money application M-Pesa provided by the Kenyan company Safaricom is a paradigmatic example of the operations of platform capitalism. Yet, the flexibility narrative attributed to service platforms (including payment) has hardly been addressed with a special focus on its actual demand-side beyond the general on-demand logic in itself. We will therefore focus on the flexibility narrative from the clients' side and will argue that the platformization of basic needs, such as water and care, makes it more difficult or precarious to meet and secure these needs.

Service platforms seem to become ubiquitous elements of day-to-day existence. At the same time, they pretend to offer *universal* technological solutions and answers generally applicable to neoliberal societies severely affected by austerity measures and the accompanying privatization of infrastructures on the one hand, and individualized precarization and responsibilization on the other. Precarious flexibility and everyday crises can be found across the Global North and South – as these seem to be *ordinary phenomena* and *travelling concepts* (Robinson 2006; 2016). Cities, both in the Global South and the Global North, have been particularly hit by a restructuring of public services and welfare due to austerity and the structural inequalities of neoliberalism (Harvey 2012). Austerity thus needs to be addressed across the Global North/South divide but also across the urban/rural divide, as seemingly fixed ideas and categories are being redefined as a result of various crises. We will therefore draw on a case study of fintech in the shape of mobile money – M-Pesa-enabled PAYGo (pay-as-you-go) water dispensers implemented in communal water systems in rural Kenya to commodify water – and reflect on platformed care services in the Global North. Rural Kenya is discursively framed by international development organizations as being excluded from formalized markets and financial systems, which serves as legitimization for its inclusion (Berndt/Boeckler 2017). Our underlying objective is to think from the South and to "see familiar things in different ways" but also to see "unfamiliar things as reflective of elsewhere" (Thieme 2018: 536).

Against this background, we will proceed as follows: after introducing the emergence of platform-mediated services and their master flexibility narrative (see below), we introduce care platforms in the Global North (see the subsequent chapter). We then turn to fintech and water-to-go in Kenya in detail. Finally, we reread platformed care services as reflective of elsewhere to provide a foundation for discussing the extent to which universal platform narratives do not offer universal solutions. Furthermore, digital service platforms themselves do not provide any reliable solutions for meeting basic needs at all – not despite but because of their privatized infrastructuralization.

Platform-mediated services and goods

Platforms of the on-demand economy are specialized in arranging individual services between *peers* by means of transaction fees (such as home care and cleaning but also food delivery and water-to-go). They operate on the basis of outsourcing labor, utilities, and maintenance costs and thus do not depend on large capital investments (Srnicek 2017). The so-called digital revolution and the expansion of its infrastructure as part of the internet boom of the 1990s have provided these platforms' structural background conditions, while, after the financial crash of 2007/08, low interest rate policies increased investment incentives: "This post-crash landscape has also provided the perfect conditions for new flows of (venture) capital in the form of digital platforms that want to operate core services related to how we live, how we work, how we travel, how we consume" (Sadowski 2020: 449). The current prominence of platforms is therefore anything but accidental. It is tied to ICT, the flexibilization of social relations and the commodification of basic services and needs.

Care platforms in the Global North

In Western societies, the neoliberal restructuring of labor relations is one of the enabling conditions for platforms related to domestic care services. It also fuels their demand through increasing the *domestic time squeeze* (Huws 2019), which involves processes of commodification, decommodification, and recommodification of care work. The growing commodification and externalization of care work is a result of the increasing participation of women in professional paid work without men taking over an equal share in care work at home. This is paired with a social situation in which more and more people need additional income, turn to side jobs and multiply the supply-side. The decommodification of care, moreover, has been linked to the emergence of public health and childcare services in Western welfare societies. As such, the recommodification and reprivatization of care work is an outcome of public service cuts due to the neoliberal restructuring of labor and welfare in general, and of austerity programs in particular:

> "The result is a time squeeze that puts pressure on the quality of life both at home and at work and also impacts personal relationships and psychological, as well as physical wellbeing. Add to this the effects of the austerity policies imposed by many governments in the aftermath of the 2008 global financial crisis, and the result for many households, at least in the West, has been a time/money crisis." (Huws 2019: 18)

The combination of time *and* money crises has resulted in situations in which an increasing number of people have to rely on services on demand. As Huws (2019; Huws et al. 2019) has stressed, summarizing her research conducted in 13 European countries, platform-mediated care services are requested nowadays not only by people with higher incomes but across all classes. People with lower incomes living under precarious conditions thus also experience situations of *time crunch* that force them to resort to buying care services.

Although the flexibility narrative tied to care platforms, in the sense of convenient on-demand services, addresses people across all income groups, public and academic attention is mostly tied to workers' assumed flexibility and its consequences (see, e.g., Berg et al. 2018; Heiland 2021; Schwiter/Steiner 2020; van Doorn 2017; Woodcock/Graham 2019). In this chapter, we go beyond workers' (supposed) flexibility to stress the narrative of *users' flexibility*, i.e., of the *convenience of basic needs services on demand* and how this narrative intensifies the commodification of services and the infrastructuralization of care platforms.

Since the reprivatization of public services and the platformization and marketization of care work are considered as both technological and societal solutions to austerity regimes, they need to be read against landscapes of neoliberal capitalism and its *crisis of care* (Fraser 2016; Tronto 2017). The marketization of care has resulted in its scarcity and the global financial crisis since 2007/08 has given full expression to what is now described as a care crisis: lower wages, flexible part-time employment, and diminishing job security, which is paired with a much higher share of unpaid care work at home due to cuts in welfare programs. The marketization of care obstructs the fact that care is a basic need of – and for – all people. However, care – and care services – have been mostly ignored in geographical research on austerity going beyond the general critique of public service restructuring and individualizing responsibilities (see Theodore 2020 for a recent overview).

Payment platforms in the Global South and water-to-go

The marketization and platformization of water delivery in the Global South via PAYGo dispensers have to be situated in the broader agenda of *financial inclusion*. The financial inclusion agenda has been pushed forward by a *fintech-philanthropy-development complex* (Gabor/Brooks 2017), consisting of organizations such as the World Bank, the Bill & Melinda Gates Foundation, the Alliance for Financial Inclusion representing regulators in the Global South, the GSM Association as an industry trade body that represents the interests of 750 mobile operators globally (among others of Safaricom), the financial inclusion think tank Consultative Group to Assist the Poor (CGAP) and by private companies such as Vodacom or Mastercard. Soederberg (2013) argues that the agenda for financial inclusion has been driven after the financial crisis in 2008 to overcome a global recession, stabilize the global financial system and find new possibilities of investment for a global finance-led capitalism targeting poverty as the new frontier of capital accumulation. It plays out in the arena of "bottom billion capitalism" (Roy 2012: 132) and its win-win logic that what is good for business is also good for society. So, while credit card companies or mobile money providers are eager to gain from transaction fees (Mader 2016), the agenda for financial inclusion assumes that "the unbanked poor" (Langley/Leyshon 2021) can be lifted out of poverty by granting them access to formal financial services such as credit, insurance, and money transfers. Thereby, it is argued, fintech projects, such as mobile money applications, can provide a valid alternative for mainstream banking.

Fintech found its way into water provision in the Global South through PAYGo water dispensers. PAYGo dispensers are designed to be installed in water kiosks, the common mode of water supply for the poorer population in urban as well as rural areas in the Global South. In so-called informal areas in cities, the kiosks are usually connected to the urban water network, whereas, in rural areas, they are connected to boreholes. While users who come to fetch water with jerry cans used to pay in cash to kiosk attendants, the latter are now to be displaced by the dispensers. PAYGo machines are equipped with Internet of Things (IoT)-based remote monitoring systems and combine prepaid with mobile money applications as a means of payment. Users utilize their mobile phones to recharge the smart cards that are provided to pay with at the dispensers.

As the argument goes, water systems in rural areas in the Global South break down soon after installation because of inadequate operation and maintenance due to a lack of revenue collection and management (IRC/VIA Water 2016). Utilizing PAYGo dispensers for inclusive business models that target 'the poor' as customers could thus result in the financial sustainability, i.e., cost recovery, of water systems while enabling a more convenient tapping experience for the users. In line with the win-win logics of ethical capitalism, the telco industry, in the form of the GSMA, and CGAP openly celebrate the interlinkage of mobile money and water as the most essential of all goods as "a powerful and sticky introduction to mobile bill payments" (CGAP/GSMA 2019: 14).

Gabor and Brooks (2017) identify the interlinkage of upcoming digital technologies and the digitization of finance and the responsibilization of individuals. Data generated from fintech applications allow for governing "risky" populations and "shape financial subjectivities" (Gabor/Brooks 2017: 3). This observation interlocks with a shift in development discourse from the failure of markets to the failure of individuals. In other words, poverty and the lack of fulfillment of basic needs is not a matter of structural inequalities but a matter of wrong individual behavior (Berndt/Boeckler 2016). Digital technologies such as PAYGo dispensers can now 'nudge' individual irrational behavior. As they are implemented to empower their users to become budgeting individuals, they are supposed to contribute to financial self-government.

In the following, we will demonstrate how care and payment platforms and their accompanying flexibility narratives enable a shift from the public or communal provision of basic needs to these needs becoming an individualized and privatized affair. In order to advance the debate on the platformization of basic needs, austerity must be addressed across the Global North/South divide and the urban/rural divide. For this paper, we thus apply the perspective *thinking from the South* with the objective to *see familiar things in the Global North in different ways* and now turn to the platformization of care services and their supposed convenience for clients.

Platformization of care services

The (re-)commodification of domestic care work through platforms is a result of the financial crisis for (at least) three reasons: (1) formerly public care services, such as health care and child and senior care, were privatized after 2008, (2) more and more people needed a second or third income *and* had less time for domestic work, and (3) setting up digital platforms was and is not dependent on large capital investments but rather on existing *assets*, such as working bodies to be *shared between platform peers* (Bauriedl/Strüver 2020). Care platforms as part of the on-demand economy encourage workers' flexibility in terms of when, where, and what they work on and the expected income they receive for that work. However, they do not prevent the precarity and vulnerability that is typically associated with flexible working conditions as they put workers in a constant competition concerning speed, rating results, and the wages of their gigs (Woodcock/Graham 2019). Yet, while platform workers' supposed flexibility has been addressed widely, the actual demand-side often remains hidden. However, care service platforms also advertise this flexibility to *clients* in terms of when, where, and what services they 'want' and need. Moreover, due to the affordances of app-mediated services, the platforms market this as 24/7 mobile availability, i.e., anytime and anywhere – as care-to-go.

In the 21st century, care service work no longer rests on care work as a social service based on "a triadic relationship between carers, the state, and people cared for" (Flanagan 2019: 66). It rather rests on the neoliberal paradigm of caring as "an entrepreneurial activity that should be properly organised through markets and competition" (ibid.). It thus encompasses ideas of empowering clients because they have the freedom of choice. The commodification of care is a result of neoliberal policies favoring market-based competition to enhance efficiency and lower costs to the benefit of care service users. As there is not much empirical research on the flexibility narrative tied to platforms' demand-side yet, we, in the following, focus on the Global North in general, and on an Australian case study in particular. The benefit for service users is, for example, emphasized in the policy documents related to the Australian care reform, which was analyzed in detail by Fiona Macdonald (2021: 80f., 147ff.). These documents stress the necessity of workers' flexibility in order to meet clients' demands for such flexibility. At the same time, the platforms advertise choice and flexibility (*who, when, where, and how long you want*) to prospective clients.

However, Macdonald argues that paid care services first of all result in *individualizing risks* for both workers and clients. She illustrates this with a comprehensive study of Australian policies that individualize care as a cash-for-care scheme. This scheme turns care recipients into clients who are responsible for purchasing services for their needs via platforms in times of diminishing public care services on the one hand, and a public discourse of efficient care *because* of competition on the other. Cash-for-care schemes thus intensify the privatization, marketization, and commodification of care as the individual clients have the freedom of choice, i.e., are made responsible to look for the 'best' in the sense of the most efficient carer: "Cash-for-care or individualised funding schemes are also referred to as consumer-directed care or self-directed support, reflecting the underlying idea that this type of scheme can empower service users by placing them in control of the services and supports they need for day-to-day living." (Macdonald 2021: 21)

Having the freedom of choice is clearly a neoliberal metanarrative. As both narrative and politics, it is also linked to the idea of the homo oeconomicus. Increasing the flexibility for clients and their choices – *who you want, when and where you want a care giver* – is advertised as clients' empowerment. However, this type of empowerment rests, first, on previous disempowerment through welfare cuts (disempowerment due to missing public care services), second, on access to technology and, third, on technology based on consumer capitalism (Levina 2017). Each type of empowerment is radically different from providing or securing basic needs.

As stated earlier, care services mediated by platforms are increasingly *on demand* across all classes and this "points to a picture in which the consumption of household services via online platforms is a regular aspect of daily life for citizens across all income bands rather than a luxury for the rich" (Huws et al. 2019: 7-8; see also SenIAS 2017).

As digital platforms seemingly *optimize* the flexibility of service labor (van Doorn 2017) and claim to *formalize* caring relations (Ticona/Mateescu 2018; Huws 2019; Flanagan 2019), the flexibility narrative is tied to the commodification and infrastructuralization of care platforms, but this does not meet the needs of all people. People in precarious situations often do not have the freedom of choice. The privatization and platformization of care services and relations thus leads to a situation in which some people do not have a choice – and are not cared for – at all. Applying Tronto's (2017: 29f.) summary of neoliberalism's three ways to account for care, we can thus state that care service platforms intensify these ways, as they individualize the responsibility for care, locate care in private households again and consider care as a market problem, which can be optimized with platform-mediated care services.

Platformization of water services and infrastructure in Kenya

While PAYGo water dispensers can be integrated with any mobile money application, Safaricom's M-Pesa is the obvious choice in Kenya. M-Pesa has been hailed as a panacea for poverty reduction within the international development community (Suri/Jack 2016). However, Bateman et al. (2019b) argue that "M-Pesa (…) provides us with a valuable case study of how contemporary platform capitalism operates in neoliberal Africa". Following a project by the UK's Department for International Development to improve private sector participation in financial services development, Safaricom launched M-Pesa in 2007. The mobile money application allows its users to deposit, transfer, and withdraw money from a broad network of agents. M-Pesa transactions can be performed by utilizing smartphones as well as basic phones as it allows sending money via SMS. While Safaricom earns money, among other ways, by charging a commission for each of the tiny transactions that go through its platform, it is famous for achieving impressive profits (US\$687 million in 2021). Safaricom is by large Kenya's biggest private company today and controls more than 60 % of the Kenyan market of mobile subscriptions, which repeatedly has led to political debates about its monopolist position (Otieno 2020). The Kenyan government holds a 35 % stake in the company, whereas the rest goes to foreign investors, among them the British Vodafone, who, with a 40 % stake, is the majority shareholder.

The entwinement of PAYGo dispensers with mobile money applications is being advertised as useful because, first, it eradicates the handling of cash and thus caters for the efficiency of the water system. Because non-revenue water is reduced and every transaction is tracked with transparent, remote monitoring systems, water systems finally become cost recovering and thus financially sustainable (CGAP/GSMA 2019). Second, as its proponents have promised, PAYGo also benefits the water users. Harnessing the connectivity of smart devices, PAYGo, or "pay on demand" (Mastercard 2020), fosters digital and financial inclusion. Being supposedly adapted to the living circumstances of 'the poor', PAYGo, as has been promised, is inclusive because it is "affordable and convenient for those with irregular incomes" (GSMA 2017: 5) and, opposed to monthly billing, allows 'the poor' to buy "what they can, when they can, when they need it" (Mastercard 2020: 4). It empowers users by granting them "valuable control" (CGAP 2018) over their consumption. Instead of having to rely on kiosk attendants, who close the kiosk for lunch breaks and at night, the "convenience of mobile payments" (CGAP 2018) enables the user to fetch water at any and in less time by avoiding queues at the kiosk. The literal imagination of "pay-as-you-drink" (CGAP 2018) not only portrays water as a commodity. The mobile money enabled PAYGo system also invokes the ones to be served as digitally included customers who are enabled and free to obtain water at their own convenience and *en passant*, simply by placing self-recharged smart cards on intuitive user interfaces.

The declaration of water as a commodity in the name of the cost recovery of water systems in the Global South is nothing new – it was already introduced in the 1990s, in line with structural adjustment. "Community management" (IRC 2003), i.e., rural communities independently managing their water systems with NGOs acting as implementing agencies, emerged as the default mode of rural water supply. While community management has, meanwhile, been criticized for the romanticization of communities (Bakker 2008), other authors have identified the wrong installation of boreholes through NGOs and the lack of availability of spare parts as major problems of community water systems (Harvey 2004). Indeed, many water systems collapsed shortly after their establishment, whereupon NGOs implemented new ones and fell into a role as de facto providers of water services in a project-based manner (Harvey/Reed 2007). The current push for the implementation of PAYGo dispensers ignores these issues and, instead, seeks to materially force through the commodification of water.

For the following, we draw on ethnographic material tracing a project on the implementation of PAYGo water dispensers in a village we call Kondo, in Makueni County, Kenya. In Makueni, the majority of the population depends on subsistence farming with casual labor as the major source of income (NDMA 2014). Thus, income flows are of immediate, irregular, and short-term nature. With 64 %, the poverty level is far greater than the Kenyan average of 45 % (World Bank 2012). While, from the view of the imperial capitalist system, Kondo can be regarded as a place that is precarious and marginalized, the people of Kondo's everyday practices, as we will see, center around their own ways of making do.

The project was funded by a philanthropic foundation from the UK and implemented by one of the world's biggest Water, Sanitation, and Hygiene NGOs to increase the sustainability of the water system. Typical for rural water schemes in the Global South, boreholes in Kondo are connected to water kiosks from which kiosk attendants used to sell water to users per jerry can. The water system is managed by a local water committee. The only sources of water, apart from the boreholes, are small earth dams collecting rainwater for irrigation and livestock and polluted rivers. Because the water system lacked revenue, which was blamed on corruption or incompetence on the side of either the committee or the kiosk attendants, the latter were replaced by PAYGo dispensers.

The contract the water committee in Kondo signed with Safaricom indicated that 7 % of the revenue of water sales would go to the company. Besides problematizing the profit generation of large corporations such as Safaricom by asking transfer fees of 'the poor', we want to question the flexibility narrative put forward by and show how platforms contribute to the increased privatization of water services.

Access to water as individualized entrepreneurial management

Proponents of PAYGo water dispensers argue that PAYGo empowers its users to gain control of their water consumption and budget. Moreover, advocates of M-Pesa emphasize that mobile payment even helps users 'save' money (Suri/Jack 2016) and thus contributes to lifting them out of poverty. Indeed, as one user reported: "Before the card I was afraid to keep money specifically for water, because if the cash is in your pocket, saving it for water, yet you have another urgent need… So I would take the money for water to buy sugar. Even if it is saved for water." (Benson 2017, interview)

Like Benson, some users, especially the wealthier ones, did indeed use their smart cards for budgeting for water. Beyond mere saving, PAYGo dispensers and smart cards seem to facilitate *earmarking* – specifying money for certain uses, something that is celebrated in behavioral economics as an important tool of *self-control* (Banerjee/Duflo 2012).

In comparison, the necessity to recharge smart cards, represented an additional burden for users with limited income. "It is not common in my home that I recharged the card to make water ready and there is no food", as Rose described. "So I prefer to have money somewhere, which can buy food so that the other small amount now has been put in card to buy water." (Rose 2017, interview) When using water dispensers, earmarking budget for water is not optional, as mobile payments automatically require to extend credit to the water system – budget, which is then lacking elsewhere. Narratives about the convenience and adaptedness of mobile bill payments for people with casual incomes override the fact that cash is the most immediate and 'flexible' form of payment. Accordingly, access to water not only depends on the ability of individualized entrepreneurial management, but users are faced with additional obstacles in their quest to access water.

Individualizing the costs of the digital divide

Not fitting into the imaginary of avid M-Pesa users, elderly or illiterate people, or those who are both, often were not able to carry out the process of recharging their smart card, which required to navigate through the M-Pesa menu, thereby executing the right orders and read confirmation text messages. While, before, water kiosks were non-discriminatory toward varying degrees of literacy, people who did not manage to recharge the card by themselves now had to refer to friends and relatives for help. People would recharge the cards for their elderly parents, or children who had already learned how to read would do so for their grandparents.

Those who were not equipped with such a social safety net had to find other ways to deal with the situation. Often, the only solution was to ask an M-Pesa agent – not to recharge the M-Pesa account but to recharge the smart card. Most of the M-Pesa agents, however, did not regard this as their task. Musa, a resident of Kondo, explained that, when users did ask an M-Pesa agent if they could help them with recharging their smart cards, the agent often replied that "these cards don't work" here, since recharging smart cards was not a service they were paid for by Safaricom. As a result, it became common form that people who wanted their cards to be recharged by the agents paid some small, extra amount for their service. Mobile money agents might react in many different ways to the new requests of customers to help them with services (Maurer/Nelms/Rea 2013). In the described cases, it was illiterate users who had to pay extra money in order to digitize the payments for water, thereby individualizing issues of technology literacy and further disempowering them.

Flexibility in terms of payment?

On top of the supposedly highly flexible water system, which can be accessed at any time, the GSMA has argued that the introduction of PAYGo systems reduces "fraud" (GSMA 2018: 8) and creates an "equitable" (ibid.) system where water access is independent of "status, relationships or income" (ibid.). One has to be aware, however, that *income* is a matter of concern for the people who these systems are supposed to address, namely 'the poor'.

Indeed, in the past, users did have the possibility to take credit at the water system in times of lack of budget, an option that was now foreclosed. While kiosks might now be open 24/7, one user commented: "A person will not go there [to the kiosk] without money and expect water. You have to make sure that the card is recharged." (Grace 2017, interview) In cases of lack of budget, users now had to resort to borrowing money from friends and neighbors, something that is celebrated by the telco industry as "strengthening ties" (GSMA 2018: 10). If borrowing money or water did not work, the commodification of water meant that people were effectively excluded from the water system: "Now, when there is no money, we go to the dams and rivers..." (Rose 2017, interview)

Flexibility has always played a major role in societal organization in Makueni. The region has historically been associated with multiple crises such as drought and famine – a result, among others, of forcing people into sedentary settlement structures during colonialism. In the recent past, Makueni also has been regularly affected by large-scale failure of crops due to the absence of rainfall, which usually results in the distribution of food aid by the Kenyan government. Arrangements of mutual reciprocity, in terms of mobilizing support from family, clan, church, and other networks of mutual support, have always represented an important mechanism to limit vulnerability during times of drought (Rocheleau/Steinberg/Benjamin 1995) and are still noticeable in the way water systems work today. While Frank, an NGO worker, bemoaned that the attendants might have been "tempted" to give water away for free when being confronted with a "sister", one's "father", or a "friend" (Frank 2016, interview), water users had a different view: "The attendant is better (...). With an attendant, a person can pay later. With an attendant, [a person] can express herself. Give her [the attendant] a reason why she has to pay later. She can express with a person, not with a machine." (Faith 2017, interview)

The introduction of PAYGo dispensers on the basis of their presumed flexibility for the users has disentangled the water system from the everyday concerns associated with precarious incomes and has shifted them from the public or communal to the sphere of interpersonal relationships. When Bateman et al. (2019a) argue that, with M-Pesa, we are confronted with a high-tech extractivist infrastructure that finds its equivalents in the colonial era, extraction extends beyond mere transaction fees. What is being advertised as "flexible" and "equitable" is factually highly unresponsive to the precarious life circumstances of the people in Kondo, which are always in motion. While, from the point of view of rational economic reasoning, handing out water for free is diminished as 'fraud', it can in fact be regarded as part of a mechanism of drought adaptation in an environment that is characterized by short-term temporalities, by immediacy and spontaneous events, emergencies – be they caused by drought, lack of income, or general poverty.

Outlook: Redefining neoliberalism's flexibility narrative

Platform societies are evolving across the Global South and North, rural and urban areas. In this short outlook, we aimed to discuss in which ways the flexibility narrative tied to the two platform economies introduced increases the commodification and privatization of goods and services such as water and care. By having paired two very different examples of platforms and platform societies, we also strived for a rereading of the flexibility narrative that is marketed as empowering and did this by thinking from the South.

Digital service platforms normalize the commodification and privatized infrastructuralization of basic needs such as water and care. Part of this normalization stems from the flexibility narrative of on-demand services (*water-to-go* and *care-to go*). At the same time, the normalization is part of an increasing infrastructuralization of these platforms on the one hand (see Plantin et al. 2018; Mörtenböck/Mooshammer 2021), and an intensifying individualization of the responsibility for basic needs on the other (Fraser 2016; Tronto 2017). Both have their roots in neoliberal ideologies and economies as well as in austerity policies. We have introduced this by referring to two very different types of platform-mediated 'goods and services' that are basic needs (water and care) in very different spatial contexts, where we found similar narratives, mechanisms, and social effects.

In the case of PAYGo water dispensers, in addition to more efficient management, the implementing agencies particularly emphasize the flexibility and convenient access at any time for the demand-side due to mobile bill payments. As we could demonstrate, however, mobile money enabled payment systems are non-respondent to the precarious life circumstances of 'the poor'. While they do indeed bring about saving and budgeting individuals, they complicate life for the very precarious who now have to extend credit.

They also cause extra costs for the illiterate, who are now charged extra to recharge their smart cards. Mobile money enabled PAYGo water dispensers individualizes water access, since it is now the users' responsibility to find backup solutions in the private sphere, cater for card top-ups and make budgets available.

Rural Kenya is commonly framed by international development interventions as a place where people behave in 'irrational' ways (which is the reason why they are poor) and, accordingly, have to be 'empowered' to behave in economically rational ways with the help of technological applications (Berndt/Boeckler 2017).

Thinking from Kondo, we suggest, however, to redefine neoliberalism's flexibility from who, when, where, and how long to a kind of flexibility that acknowledges mutual interdependencies and is characterized by situation specific reasoning that is sensitive to people's situated needs and vulnerabilities. Considering that circumstances of precarity can also increasingly be found in the Global North allows us to be sensitive to people's *disempowerment* resulting from the individual freedom of – and responsibility for – choice, often resulting not in individualized care but individualized responsibilities in both the North and South. The problem at stake cannot be reduced to the platform itself, but we have to consider the socioeconomic structures that enable – and rely on – platform capitalism. Against this background, we call for more collective, solidary, and caring forms of societal organization in platform societies.

References

Anwar, Mohammad Amir/Graham, Mark (2021): Between a rock and a hard place: Freedom, flexibility, precarity and vulnerability in the gig economy in Africa, in: *Competition & Change* 25(2): 237-58.

Bakker, Karen (2008): The Ambiguity of Community: Debating Alternatives to Private-Sector Provision of Urban Water Supply, in: *Water Alternatives* 1(2): 236-52.

Banerjee, Abhijit Vinayak/Duflo, Esther (2012): *Poor Economics: A Radical Rethinking of the Way to Fight Global Poverty*, New York: PublicAffairs.

Bateman, Milford/Duvendack, Maren/Loubere, Nicholas (2019a): Is Fin-Tech the New Panacea for Poverty Alleviation and Local Development? Contesting Suri and Jack's M-Pesa Findings Published in Science, in: *Review of African Political Economy* 46(161): 480-95.

Bateman, Milford/Duvendack, Maren/Loubere, Nicholas (2019b): Another False Messiah: The Rise and Rise of Fin-Tech in Africa. https://roape.net/2019/06/11/another-false-messiah-the-rise-and-rise-of-fin-tech-in-africa/ [11.06.2019].

Bauriedl, Sybille/Strüver, Anke (2020): Platform Urbanism: Technocapitalist Production of Private and Public Spaces, in: *Urban Planning* 5(4): 267-76.

Berg, Janine/Furrer, Marianne/Harmon, Ellie/Rani, Uma/Silberman, Michael Six (2018): *Digital Labour Platforms and the Future of Work: Towards Decent Work in the Online World*, Geneva: ILO Publications.

Berndt, Christian/Boeckler, Marc (2016): Behave, Global South! Economics, Experiments, Evidence, in: *Geoforum* 70: 22-24.

Berndt, Christian/Boeckler, Marc (2017): Märkte in Entwicklung: Zur Ökonomisierung Des Globalen Südens, in: Diaz-Bone, Rainer/Hartz, Ronald (eds.): *Dispositiv und Ökonomie*, Wiesbaden: Springer Fachmedien Wiesbaden: 349-70.

CGAP (2018): Pay-as-You-Drink: Digital Finance and Smart Water Service. https://www.cgap.org/blog/pay-you-drink-digital-finance-and-smart-water-service/ [23.03.2019].

CGAP/GSMA (2019): Testing the Waters: Digital Payments for Water and Sanitation. https://www.cgap.org/research/publication/testing-waters-digital-payments-water-and-sanitation/ [27.03.2020].

Flanagan, Frances (2019): Theorising the Gig Economy and Home-Based Service Work, in: *Journal of Industrial Relations* 61(1): 57-78.

Fraser, Nancy (2016): Contradictions of Capital and Care, in: *New Left Review* (100): 99-117.

Gabor, Daniela/Brooks, Sally (2017): The Digital Revolution in Financial Inclusion: International Development in the Fintech Era, in: *New Political Economy* 22(4): 423-36.

GSMA (2017): Mobile for Development Utilities: Lessons from the Use of Mobile in Utility Pay-as-You-Go Models. https://www.gsma.com/mobilefordevelopment/wp-content/uploads/2017/01/Lessons-from-the-use-of-mobile-in-utility-pay-as-you-go-models.pdf [22.03.2019].

GSMA (2018): Africa Water Enterprises: Using IoT to Monitor and Introduce Pre-Payment for Remote Water Stands in the Gambia. https://www.gsma.com/mobilefordevelopment/wp-content/uploads/2018/04/Africa-Wate

r-Enterprises-Using-IoT-to-monitor-and-introduce-pre-payment-for-remote-water-stands-in-The-Gambia.pdf [04.01.2022].

Harvey, David (2012): *Rebel Cities. From the Right to the City to the Urban Revolution*, London: Verso.

Harvey, Peter A. (2004): Borehole Sustainability in Rural Africa: An Analysis of Routine Field Data. https://repository.lboro.ac.uk/articles/Borehole_sustainability_in_rural_Africa_an_analysis_of_routine_field_data/9594875 [23.08.2020].

Harvey, Peter A./Reed, Robert (2007): Community-Managed Water Supplies in Africa: Sustainable or Dispensable?, in: *Community Development Journal* 42(3): 365-78.

Heiland, Heiner (2021): Neither timeless, nor placeless: Control of food delivery gig work via place-based working time regimes, in: *Human Relations* (June). doi: https://doi.org/10.1177/00187267211025283.

Huws, Ursula (2019): The hassle of housework: Digitalization and the commodification of domestic labour, in: *Feminist Review* 123(1): 8-23.

Huws, Ursula/Spencer, Neil/Coates, Matt/Holts, Kaire (2019): The Platformisation of Work in Europe: Results from Research in 13 European Countries. https://www.eurofound.europa.eu/de/data/platform-economy/records/the-platformisation-of-work-in-europe-results-from-research-in-13-european-countries [27.08.2021].

IRC (2003): *Community Water, Community Management: From System to Service in Rural Areas*, London: ITDG Publishing.

IRC/VIA Water (2016): The 'End of Ownership' of Water and Sanitation Infrastructure? https://www.ircwash.org/resources/end-ownership-water-and-sanitation-infrastructure-background-paper-joint-irc-water-event [20.02.2019].

Langley, Paul/Leyshon, Andrew (2021): The Platform Political Economy of FinTech: Reintermediation, Consolidation and Capitalisation, in: *New Political Economy* 26(3): 376-88.

Levina, Marina (2017): Disrupt or Die: Mobile Health and Disruptive Innovation as Body Politics, in: *Television & New Media* 18(6): 548-64.

Mader, Philip (2016): Card Crusaders, Cash Infidels and the Holy Grails of Digital Financial Inclusion, in: *Behemoth* 9(2): 50-81.

Macdonald, Fiona (2021): *Individualising Risk. Paid Care Work in the New Gig Economy*, Singapore: Springer.

Mastercard (2020): Pay on Demand: The Digital Path to Financial Inclusion in Africa. https://www.mastercard.com/news/media/urykzcqm/mastercard-africa-pay-on-demand-white-paper-march-3-2020.pdf [25.07.2021].

Maurer, Bill/Nelms, Taylor C./Rea, Stephen C. (2013): 'Bridges to Cash': Channelling Agency in Mobile Money, in: *Journal of the Royal Anthropological Institute* 19(1): 52-74.

Mörtenböck, Peter/Mooshammer, Helge (2021): *Platform Urbanism and Its Discontents*, Rotterdam: nai010 publishers.

NDMA (2014): Makueni County. Drought monthly bulletin for September 2014. https://reliefweb.int/sites/reliefweb.int/files/resources/Makueni-September-2014.pdf [27.07.2021].

Otieno, Julius (2020): Senators Reignite Push to Split Safaricom. https://www.the-star.co.ke/news/2020-11-18-senators-reignite-push-to-split-safaricom [04.01.2021].

Plantin, Jean-Christophe/Lagoze, Carl/Edwards, Paul N./Sandvig, Christian (2018): Infrastructure Studies Meet Platform Studies in the Age of Google and Facebook, in: *New Media & Society* 20(1): 293-310.

Robinson, Jennifer (2006): *Ordinary Cities: Between Modernity and Development*, London: Routledge.

Robinson, Jennifer (2016): Thinking cities through elsewhere: Comparative tactics for a more global urban studies, in: *Progress in Human Geography* 40(1): 3-29.

Rocheleau, Dianne E./Steinberg, Philip E./Benjamin, Patricia A. (1995): Environment, development, crisis and crusade: Ukambani, Kenya, 1890-1990, in: *World Development* 23(6): 1037-51.

Roy, Ananya (2012): Ethical Subjects: Market Rule in an Age of Poverty, in: *Public Culture* 24(1 (66)): 105-8.

Sadowski, Jathan (2020): Cyberspace and cityscapes: On the emergence of platform urbanism, in: *Urban Geography* 41(3): 448-52.

Schwiter, Karin/Steiner, Jennifer (2020): Geographies of care work: The commodification of care, digital care futures and alternative caring visions, in: *Geography Compass* 14(12). doi: https://doi.org/10.1111/gec3.12546.

Senatsverwaltung für Integration, Arbeit und Soziales Berlin (SenIAS) (2017): Der Job als Gig. Digital vermittelte Dienstleistungen in Berlin. https://www.arbeitgestaltengmbh.de/assets/projekte/Joboption-Berlin/Der-Job-als-Gig-Expertise-Digital-November-2017.pdf [22.08.2021].

Soederberg, Susanne (2013): Universalising Financial Inclusion and the Securitisation of Development, in: *Third World Quarterly* 34(4): 593-612.

Srnicek, Nick (2017): *Platform capitalism*, Cambridge, MA: Polity Press.
Suri, Tavneet/Jack, William (2016): The Long-Run Poverty and Gender Impacts of Mobile Money, in: *Science* 354(6317): 1288-92.
Theodore, Nik (2020): Governing through austerity: (Il)logics of neoliberal urbanism after the global financial crisis, in: *Journal of Urban Affairs* 42(1): 1-17.
Thieme, Tatiana Adeline (2018): The hustle economy: Informality, uncertainty and the geographies of getting by, in: *Progress in Human Geography* 42(4): 529-48.
Ticona, Julia/Mateescu, Alexandra (2018): Trusted strangers: Care platforms' cultural entrepreneurship in the on-demand economy, in: *New media & society* 20(11): 4384-404.
Tronto, Joan (2017): There is an alternative: homines curans and the limits of neoliberalism, in: *International Journal of Care and Caring* 1(1): 27-43.
van Dijck, José/Poell, Thomas/de Waal, Martijn (2018): *The platform society: Public values in a connective world*, Oxford: Oxford University Press.
van Doorn, Niels (2017): Platform labor: On the gendered and racialized exploitation of low-income service work in the 'on-demand' economy, in: *Information, Communication & Society* 20(6): 898-914.
Woodcock, Jamie/Graham, Mark (2019): *The Gig Economy: A Critical Introduction*, Cambridge: Polity.
World Bank (2012): Data Kenya. https://web.archive.org/web/20131211044508/http://data.worldbank.org//country//kenya [27.07.2021].

SPATIAL AND SOCIAL EFFECTS
OF PLATFORMIZATION

#FairDelivery?
Potential for and Limits to Alternative Platformization

Yannick Ecker

Introduction

Why should we think of intermediary websites that do not rely on venture capital, rent-based accumulation, and algorithmic matching as platforms? Participants at an online conference on platform urbanism (PU) at the University of Graz in March 2021 raised several such critical questions while discussing diverse platforms in sectors such as care, delivery, and short-term rentals. Viewed as an emerging mode of producing the urban, the concept of PU increasingly supplants the smart city as a conceptual framework for analyzing changing urban realities (Barns 2019; Bauriedl/Strüver 2020; Leszczynski 2020; Sadowski 2021). However, the recent extensive and multifaceted examination of platform economies and practices in urban studies and human geography comes with the danger of neglecting to thoroughly define and reflect on implicit assumptions – the latter being of upmost relevance for accurate analyses, as Ticona and Mateescu's (2018) critique of the dominance of the *Uberization narrative* has shown.[1]

Reflecting on implicit assumptions has become even more important as social grievances connected to the rise of platform economies have led to calls for *platform cooperativism* (Scholz 2016) and *platform municipalism* (Thompson 2021). Such projects promise alternatives to "end[ing] up with unaccountable and undemocratic organizations managing key digital infrastructures of our cities" (Graham 2020: 3). They seek to address issues that are most frequently

---

1   The authors argue that equating lean platformization with the spread of Uber's business model leads to the neglecting of aspects specific to care work. These include the feminization and racialization of labor and specific challenges, such as informality and invisibility, associated with labor in domestic spaces.

associated with lean platforms of the urban on-demand economy, such as Lieferando, Helpling, and Uber. These platforms specialize in brokering individual services (such as care, cleaning, grocery shopping, or food delivery) and operate based on maximized outsourcing – of labor and fixed capital but also of training and maintenance costs – to pursue strategies of rapid expansion driven by venture capital (VC; Srnicek 2017: 75ff.).

The *alternative* in alternative platformization must, thus, be assessed by addressing these issues and questions as to how alternative platforms differ or should differ from existing corporate ones: what are the necessary conditions for calling a socio-technical ensemble a platform? Moreover, what is not part of the platform logic but rather of the capitalist logic specific to corporate platforms and how might alternative platforms be different? Thoughts similar to those expressed in these questions and the question that opened this paper troubled us in a recent research project on the self-proclaimed "sustainable food delivery platform" Velofood in Graz, Austria (Ecker/Strüver 2022). Neither the financial model and strategy of this owner-run platform nor the mode of organizing its bicycle-based courier fleet seemed to fit commonplace assumptions associated with lean platforms.

Focusing on the European context and lean platforms, I therefore aim to offer in my contribution a deeper understanding of this problem by linking two distinct threads. Firstly, I present an overview of the definitions of *platform* frequently employed in current academic debates. Secondly, I draw on our case study in Graz, exploring how the examined food delivery platform differs from more conventional ones. In the conclusion, I summarize assumptions about the socio-technological aspects of platformization and present a framework for reflecting on alternative platforms.

The platform in platform urbanism

With the spread of lean platform services in urban spaces, the importance of digital platforms for the mediation of social and economic relations has increased. Hence, urban geographers increasingly apply the concept of PU to analyze the ways platformization alters the production of urban space (Barns 2019; Leszczynski 2020; Hodson et al. 2021). In this framework, the meaning of *platform* extends beyond its technological definition as a programmable interface (Helmond 2015) to encompass the platform as an organizational form for a data-based business model (Srnicek 2017; van Doorn/Badger 2020) and a mode of governing (Barns 2019; Altenried 2020).

Often drawing on Srnicek's 2017 book *Platform Capitalism*, authors writing on PU define the platform as a digital medium of interaction – an infrastructure allowing two or more parties to interact – or, more abstractly, as a system "comprising a set of stable core components or services, linked to an evolving set of peripheral components or services" (Lee et al. 2020: 117). In the case of lean platforms, this interaction typically takes the form of a transaction of labor power between customers and workers or third parties, such as restaurants. A closer look reveals that such platforms are themselves peripheral services linked to infrastructural platforms such as Google Maps, PayPal, and so on (van Dijck/Poell/de Waal 2018).

The analytical strength of the concept of PU lies in its focus on the mediating role of platforms. In contrast to rather "ill-defined" terms (Lee et al. 2020: 117), such as *smart city*, PU situates the analysis of the datafied city in everyday practices such as shopping, cleaning, housing, dating, or holiday planning. Taking the infrastructural role of platforms seriously, PU focuses on the infrastructural power these platforms develop as mediators of such socio-spatial practices (Bauriedl/Strüver 2020; Bissell 2020; Strauss 2020; Barns 2019). Platforms are viewed as emerging *urban institutions* – or *strategic terrains* – that distribute agency in a differential and unequal manner (van Doorn 2020; Ecker/Strüver 2022).

A necessary precondition for understanding a part of urban infrastructure as a platform herein is its functioning as a medium of interaction. However, further assumptions are often articulated. These derive especially from the expanded meaning of platform as a form of company and are heavily influenced by the fact that lean platforms have become the paradigmatic cases used to discuss platformization in cities. Hence, these assumptions concern aspects of their business models, such as the algorithmically controlled organization of labor, maximized outsourcing, the collection and valorization of data, and a VC-driven logic of rapid scalability. In what follows, I discuss these interconnected aspects (dynamics and ownership, function of data extraction, and labor organization) and their strategic interrelation (platform politics), thereby creating the basis for an analytical framework that differentiates the platform as an organizational form from the lean platform arising in many of today's cities as a result of VC-driven platformization. This systematization provides a tool for an analysis of current processes of platformization and enables the mapping of alternative platform futures.

Ownership and dynamics: Network effects and monopolistic tendencies

First, certain dynamics are associated with platforms. Network effects are frequently used to explain the rapid expansion of platforms and are key factors contributing to monopolistic tendencies (see, for example, Srnicek 2017: 45; Lee et al. 2020: 118; van Doorn/Badger 2020: 1489). Simply put, the term relates to a self-reinforcing tendency in network formation: as more connections are made, the network becomes more useful for additional nodes, leading to further connections.

Such network effects are closely linked to strategies of growth-before-profit. These strategies are associated with many platforms' VC-backed business models, which rely on monopolizing data and market segments. Studies on PU make an important contribution here, embedding the currently booming business model and practices of lean platforms in space and time. Authors draw attention to the fact that it was not only technological developments (of the internet, computer technologies, etc.) that facilitated platformization; rather, flexibilization of labor relations (Zwick 2018) and increasing financialization since the 1970s have played important roles. These processes prepared the ground for the emergence of business models relying on large amounts of VC and the labor of precarious urban populations in the aftermath of the 2008 financial crisis (Sadowski 2021).

While these dynamics are frequently assumed as general features of platforms per se, our research on the alternative food delivery platform Velofood helps to reflect on these observations by questioning quasi-deterministic assumptions regarding network effects and the importance of the number of connections in a network alone. Velofood focuses on a higher-priced and more ecologically sustainable market segment than its competitors Mjam and Lieferando and has only about a third of the number of restaurants mediated by its competitors; nevertheless, Velofood survives against its VC-backed international counterparts in Graz. As an owner-run company, it does not meet the criterion of collective ownership present in worker cooperatives and is subject to the will of the individual owner. As of 2021, however, this also means that there is no VC-induced pressure to expand. In an interview with us, the Graz-based company's management explicitly claimed to focus on capitalizing on the local, higher-priced market segment instead of scaling up and replicating the model elsewhere. The example serves as a reminder that not all connections in a network are equal and that the number of connections alone is not all that matters. Networks, instead, exhibit meaningful qualitative differences that are important to explain platform dynamics and opportunities for alternative platforms.

Furthermore, the example of the owner-run platform Velofood stresses the need to question network effects as a technologically deterministic process driving monopoly formation and quests for *functional sovereignty* (Sadowski 2021) in certain service segments of the platform economy. Considering the historical conjuncture in which most lean platforms have emerged helps to illustrate that they evolved as assets in a financialized economy. Although the technological logic amplifies monopolistic tendencies, it is the VC-backed business model and stock-market oriented ownership model that necessitate growth-before-profit strategies and attempts to monopolize market segments. Neither Velofood nor worker cooperatives elsewhere (e.g., co-ops within the CoopCycle federation) follow this logic.

The function of data extraction: Valorization and control

Second, there are various interpretations of the role of data in the political economy of platformization. For authors drawing on Srnicek (2017), data represents the new raw material necessary for the continued existence of capitalism in the 21st century; the platform is the corresponding business model harnessing this force of production. Zuboff (2019) assigns data a similar degree of importance, although, instead of framing platforms as innovations on the side of production, she focuses on their function as "means of behavior modification" and control, stressing the role of platforms as politico-economic technology over a merely economic function. Other researchers view data as less central. For example, Staab (2020) argues against viewing the extraction of user data as essential to the definition of platforms and as an accumulative logic sidelining the exploitation of labor and natural resources as the main sources of value. Instead, the author argues that platforms are based on the (old) accumulative logic of extracting rent from *proprietary markets*. Collected data on users, competitors, and so on serves secondary functions such as (a) monopolizing data on market developments (information control) or (b) controlling access to and competition within platform ecosystems (access control). However, both the socio-spatial implications of a changing mode of rent-based accumulation and the politics and behavioral implications of mass data collection and surveillance are important in theorizing PU (Elwood 2021; Sadowski 2021).

Hence, it has been puzzling to see the peripheral importance data plays for the local delivery platform Velofood. Data might be valorized in a number of ways, but this company practices none of those methods. Customer data could be used for (a) advertising, (b) marketing to restaurants (e.g., as a consultancy service), (c) entering the restaurant market (e.g., with its own ghost kitchens), or (d) developing an algorithm that can be valorized as an asset by financial markets. In contrast, the management offers insights and advice to partner restaurants based on orders for free. Data also does not play a central role in the management of the workforce. The smartphone applications used for communication and delivery work do not break down the labor process into micro-tasks that are tracked and distributed algorithmically. The ordering and delivery processes still require the transmission of a large continuous flow of data – a fact that drew attention to itself when server and app functions crashed due to increased use during COVID-19-related lockdowns. However, the way the data is handled cannot be described as extractivist using the narrower meaning of extractivism: an exploitative process drawing data from a primary circuit to be sold in a secondary circuit.

Besides, although smaller platforms such as this example from Graz cannot be seen as means of behavioral control, we could nonetheless identify changes in practices among parties participating in the platform ecosystem. Driven by platformization and accelerated by COVID-19-related lockdowns, several restaurants adapted their operations to increased platform sales. Such changes ranged from reorganizing labor processes in restaurants to opening new sites for delivery and pick-up only. Here, we observed a 'recalibration' of practices – although the company may not consciously intend to recalibrate practices of market participants, the platform terrain incentivizes and disincentivizes certain changes in the market.

Organizing labor: Algorithmic control and social subjection

Third, lean platforms are assumed to be based on a model that maximizes the outsourcing of labor costs and uses algorithmic management (Altenried 2020). There are two complementary aspects to this model of organizing labor. On the one hand, (nominal) independent contractors are frequently used to undercut labor standards (regarding wages, safety, etc.) and to outsource risks (van Doorn 2017). On the other hand, digital technologies are used to break down the labor process into tasks and allow algorithmic control of processes such as performance tracking or shift planning. This algorithmic control allows the disciplinary power associated with the factory as an enclosed space to spread throughout the urban fabric, for example, into public streets, private homes, and so on (Altenried 2020). This *digital Taylorism* is frequently identified as necessary to enable platform companies' growth strategies, and, as some authors argue, it may be that platforms cannot be profitable without this extensive outsourcing of costs (for this argument, see Srnicek 2017: 121).

However, to assess the potential of alternative platforms, it is necessary to determine whether this model of organizing labor is necessary for a platform to be feasible or whether it is merely a feature of capital-driven platformization. As Flanagan (2019) argues, considering the historical context of precarious service work helps to improve our understanding of platformization. Although managers of food delivery aggregator platforms such as Deliveroo or Lieferando tend to present their businesses as innovations, they show their awareness of this historical context when drawing on the image and work ethic of bicycle messenger culture for advertising purposes (for research on bicycle messengers, see, for example, Kidder 2006). The Graz-based delivery company Velofood, in fact, continues to organize the labor process using a model that is typical for this industry.[2] As with many other messenger services, (nominal) independent contractors rely on constant communication via a walkie-talkie app and a dispatching team to coordinate deliveries. While delivery companies such as Lieferando, Mjam, and Velofood face similar coordination problems when it comes to their deliveries, Velofood's approach focuses more on interpersonal communication and teamwork. This does not necessarily mean that its model ensures better working conditions – in fact, the anonymity and depersonalized labor process in an algorithmic system might be beneficial in meeting certain needs relating to, for example, language skills, saved time, and interpersonal and emotional stress. However, the continued existence of the model serves as a reminder of the fact that there are different ways to organize platform labor. Additionally, at least in the delivery

---

2   There is another important difference between Lieferando and Velofood that cannot be overstated, as academic research frequently misrepresents the platform. A platform such as Lieferando operates as an aggregator platform – in most cases, planning and executing delivery is left to restaurants and their precariously employed delivery workers. This is especially true when we look beyond the case of Graz. Lieferando's delivery share among processed orders is below 20 % in most national markets and only 7 % in the German market (Just Eat Takeaway.com 2021: 21). Typically, such companies simply aggregate food delivery options and charge delivery commissions, while companies such as Velofood actually offer food delivery.

sector, successes such as pushbacks against fake independent contracting and the establishment of the first collective bargaining agreements and workers' councils have been achieved in many European contexts such as Spain, Germany, and Austria. Extreme forms of digital Taylorism might thus be viewed as impermanent features of platformization as labor organizations succeed in inscribing workers' interests into platform terrains.

Platform politics: What, how, and for whom?

Fourth, each platform has its own *platform politics*[3] consisting of an answer to the following question: which problems does the platform address, in what way, and for whom? Most lean platforms are based on a specific aspect of reproductive labor for which they offer a commodified response to those who can afford it (Huws 2019). Addressing platform politics is essential when considering alternative platform futures – is the way a company, such as Lieferando, addresses the issue of food provision an adequate systemic response that factors in the needs of all parties involved (workers, restaurant staff, customers, urban traffic, etc.)? The answer is frequently negative, as many platforms "seek control and reward while abdicating responsibility to those who perform the labor that powers them" (Graham 2020: 2f.). Such strategies of disembedding and shedding of responsibility adversely affect systems of vocational training (e.g., formal education for taxi drivers), regulation (e.g., existing price mechanisms, labor standards), urban infrastructure (road traffic, etc.) and other stakeholders in a given industry (e.g., restaurants).

While Velofood incorporates sustainability practices (e.g., bicycle delivery only, biodegradable packaging, favoring vegetarian and vegan restaurants) into its answers to the aforementioned questions, its platform politics are similar to those embodied in aggregator platforms such as Lieferando: it offers the promise of a commodified response in the field of social reproduction (Ecker/Rowek/Strüver 2021). A restaurateur stressed this similarity when

---

3   Although the term *platform politics* has already been featured prominently in a 2013 edition of *Culture Machine*, I am using it with reference to Srnicek (2017: 46f.), who uses it in passing: "Finally, platforms are also designed in a way that makes them attractive to its [sic] varied users. While often presenting themselves as empty spaces for others to interact on, they in fact embody a politics."

explaining to us that Velofood has "basically just copied the concept from Vienna [...] This is basically exactly the same concept as Foodora. They have those tablets, which they have in the restaurants, [and they] have a menu [...] This is really the same everywhere." Restaurateurs view delivery platforms ambivalently because they offer limited economic profitability due to high fees, the disruption of labor routines, and packaging costs (Ecker/Strüver 2022). From this point of view, the question of what Lieferando would look like if it were a cooperative seems secondary to the question of whether there could be different platform politics that would, for example, be more favorable to smaller restaurants or produce less traffic and waste. When imagining alternative platform politics, authors can also learn from feminist critiques regarding the history of the automation of domestic work (Srnicek/Hester 2021). Lean service platforms reproduce the individualization of reproductive labor inherent in older techno-solutionist approaches that sought to replace the labor of servants and family members with machines instead of fundamentally questioning the gendered division of labor.[4]

Focusing on platform politics helps to reveal assumptions about how a social problem is imagined through particular platforms and to identify what role platforms might play in systemic responses. The platform politics of VC-driven platforms are almost exclusively centered on isolating a part of reproductive labor, turning it into a buyable service and marketing this labor as an individualized response to a social problem and as a vehicle to attract VC. Still very little is known about ways platforms could offer collective and systemic answers to address questions of ecological sustainability or the current spatial and gendered division of labor.

Conclusion

Overall, discussing an alternative delivery platform that is not focused on data extractivism, algorithmic management, and VC-backed expansion provides a basis for reflecting on how most current platforms function and how alternative platforms might function. The discussion can be summarized as a set of questions and a resulting framework that is useful as a toolkit for future analyses (see Fig. 1).

---

4   Platforms even fall short of these approaches by adding the regressive aspect of not promising automation but offering to replace labor with (other) precarious labor.

Figure 1 Framework for mapping alternative platforms

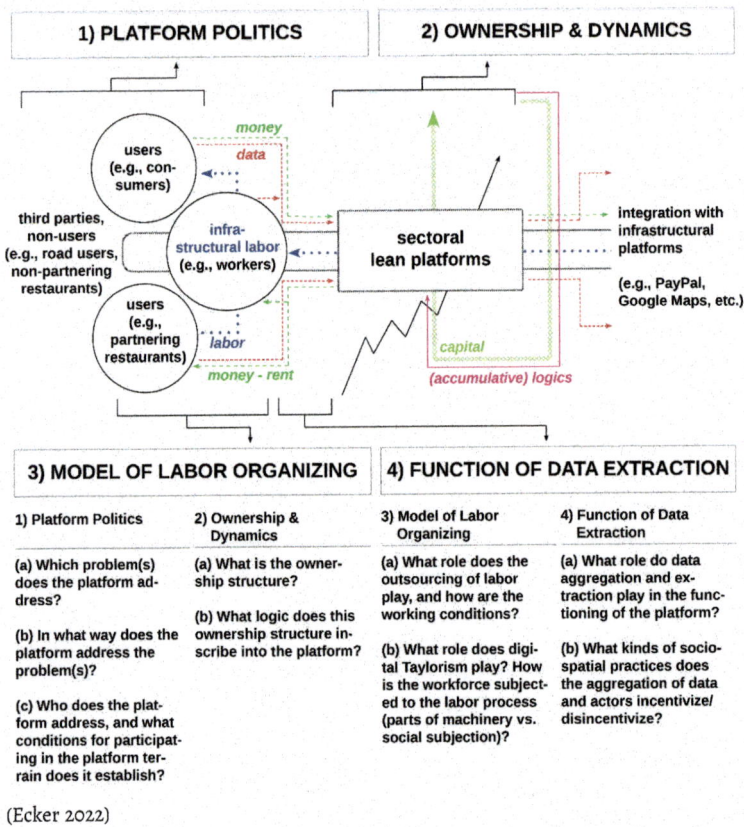

(Ecker 2022)

Discussing our case study from Graz reveals common features of lean platforms while also revealing that some features commonly associated with platforms are specific to capital-driven platformization and not necessarily part of platformization per se. This might help us address questions such as the one raised at the beginning of this paper. It can make sense to analyze certain parts of digital infrastructure through the lens of platformization even if they do not exhibit some commonly assumed core characteristics. The reflection offers two arguments for this: (a) platformization without some of the features of capital-driven platformization can provide insights as to how alternative platforms might function and offer inspiration for features that unions or policymakers could demand from VC-backed platforms (e.g., free access to aggregated data collected by the platform or a labor process wherein workers are not reduced to the role of underpaid "cogs in the food delivery machine"[5]); and (b) sectoral platforms such as Velofood may not function as programmable platforms in the computational sense, but they still channel users toward infrastructural platforms and create a terrain that is shaped by their platform politics, in turn shaping the agency of participating nodes.

Furthermore, this contribution highlights the importance of platform politics. An alternative model with respect to labor processes and strategy may still reproduce the same systemic response capital-driven platforms offer: a commodified response to the crisis of social reproduction. Hence, my reflection enhances speculations about alternative platform futures by including questions concerning the platform service itself.

These two aspects lead to a third concern: there seems to be little hope that dominant lean platforms such as Lieferando, Uber, or Helpling will be replaced if alternative platforms do not follow an expansionist logic and do not use other core features of capital-driven platformization that allow rapid scalability, such as the outsourcing of risks. Many analysts expand upon this point by arguing that lean platforms will be a short-term phenomenon because they are not economically viable enough (Srnicek 2017: 120ff.). The question about platform politics adds doubt to this already uncertain future perspective about whether an alternative platform that embodies the same platform politics but addresses some concerns with respect to data extraction or working conditions – i.e., 'a fair Lieferando' – should be seen as a satisfying result when imagining alternative platform futures. Instead, such reflections point in another direction: alternative platform futures might consist of qualitatively different responses. Such platforms might embody responses that recalibrate "the way in which we, as citizens, seek to know, interact, document and traverse" (Barns 2019: 10) in ways that rearticulate the spatial and gendered division of labor. Thereby, they might offer more equitable systemic responses to questions related to social reproduction.

---

5   Quote from a delivery worker at a union rally at the Deliveroo headquarters in Berlin attended by the author on June 28, 2017.

References

Altenried, Moritz (2020): The Platform as Factory: Crowdwork and the Hidden Labour behind Artificial Intelligence, in: *Capital & Class* 44(2): 145-58.

Barns, Sarah (2019): Negotiating the Platform Pivot: From Participatory Digital Ecosystems to Infrastructures of Everyday Life, in: *Geography Compass* 13(9). doi: https://doi.org/10.1111/gec3.12464.

Bauriedl, Sybille/Strüver, Anke (2020): Platform Urbanism: Technocapitalist Production of Private and Public Spaces, in: *Urban Planning* 5(4): 267-76.

Bissell, David (2020): Affective Platform Urbanism: Changing Habits of Digital on-Demand Consumption, in: *Geoforum* 115(October): 102-10.

Ecker, Yannick/Rowek, Marcella/Strüver, Anke (2021): Care on Demand: Geschlechternormierte Arbeits- und Raumstrukturen in der plattformbasierten Sorgearbeit, in: Altenried, Moritz/Dück, Julia/Wallis, Mira (eds.): *Plattformkapitalismus und die Krise der sozialen Reproduktion*, Münster: Westfälisches Dampfboot: 113-29.

Ecker, Yannick/Strüver, Anke (2022): Towards alternative platform futures in post-pandemic cities? A case study on platformization and changing socio-spatial relations in on-demand food delivery, in: *Digital Geography and Society* 3. doi: https://doi.org/10.1016/j.diggeo.2022.100032.

Elwood, Sarah (2021): Digital geographies, feminist relationality, Black and queer code studies: Thriving otherwise, in: *Progress in Human Geography* 45(2): 209-28.

Flanagan, Frances (2019): Theorising the Gig Economy and Home-Based Service Work, in: *Journal of Industrial Relations* 61(1): 57-78.

Graham, Mark (2020): Regulate, replicate, and resist – the conjunctural geographies of platform urbanism, in: *Urban Geography* 41(3): 453-57.

Helmond, Anne (2015): The Platformization of the Web: Making Web Data Platform Ready, in: *Social Media + Society* 1(2). doi: https://doi.org/10.1177/2056305115603080.

Hodson, Mike/Kasmire, Julia/McMeekin, Andrew/Stehlin, John G./Ward, Kevin (eds.) (2021): *Urban Platforms and the Future City. Transformations in Infrastructure, Governance, Knowledge and Everyday Life*, Oxon/New York: Routledge.

Huws, Ursula (2019): The Hassle of Housework: Digitalisation and the Commodification of Domestic Labour, in: *Feminist Review* 123(1): 8-23.

Kidder, Jeffrey L. (2006): "It's the Job That I Love": Bike Messengers and Edgework, in: *Sociological Forum* 21(1): 31-54.

Lee, Ashlin/Mackenzie, Adrian/Smith, Gavin J.D./Box, Paul (2020): Mapping Platform Urbanism: Charting the Nuance of the Platform Pivot, in: *Urban Planning* 5(1): 116-28.

Leszczynski, Agnieszka (2020): Glitchy vignettes of platform urbanism, in: *Environment and Planning D: Society and Space* 38(2): 189-208.

Just Eat Takeaway.com (2021): Annual Report 2020. https://www.justeattakeaway.com/investors/annual-reports/ [14.08.2021].

Sadowski, Jathan (2021): Who Owns the Future City? Phases of Technological Urbanism and Shifts in Sovereignty, in: *Urban Studies* 58(8): 1732-44.

Scholz, Trebor (2016): *Platform Cooperativism. Challenging the Corporate Sharing Economy*, New York, NY: Rosa Luxemburg Stiftung.

Staab, Philipp (2020): *Digitaler Kapitalismus. Markt und Herrschaft in der Ökonomie der Unknappheit*, Berlin: Suhrkamp.

Strauss, Kendra (2020): Labour Geography III: Precarity, Racial Capitalisms and Infrastructure, in: *Progress in Human Geography* 44(6): 1212-24.

Srnicek, Nick (2017): *Platform capitalism*, Cambridge/Malden: Polity.

Srnicek, Nick/Hester, Helen (2021): Zuhause im Plattformkapitalismus, in: Altenried, Moritz/Dück, Julia/Wallis, Mira (eds.): *Plattformkapitalismus und die Krise der sozialen Reproduktion*, Münster: Westfälisches Dampfboot: 94-111.

Thompson, Matthew (2021): What's so new about New Municipalism?, in: *Progress in Human Geography* 45(2): 317-42.

Ticona, Julia/Mateescu, Alexandra (2018): Trusted Strangers: Carework Platforms' Cultural Entrepreneurship in the on-Demand Economy, in: *New Media & Society* 20(11): 4384-404.

van Dijck, José/Poell, Thomas/de Waal, Martijn (2018): *The platform society*, New York/Oxford: University Press.

van Doorn, Niels (2017): Platform Labor: On the Gendered and Racialized Exploitation of Low-Income Service Work in the 'on-Demand' Economy, in: *Information, Communication & Society* 20(6): 898-914.

van Doorn, Niels (2020): A New Institution on the Block: On Platform Urbanism and Airbnb Citizenship, in: *New Media & Society* 22(10): 1808-26.

van Doorn, Niels/Badger, Adam (2020): Platform Capitalism's Hidden Abode: Producing Data Assets in the Gig Economy, in: *Antipode* 52(5): 1475-95.

Zuboff, Shoshana (2019): *The Age of Surveillance Capitalism: The Fight for a Human Future at the New Frontier of Power*, New York: PublicAffairs.

Zwick, Austin (2018): Welcome to the Gig Economy: Neoliberal Industrial Relations and the Case of Uber, in: *GeoJournal* 83(4): 679-91.

Riders United Will Never Be Divided?
A Cautionary Tale of Disrupting the Platformization of Urban Space

Barbara Orth

Introduction

Digital platforms have become a staple of everyday life, a trend reified by the Covid-19 pandemic. While providing conveniences to their users and consumers, these technology companies arguably have various detrimental effects on society: communication platforms, for example, are criticized for enabling surveillance by collecting big data sets while digital service platforms stand accused of eroding labor standards. Both data protection and labor standards hinge on effective government regulation, yet public oversight of platform companies is still piecemeal.

What is more, the algorithms and the code used by platform companies are also jealously guarded business secrets, rendering algorithmic decision-making a black box. In lieu of being able to reverse engineer code to understand the effects of these decisions on urban space, geographers have proposed workaround methods such as proxying (Fields/Bissell/Macrorie 2020) or studying 'glitches' (Leszczynski 2020) to scrutinize digital platforms. Especially labor-mediating platforms lend themselves to being studied this way: after all, "[...] it is not necessary to know how the machine works to know if you are getting a raw deal when it comes to payday, or when you have to deal with a bullying manager or keep up with an ever-increasing pace of work" (Moore/Joyce 2020: 942). To put it simply, while the source code platforms run on is not openly available, exploring platform operations at the scale of the everyday and through the lived experience of workers can help us make sense of the transformations brought about by platform capitalism, and thus produce knowledge to inform public debate over regulatory frameworks.

In my contribution to this volume, I follow this line of inquiry by analyzing the labor organizing efforts that took place at the Berlin-based platform Gorillas in 2021. Gorillas is the *enfant terrible* of the local start-up scene: the company became the first German start-up *ever* to achieve *unicorn status* – the Silicon Valley term for a start-up that reaches a valuation of one billion dollars (Partington/Lewin 2021). While the start-up scene is in awe, the exceptional pace of business growth and influx of investor capital has sparked discontent among the company's workers. Since February 2021, Gorillas workers have pursued various strategies to struggle for better working conditions, including initiating a *works council*, calling for wild cat strikes, i.e., strikes without the involvement of a union, and facing Gorillas management in court.

My analysis of this ongoing conflict situates the struggle over labor rights at Gorillas within other organizing efforts in the platform economy. The empirical material includes both formal research interviews and informal conversations with workers as well as an engagement with workers' publicly available digital communications. Since many of the collective actions have been documented on social media as they unfolded, social media posts provide a detailed timeline and a chronicle of the events. In the first section, I lay out the specifics of the local platform economy in Germany's capital Berlin and introduce Gorillas. I then recount the collective struggle over working conditions at the company and draw on research on previous platform economy organizing to highlight similarities and differences between Gorillas and these movements. I argue that a particular combination of external circumstances and successful organizing strategies enabled a relatively small group of workers to, at least temporarily, disrupt a growing billion-dollar business. While the collective actions at Gorillas, therefore, illustrate how local conditions can be successfully leveraged to disrupt a platform's operations from below, the paper cautions against generalizing from the Gorillas experience – given the unpredictability of venture capital-driven markets – it remains a cautionary tale.

Situating the case of Gorillas in Berlin's platform economy

As the pandemic is reaching its two-year anniversary, the logistics and delivery sectors have emerged as some of the clear economic winners of this period. In addition to record profits for Amazon and DHL (DHL Group 2021; Weise 2021), the lockdowns also benefited online retail in the food and grocery sector. In Germany, online food shopping has increased by 60 % since the pandemic started (HDE 2021: 8). Spurred by this growth, venture capitalists have heavily invested in food delivery platforms: two internationally established ready-to-eat-meal-delivery brands, UberEats and FoodPanda, have (re-)launched in Berlin in 2021 to contest the local monopoly of Lieferando and Wolt. In addition to the well-established model of delivering meals prepared in restaurants or dark kitchens, consumers' increased appetite for food delivery has also produced new business models in grocery retail.

In this new segment, local platforms Gorillas and Flink as well as the Turkish platform Getir compete with supermarkets to deliver groceries to a customer's doorstep within a very short time, often less than ten minutes. Advertisements for these platforms and their warehouses have become ubiquitous across the city's central residential neighborhoods. Gorillas launched shortly after the first Covid-19 lockdown in May 2020, and quickly expanded. It not only sells groceries at largely the same retail prices as large supermarket chains, but it also offers a much faster service than supermarkets – for a relatively small delivery fee of €1.80 (Gode 2021). To ensure these extremely fast deliveries, Gorillas operates through an infrastructure of small warehouses staffed by e-bike couriers, so-called *riders*, and warehouse workers, known in the company lingo as *pickers*. When a customer places an order through the Gorillas app, staff at the nearest warehouse quickly get to work: a picker collects the ordered products from the shelves, and hands them over to a rider. The rider puts the goods in a backpack, gets on an e-bike, and delivers the order to the customer's doorstep. In contrast to the archetype of meal-delivery, where workers were considered freelance *partners*, who had to own their own bikes and were paid per *gig*, Gorillas offers its workers employment contracts and e-bikes to enable fast deliveries. These *perks* made working for Gorillas as a rider or picker a comparatively good option for many workers at first – especially since most of the Gorillas workers have recently migrated to Berlin and have very limited options on the job market. Given the choice between these options, my interlocutors compared working conditions at Gorillas favorably to other jobs they could get on other labor platforms or in the hospitality and tourism industries. While Gorillas employment contracts have their own challenges, they do offer workers the benefits of employee status including sick leave, paid vacation, and, for the most part, health insurance coverage[1]. A former Gorillas worker I interviewed explained:

> "[...] I was super happy with the job because [...] I always [used to] work in contact with customers like bar, restaurants, also customer care and stuff. With Gorillas I didn't have to see any customer. [...] And it was a really nice environment [...] and the salary was really good. [...] I wish to find another job again, a good job, well paid like Gorillas."[2]

As the company raised more and more capital and grew at an exponential rate, however, the stark contrast between the company's available budget and its refusal to spend any of it on pay raises or better-quality equipment eventually sparked frustration among the workers. Some had believed in the start-up culture promise to *work hard until you make it*. Yet, even after Gorillas had 'made it', nothing changed substantially for them.

#WeWantSantiBack: Labor organizing efforts at Gorillas

In addition to the tension between the start-up's astonishing success with raising ever more capital and the working conditions on the shopfloor, the weather played an important role in sparking the first labor organizing efforts at Gorillas. During an extremely cold and snowy week in February 2021, riders faced icy roads which made their jobs more dangerous than usual. On February 9th, riders at three different Gorillas warehouses went on strike after being forced to deliver goods despite heavy snowfall that day. A day later, the Gorillas Workers Collective (GWC)[3] began tweeting about working conditions, starting a new Twitter account, @GorillasWorkers, which called for additional strikes (GWC 2021a). Ceding to the strike pressure, Gorillas management decided to temporarily shut down operations. After this initial success in halting deliveries until the snow subsided, the GWC also began advocating on behalf of warehouse pickers, who up until this point still had to come in for

---

1   In Germany, the type of employment contract determines whether it includes statutory health insurance. So called *student worker* contracts or *mini jobs* – both specifically precarious employment forms exempted from many of the German labor standards – do not cover health insurance.

2   Interview with former Gorillas worker, conducted in June 2021.

3   There are different accounts as to when exactly the GWC was formed. Different workers have indicated different starting times.

their shifts. The GWC demanded pickers, too, ought to be given paid time off (GWC 2021b). Shortly after this incidence, the GWC began to voice additional grievances:

> "Riders, did you know that we all earn a different hourly wage? While most get 10,50€/h, there are some earning 11,25€/h, 11,50€/h and 12,00€/h. This is not regulated in written [sic] by any ascending wage structure in our contracts. #equalpay4equalwork #gorillas #berlin" (GWC 2021c)

During the following weeks, additional issues were discussed between the workers and online. The GWC created its own Telegram[4] channel which has over 1.000 subscribers. The activists use this channel to collect information about problems such as the lack of appropriate gear for deliveries during cold and rainy weather, problems with faulty or late wage payments, safety issues related to Covid-19 and bike defects, and concerns over workers' privacy when CCTV was installed in several warehouses. Polling their co-workers about workplace grievances gave the GWC a sense of how widespread these issues were beyond the warehouses they themselves were familiar with.

At the end of March 2021, another concern came to the fore: the precarity of employment contracts issued by Gorillas. By default, all Gorillas workers receive a contract that is limited to one year and includes a six-month probation period. In Germany, employers can contractually mandate probation periods of between three to six months. During this time, an employee can be terminated easily and almost immediately without any reasons given, typically with a notice period of two weeks. After the end of the probation period, much stronger labor protections apply; employers need to cite reasons for terminating a contract and adhere to longer notice periods (the specifics depend on the industry and the type of contract but typically would include a three-month notice period) (BMAS 2021). Given this legal framework, long probation periods – as well as limited contracts – are a way for employers to sidestep labor protections.

When a rider who was a core member of the GWC was fired towards the end of his probation period (GWC 2021d), workers began to question the legitimacy of probation periods that covered half of their entire employment period. To challenge these precarious, albeit legal, hiring practices, three GWC activists initiated procedures for the formal election of a *Betriebsrat* (works

---

4   Telegram is a messenger app widely used in Germany.

council)[5] in early June (GWC 2021e). In mid-June, however, yet another rider, Santiago, was dismissed shortly before his probation period ended. Riders again went on strike, and this time, news of the campaign to reinstate Santiago generated attention both in the traditional media as well as on social media. The GWC successfully forged ties with journalists, unionists, and other activists, and this support base joined the physical picket lines and helped spread the hashtag #WeWantSantiBack online. As the campaign gained momentum, it spawned solidarity actions from other Gorillas warehouses in Germany and beyond. Throughout June and July 2021, several wildcat strike actions took place, and workers temporarily blocked warehouses across Berlin. In mid-July, the German Minister of Labor intervened to mediate between the parties. At a joint meeting between Gorillas managements, the minister, and the workers, the GWC presented a list of 19 demands that included payment of outstanding wages, a reduction in the length of probation periods, air conditioning for warehouses, and the issuing of work phones, to name but a few (see GWC 2021f for the full list). At the time of writing in December 2021, Gorillas management seems not to have met any of these demands. However, between September and December 2021, workers won several lawsuits relating to the limitations and the long probation periods of Gorillas employment contracts (Arbeitsgericht Berlin 2021a; GWC 2021g). Furthermore, Gorillas had sued the GWC, disputing the legality of their attempt at forming a works council. In November 2021, the Berlin Labor Court dismissed the company's lawsuit and confirmed the workers' right to form a works council (Arbeitsgericht Berlin 2021b). Following from this, the court also affirmed the temporary protection of those who were directly involved in preparing works council elections: under German law, they cannot be fired, not even during probation. Hence, the court judged the termination of GWC members who had been dismissed, likely in retaliation for their labor organizing, illegal. As a result, the company was ordered to reinstate these workers (GWC 2021i).

---

5   In Germany, all companies that have more than five employees are legally entitled to have a works council (*Betriebsrat*). A works council represents all workers of the company in disputes with management and provides oversight during hiring and firing processes (ETUI 2016).

Riders United: Platform organizing at large

The workers at Gorillas arguably attracted so much attention because labor organizing in the platform economy is considered extremely difficult. Mainstream unions have long struggled with the fragmentation of work under neoliberalism, and unionizing workers in Germany's expansive low wage sector – one of the largest in Europe (Grabka/Schröder 2019) – has been a long-term issue not least because migrant workers make up a significant portion of this workforce and unions have long struggled to include them (Bojadžijev 2008; Krings 2021). Rather than posing entirely new challenges, platform labor amplifies these existing difficulties. Unionizing platform workers is to organize a highly fragmented workforce with few interpersonal relationships: many platform workers neither meet nor know their co-workers, nor do they have a human-being for a supervisor. Many work as *independent partners*, i.e., freelancers who have to provide their own work equipment and are paid for one gig at a time. In addition to the anonymity of social relations, building union power with no physical workplace infrastructure to rally workers around is challenging, with domestic and home workers being another case in point (Shinozaki 2015). For these reasons, established unions have so far largely failed to achieve a significant rate of unionization amongst platform workers (Woodcock 2021).

With most platform workers not being union members, labor organizers cannot fall back on union strike budgets to cover lost income. Without a strike budget, stopping work to protest working conditions means forgoing immediate wages and tips in the hope of increased future income. However, this calculation is often hardly possible for platform workers: platform workers tend to be 'hustlers' piecing together a meager livelihood from their work and usually have no savings to fall back on (Ravenelle 2019). What is more, being largely a migrant workforce, they tend to be excluded from social welfare and unemployment benefits, and, depending on immigration status, they often need to earn a steady income to remain in the country (Lam/Triandafyllidou 2021).

Despite these challenging circumstances, Gorillas is not the first time platform workers collectively struggle for improvements. Platform workers have been striking against changes in payment systems across Europe in London, Toronto, and Turin, as well as in India and China, since at least 2016. Berlin itself has seen platform economy organizing before when food couriers at Deliveroo and Foodora – both platforms that specialize in delivering ready-made meals – founded the syndicalist union DeliverUnion in 2017 (New Syndicalist 2019).

Notwithstanding ongoing organizing efforts at Gorillas, I want to propose that the case of Gorillas differs from other attempts at organizing platform workers. Collective actions serve as an illustration of just *how many* factors need to come together to leverage worker power. Some of these factors are external to the organizing factors and include the timing of the protests and the spatializations of grocery delivery models as well as the visa regime that produces a certain type of worker at Gorillas. Other components of the successful collective action are created by the workers themselves, such as their ability to successfully leverage advantages created by these external circumstances and foster community ties that carried the protests forward. This specific combination of circumstances gave workers leverage to organize at Gorillas but is not necessarily replicable. To contextualize the success of collective actions at Gorillas thus is not to underestimate the considerable amount of work the GWC and its allies put in, nor to belittle the importance of building worker power vis-à-vis platform companies. Yet, to better understand the prospects of labor organizing against platform companies, it is crucial to situate the case within the broader frame of a venture-capital driven sector of the economy. I will turn to each of these aspects to examine how they make the organizing efforts at Gorillas different from previous organizing efforts in the platform sector.

Contextualizing the collective actions at Gorillas

Starting with the external circumstances, it is, first, important to note the timing of the protests: the push to form a works council, as well as the first wave of strikes, coincided with a particularly quick expansion of the platform economy in Berlin. As a result, Gorillas workers benefited from an industry pivot: since the rapid growth of the food delivery sector, platform riders have been offered employment contracts rather than being subjected to the gig model. Both the recently launched grocery-delivery start-ups, as well as the established ready-to-eat platforms, have largely shifted from per-drop payment to offering a mix of hourly pay and bonuses. So unlike previous gig workers that went on strike, Gorillas workers did not have to sacrifice their primary income entirely. And thanks to its large support base, the GWC was also able to crowdsource a budget to cover lost tips, which form a considerable portion of workers' income. The #WeWantSantiBack campaign likewise coincided with major business news: Gorillas' main corporate competitors Flink and Getir received large amounts of investment capital at funding rounds in June 2021 and immediately started recruiting as many riders and pickers as they could (Stothard 2021). As companies outbid each other for workers to scale as fast as possible, there were, and still are, many job openings in the industry. At the time of writing, delivery companies in Berlin offer roughly the same salaries and conditions, including employment contracts, payment above minimum wage with a starting salary of €10.50/hour, and often also an e-bike. Benefits that previously made Gorillas stand out to the first applicants are now more or less the industry standard. These fairly uniform conditions across delivery platforms in Berlin also meant retaliation by management – terminations and not renewing contracts when they expired – was somewhat buffered. Given the number of job openings in the sector, everyone who got fired because of their workplace activism and wanted to continue working in the delivery sector was able to do so easily.[6] In short, the fact that several companies with similar business models launched in Berlin at the same time, and demand for staff was high, workers in the city occupied a better bargaining position than previous platform workers found themselves or currently find themselves in other cities.

Second, the ability to take the risk of losing one's job and being forced to look for another one – either in the industry or beyond – is possibly also related to the demographics of the Gorillas workforce. As mentioned earlier, digital labor platforms overwhelmingly attract migrant workers in Germany (Altenried 2021; Schaupp 2021). While Gorillas is no exception to this general tendency in platform work – warehouse and delivery workers are mostly recent arrivals to Berlin – in some important ways, Gorillas workers *do* differ from both the 'migrantized' workforce in non-platform jobs and from other platform workers who are also migrants. Recent research on platform work in Canada, for example, points to a large prevalence of migrant workers on employment visas, which make it difficult to change jobs (Lam/Triandafyllidou 2021). The Gorillas workers I encountered, on the other hand, are by and large not on such visas. Instead, Gorillas workers are often either dual citizens of both a non-EU and an EU country – and hence able to work and move freely under the Schengen agreement – or they hold student or working holiday visas. Under these latter visa categories, one's immigration status is not tied

---

6 Interview with GWC member, conducted in October 2021.

to a specific employer; in the cases of students and EU citizens, their immigration status is not conditional on generating an income at all as long as they can support themselves financially. Consequently, losing a particular job then does not immediately risk Gorillas workers' ability to stay in Germany. While fulfilling contract-hour targets or financial targets in employment visa categories is often needed simply to secure an individual's ability to stay in the host country, it is also often a prerequisite to bring family members or pay off a migrant's journey (Bauder 2006; Könönen 2019). Student and working holiday visas, on the other hand, tend to be issued exclusively to young people in their 20s or early 30s. In contrast to employment visas or asylum stipulations, working holiday visas rule out bringing a spouse or other dependents to Germany. Likely because of these visa regimes, none of the workers I spoke to – regardless of their gender – had any financial responsibilities towards dependents in Germany. While some workers send money to their families abroad, in Germany they only had themselves to support, and migration projects were individual lifestyle projects rather than joint family decisions. Nor were the workers I interviewed required to meet specific income targets to be able to stay in the country, pay for their journey, or apply for family reunion. Considering these circumstances, I would argue, it was more feasible for Gorillas workers to take risks with organizing than it is for most migrants in comparable low-wage jobs. The combined factors of not being subjected to immigration-related labor requirements and being young and unattached meant that Gorillas workers are overall comparatively better positioned to fight for labor rights.

Third, in addition to the timing and the demographics of the Gorillas workforce, the organizing efforts also benefited from the particularities of grocery delivery logistics, namely its spatialization. All grocery delivery startups that have launched in Berlin in the past two years promise extremely short delivery times, in most cases less than ten minutes. The almost instant delivery makes them distinct from the scheduled delivery services offered by supermarket chains, and it is even faster than ordering from a restaurant through a meal-delivery app. To deliver this fast is extremely challenging given that the so-called 'last mile' in logistics is the most expensive part of the supply chain and computationally also the most difficult problem to solve (Altenried 2019). The new grocery delivery models approach this problem by relying on both a reduction in complexity and a very localized infrastructure.

In the meal-delivery business, companies must mediate workers and two dynamic variables, the restaurant's location, and the customer's location. In grocery delivery, however, the pick-up location remains fixed as riders only deliver products within a specific radius of each warehouse and return to the same warehouse after every delivery[7] – the only changing variable is the customer's location. This reduction in complexity not only serves a business rationale, it also lends itself to collective action: it is much more feasible to picket individual warehouses than it would be to block off hundreds of restaurants or dark kitchen locations. To keep distances between a customer's location and a warehouse short, platform-operated warehouses are directly located in residential neighborhoods rather than on the outskirts of cities, where rent for industrial warehouses tends to be cheaper. The built environment of residential neighborhoods, however, limits the size of platform-operated grocery delivery warehouses compared to industrial supermarket warehouses[8]. Picketing these physically small warehouses with one or two entrances, of course, requires fewer workers than attempting to block off an entire regular-sized industrial warehouse. With these factors combined, the spatial organization of grocery delivery platform logistics makes disruption of the supply chain attainable.

Fourth, thanks to the spatial configuration of grocery delivery, Gorillas workers were able to co-produce social infrastructures. Importantly, these social infrastructures are what make or break organizing efforts at companies. Given the fragmentation of digitally mediated labor, planning collective actions requires co-workers who do not know each other and are subjected to digital surveillance and algorithmic management to build trust and relationships (Bronowicka/Ivanova 2020; Leonardi et al. 2019). For these reasons, previous ride-hailing and food courier organizers relied on reaching out to workers in public spaces where they are identifiable by their platform-branded backpacks (Tassinari/Maccarrone 2020; Woodcock 2021). In the case of Gorillas, however, warehouses provided a ready-made physical space for workers to cultivate these relationships by 'hanging out' between deliveries. As one picker I interviewed recounted, "We put [on] music, we make coffee and eat all the time."[9] The company even advertised warehouses as the "homebase for all riders to catch up with the crew, take a break and unwind" and

---

7   Some companies also dispatch workers with two to three orders at a time, but workers still regularly return to a warehouse during their shift.
8   The price of real estate in central urban districts likely also plays a role but it would go beyond the scope of this article to discuss this aspect in detail.
9   Interview with former Gorillas worker, conducted in June 2021.

even organized company-sponsored parties there to foster warehouse communities (Gorillas Company 2021a; 2021b). In addition, Gorillas used to assign riders and pickers shifts at different but recurring warehouses[10]. This allowed workers to get to know co-workers at multiple warehouses located in different parts of the city, and information could be easily shared between different warehouse communities. As a result, the GWC was able to draw on strong informal group dynamics and social infrastructures that had formed in the first months of the company's existence. The importance of this early external advantage became even more apparent in the aftermath of the summer 2021 strikes when management reassigned GWC activists to entirely new warehouses. In these new locations, the organizers had to begin building mutual trust with their fellow workers from scratch, which impacted their ability to organize.[11]

In addition to the strength of social ties fostered in physical space, the workers also created a rich digital space to socialize. Most platforms, including Gorillas, do not have features for workers to contact each other through the app they work on. As van Doorn (2017) argues, this is not a "bug but a feature": app developers deliberately design digital labor platforms in a way that shields companies from being held accountable for workplace issues. To overcome this widespread problem, platform workers often rely on other digital meeting places on social media to communicate with each other. Examples include Reddit threads, Facebook groups, or WhatsApp group chats, in which workers discuss covering each other's shifts, warn each other about bad-faith customers, sexual predators, or scams (van Doorn 2020b; Tassinari/Maccarrone 2020). Woodcock (2021: 2) points to these digital spaces as "digital watercoolers" because they serve the same social purpose as coffee rooms or watercoolers in office environments: a space for co-workers to meet informally, share workplace gossip, and chat about problems.

During the organizing drive at Gorillas, the satirical Instagram account @gorillasriderlife2 served as an increasingly frequented digital watercooler. Founded by a group of apolitical riders, it was at first neither related to the GWC nor the company itself. It was not started with a view to organize workers but merely to provide a space for workers to vent about their work-life online. The account provided comic relief through shared memes and jokes

---

10   In March 2021, this policy was changed and now workers are assigned to a single warehouse (GWC 2021h).
11   Interview with GWC member, conducted in October 2021.

about being a rider at Gorillas. The created content was relatable to workers' everyday work-life, whether they were already politicized or not, drawing nearly 3.000 followers (Gorillas Rider Life 2021). As the campaign for better working conditions progressed, however, the GWC and the riders behind the Instagram account began collaborating. The @gorillasriderlife2 account thus became a two-way communication channel for the GWC. Thanks to the account's large follower base amongst Gorillas workers, information about collective actions could be spread easily and fast, and, in turn, the GWC was also able to poll workers about their grievances and crowdsource demands.

In sum, the spatial organization of grocery-delivery both enabled physical strike action as well as important social infrastructure among workers that the other, less radical approaches, could take advantage of. The social media accounts, for example, led to collaboration with different labor and migrant justice groups. After getting connected through Twitter, these groups supported the early GWC activists in their push for works council elections. Through these joint efforts, the GWC was able to mobilize nearly 200 workers to come to the first election necessary for establishing a works council[12]; and later to attract trade union and labor activists to accompany workers to their court hearings.

Even though the struggle is ongoing, it is possible to relate the Gorillas example back to previous organizing efforts in the platform economy and point to both similarities and differences. Drawing on their ethnographic observations of delivery strikes across the UK in 2018, Cant and Woodcock (2020) suggest that organizing efforts within the platform sector were only successful if they followed two principles. Those were, one, making strategic use of existing informal group structures and, two, rallying around winnable workplace-specific grievances. The organizing efforts at Gorillas fit both tenets: the GWC successfully drew on social ties that had already existed in physical space and created additional digital spaces to bolster these connections. Moreover, the early strikes in February 2021 had a specific and winnable goal, i.e., to stop deliveries until the snow subsided. Given that the weather was a short-term phenomenon, Gorillas management could pragmatically agree to a temporary work stoppage seeing as it cost the company less than longer-term concessions likely would. The first organizing goal was therefore very

---

12   The process of forming a works council requires several steps: a first election to vote on candidates for an *electoral board*. The electoral board is then tasked with preparing the main elections for the works council.

clear and time-bound, and the spatial layout of the warehouses made it feasible. The GWC's organizing strategy thus enabled the workers to replicate previous positive experiences with organizing in the platform sector.

However, this success also hinged on factors beyond the activists' control: the changes in the industry that led to employment contracts rather than freelance gigs; the launching of competing platform companies in Berlin that coincided with the organizing efforts; the particular vulnerability to delivery disruptions inherent in the grocery delivery model; as well as the workers' comparative privilege as social-media savvy, young migrants who were able to take risks with organizing because the worst-case scenario of losing their job did not result in deportation or failing financial responsibilities towards others. Lastly, September 2021 also saw a triple election in Berlin[13], and the timing of the campaigns during this super-election year may have also added to a particular political climate that was ripe for agitation and media attention. As the organizing has since progressed, the erstwhile campaign focus has broadened into a long list of demands, which have not been met so far. It remains to be seen whether these much more ambitious goals, such as having a dedicated visa team at Gorillas Human Resources to help workers with immigration procedures, will eventually be achieved.

Conclusion: A cautionary tale

Overall, the case of Gorillas may substantiate a geographic reading of platforms as "simultaneously embedded and disembedded from the space-times [they] mediate" (Graham 2020: 7). Thanks to tremendous amounts of capital, platform businesses seem disembedded from the constraints of regular businesses and out of reach of regulators. They neither need to turn a profit nor sustainably use their resources, including their workforce, as long as fresh capital abounds. At the same time, however, the case of Gorillas also shows that the company's very business model relies on a neighborhood-based network of warehouses, embedding the platform at a very local level. And this embeddedness opens opportunities for collective action to disrupt the business effectively at this scale in a way that previous meal-delivery organizing

---

13   Seats in three different levels of government were up for election: the federal parliament (*Bundestag*), Berlin's City Council (*Senat*) as well as seats at the municipal level (*Bezirk*).

efforts could not have. At the time of writing, several wins have transpired: the Berlin Labor Court ruled in favor of the workers who had been fired in connection to their organizing efforts; the court has also confirmed workers' rights to form a works council and ruled the limitations on workers' contracts illegal. Outside the legal realm, Gorillas as a company has been widely criticized in the press and decried as a bad employer. Whether or not this has hurt the company's efforts to acquire new customers is difficult to assess. However, the bad press has marked them out as a target for other local activist groups: in August 2021, an anonymous group poured glue into the locks of five Gorillas warehouses during the night, delaying deliveries the following morning. The activists cited "unfair working conditions" and "solidarity with Gorillas workers" as their motives (Kluge 2021). Lastly, the case of the fighting workers at Gorillas also has potential to reach beyond the platform economy. Wild cat strikes are a challenge to Germany's model of industrial relations based on social partnerships and dialogue in which worker-initiated strike actions without union representation are deemed illegal. Given the mixed results of pursuing social dialogue mechanisms in the platform economy (Frenken et al. 2020; Johnston 2020) and beyond, the more radical tactics of the GWC's organizing efforts may well become a tale to inspire a new generation of labor organizers.

However, I have argued such a tale should be treated with caution. Only the fortunate combination of external factors and internal factors led to a temporarily successful disruption of the platform's operation. To reiterate these points: external factors beyond the workers' control have included the timing of the protests; the demographics of the Gorillas workforce; and the spatial organization of grocery delivery and its susceptibility to service disruptions. Factors internally fostered by workers were strong community ties and workers' ability to create digital watercoolers to strengthen the existing sense of community. The GWC's skillful use of social media also gathered a large network of outside supporters and attention from unions and politicians during an election year. It was this – perhaps unique – combination of factors that facilitated collective action at Gorillas.

Comparing this specific case again to the wider context of platform worker movements, it is important to lastly highlight the volatility of this venture-capital driven sector. The fate of the previously mentioned grassroots initiative DeliverUnion in Berlin can serve as an example: DeliverUnion had, to an extent, managed to overcome the challenges of anonymity and the lack of a physical work-place infrastructure. Over three years, activists worked on organizing Foodora and Deliveroo riders while Berlin witnessed a 'delivery platform war' between different food business conglomerates. When this competition culminated with a merger of Lieferando and Foodora (Ksienrzyk 2019), Deliveroo's investors saw better return-on-investment prospects in other markets and shut down Deliveroo's operations in Germany in August 2019. The investors' decisions thus abruptly upended existing organizing efforts and practically overnight, 1.000 riders and drivers lost their jobs (Lomas 2019). It was thus the investors who ultimately decided the future of these food couriers, and some workers even left Berlin entirely to follow Deliveroo abroad (Altenried 2021). Similarly, the delivery platform FoodPanda recently announced the end of its operations in Germany after less than six months of launching in Berlin (Kläsgen 2021). These examples highlight the vulnerability of worker struggles vis-à-vis capital flight (van Doorn 2020a), and, therefore, the most interesting question may be whether the strikes at Gorillas have had an impact on investors' perception of Gorillas as a start-up to throw their weight behind.

In early August 2021, DoorDash, one of the biggest players in the food delivery business, entered talks to acquire Gorillas (Partington 2021). What a takeover by a company the size of DoorDash would have meant for labor relations at Gorillas is, of course, up to speculation – and at the time of writing it had not materialized. A corporation of the size of DoorDash, however, is less dependent on constantly raising 'fresh' capital from new investors, and consequently perhaps less likely to care about service disruptions and bad press. While I have shown that workers at Gorillas may have been in a comparatively good bargaining position thus far, the almost-takeover by DoorDash revealed just how quickly the cards on the table can be reshuffled in the venture-capital driven platform economy – and the cards tend to be stacked against the workers.

References

Altenried, Moritz (2019): On the Last Mile: Logistical Urbanism and the Transformation of Labour, in: *Work Organisation, Labour & Globalisation* 13(1): 114-29.

Altenried, Moritz (2021): Mobile Workers, Contingent Labour: Migration, the Gig Economy and the Multiplication of Labour, in: *Environment and Plan-*

ning A: Economy and Space (November). doi: https://doi.org/10.1177/030851 8X211054846.

Arbeitsgericht Berlin (2021a): Entfristungsklagen beim Lieferdienst Gorillas. https://www.berlin.de/gerichte/arbeitsgericht/presse/pressemitteilungen/2021/pressemitteilung.1123153.php [10.09.2021].

Arbeitsgericht Berlin (2021b): Kein Abbruch der Betriebsratswahl. https://www.berlin.de/gerichte/arbeitsgericht/presse/pressemitteilungen/2021/pressemitteilung.1147485.php [10.12.2021].

Bauder, Harald (2006): *Labor Movement: How Migration Regulates Labor Markets*, Oxford: Oxford University Press.

Bojadžijev, Manuela (2008): *Die Windige Internationale. Rassismus und Kämpfe der Migration*, Münster: Westfälisches Dampfboot.

Bundesministerium für Arbeit und Soziales (BMAS) (2021): Arbeitsrecht – Kündigungsschutz. https://bmas.de/DE/Arbeit/Arbeitsrecht/Arbeitnehmerrechte/Kuendigungsschutz/kuendigungsschutz.html [05.12.2021].

Bronowicka, Joanna/Ivanova, Mirela (2020): Resisting the Algorithmic Boss: Guessing, Gaming, Reframing and Contesting Rules in App-Based Management, in: *SSRN Research Paper Series* (March). doi: https://doi.org/10.2139/ssrn.3624087.

Cant, Callum/Woodcock, Jamie (2020): Fast Food Shutdown: From Disorganisation to Action in the Service Sector, in: *Capital & Class* 44(4): 513-21.

DHL Group (2021): Deutsche Post DHL Group Expects Record Earnings in 2021 of More than EUR 7.7 Billion – Mid-Term Outlook Also Raised. https://www.dpdhl.com/en/media-relations/press-releases/2021/deutsche-post-dhl-group-financial-figures-q3-2021.html [14.01.2022].

European Trade Union Institute (ETUI) (2016): Workplace Representation in Germany. https://www.worker-participation.eu/National-Industrial-Relations/Countries/Germany/Workplace-Representation#_ftn2 [06.09.2021].

Fields, Desiree/Bissell, David/Macrorie, Rachel (2020): Platform Methods: Studying Platform Urbanism Outside the Black Box, in: *Urban Geography* 41(3): 462-68.

Frenken, Koen/Vaskelainen, Taneli/Fünfschilling, Lea/Piscicelli, Laura (2020): An Institutional Logics Perspective on the Gig Economy, in: Maurer, Indre/Mair, Johanna/Oberg, Achim (eds.): *Theorizing the Sharing Economy: Variety and Trajectories of New Forms of Organizing*, Bingley: Emerald Publishing: 83-105.

Gode, Solveig (2021): *Wir haben die Preise von Gorillas und Flink mit Rewes und Edekas Lieferservice verglichen – so bestellt ihr am günstigsten*, in: Businessinsider, 16.12.2021. https://www.businessinsider.de/wirtschaft/handel/so-t euer-sind-flink-und-gorillas-im-vergleich-zu-edeka-und-rewe-a/ [19.12.2021].

Gorillas Company (2021a): Sign up Gorillas Music Stream. https://www.notion.so/Sign-up-Gorillas-Music-Stream-c9a3de5deef342368cc003feeec1536f [13.09.2021].

Gorillas Company (2021b): Gorillas Manifesto. https://gorillas.io/en/manifesto [13.09.2021].

Gorillas Rider Life (@gorillasriderlife2) (2021): https://www.instagram.com/gorillasriderlife2/ [08.01.2022].

Gorillas Workers Collective (@GorillasWorkers) (2021a): https://twitter.com/GorillasWorkers/status/1359538283336916993 [13.09.2021].

Gorillas Workers Collective (@GorillasWorkers) (2021b): https://twitter.com/GorillasWorkers/status/1360192945404727298 [10.09.2021].

Gorillas Workers Collective (@GorillasWorkers) (2021c): https://twitter.com/GorillasWorkers/status/1360981133899554817 [24.08.2021].

Gorillas Workers Collective (@GorillasWorkers) (2021d): https://twitter.com/GorillasWorkers/status/1375009562781171713 [06.09.2021].

Gorillas Workers Collective (@GorillasWorkers) (2021e): https://twitter.com/GorillasWorkers/status/1375725527869353984 [06.09.2021].

Gorillas Workers Collective (@GorillasWorkers) (2021f): https://twitter.com/GorillasWorkers/status/1413087153257594881 [06.09.2021].

Gorillas Workers Collective (@GorillasWorkers) (2021g): https://twitter.com/GorillasWorkers/status/1433710343356829714 [10.09.2021].

Gorillas Workers Collective (@GorillasWorkers) (2021h): https://twitter.com/GorillasWorkers/status/1369694994475462656 [25.08.2021].

Gorillas Workers Collective (@GorillasWorkers) (2021i): https://twitter.com/GorillasWorkers/status/1471036053276397576 [15.12.2021].

Grabka, Markus M./Schröder, Carsten (2019): The Low-Wage Sector in Germany Is Larger than Previously Assumed, in: *DIW Weekly Report* 9(14): 117-24.

Graham, Mark (2020): Regulate, Replicate, and Resist – the Conjunctural Geographies of Platform Urbanism, in: *Urban Geography* 41(3): 453-57.

Handelsverband Deutschland (HDE) (2021): Online-Monitor. https://einzelhandel.de/online-monitor [02.09.2021].

Johnston, Hannah (2020): Labour Geographies of the Platform Economy: Understanding Collective Organizing Strategies in the Context of Digitally Mediated Work, in: *International Labour Review* 159(1): 25-45.

Kläsgen, Michael (2021): *Foodpanda zieht sich aus Deutschland zurück*, in: Süddeutsche Zeitung, 22.12.2021. https://www.sueddeutsche.de/wirtschaft/gorillas-flink-foodpanda-delivery-hero-rewe-1.5493948 [23.12.2021].

Kluge, Christoph (2021): *Protest Radikalisiert Sich: Türschlösser von Gorillas-Filialen in Berlin Verklebt*, in: Der Tagesspiegel, 13.08.2021. https://www.tagesspiegel.de/berlin/protest-radikalisiert-sich-tuerschloesser-von-gorillas-filialen-in-berlin-verklebt/27514660.html [13.09.2021].

Könönen, Jukka (2019): Becoming a 'Labour Migrant': Immigration Regulations as a Frame of Reference for Migrant Employment, in: *Work, Employment and Society* 33(5): 777-93.

Krings, Torben (2021): 'Good' Bad Jobs? The Evolution of Migrant Low-Wage Employment in Germany (1985-2015), in: *Work, Employment and Society* 35(3): 527-44.

Ksienrzyk, Lisa (2019): *Kein Pink mehr auf den Straßen: Foodora ist jetzt Lieferando*, in: Businessinsider, 18.04.2019. https://www.businessinsider.de/gruenderszene/food/foodora-lieferando-integration/ [13.12.2021].

Lam, Laura/Triandafyllidou, Anna (2021): An Unlikely Stepping Stone? Exploring How Platform Work Shapes Newcomer Migrant Integration, in: *Transitions: Journal of Transient Migration* 5(1): 11-29.

Leonardi, Daniela/Murgia, Annalisa/Briziarelli, Marco/Armano, Emiliana (2019): The Ambivalence of Logistical Connectivity: A Co-Research with Foodora Riders, in: *Work Organisation, Labour & Globalisation* 13(1): 155-71.

Leszczynski, Agnieszka (2020): Glitchy Vignettes of Platform Urbanism, in: *Environment and Planning D: Society and Space* 38(2): 189-208.

Lomas, Natasha (2019): *Deliveroo Is Exiting the German Market*, in: Tech Crunch, 12.08.2019. https://social.techcrunch.com/2019/08/12/deliveroo-is-exiting-the-german-market/ [02.09.2021].

Moore, Phoebe V./Joyce, Simon (2020): Black Box or Hidden Abode? The Expansion and Exposure of Platform Work Managerialism, in: *Review of International Political Economy* 27(4): 926-48.

New Syndicalist (2019): *No love for Deliveroo! A reflection on organising and mobilising in the "gig" economy*, in: New Syndicalist, 15.02.2019. https://newsyndicalist.org/2019/02/15/manchester-deliveroo-strike/ [25.08.2021].

Partington, Miriam/Lewin, Amy (2021): *On-Demand Grocery Delivery Startup Gorillas Raises €245m and Becomes a Unicorn, Nine Months after Launch*, in:

Sifted, 25.03.2021. https://sifted.eu/articles/gorillas-raises-e245m-unicorn/ [03.09.2021].

Partington, Miriam (2021): Gorillas in Talks to Take DoorDash Investment at a $2.5bn Valuation, in: Sifted, 05.08.2021. https://sifted.eu/articles/gorillas-doordash/ [06.09.2021].

Ravenelle, Alexandrea J. (2019): Hustle and Gig: Struggling and Surviving in the Sharing Economy, Oakland: University of California Press.

Schaupp, Simon (2021): Algorithmic Integration and Precarious (Dis)Obedience: On the Co-Constitution of Migration Regime and Workplace Regime in Digitalised Manufacturing and Logistics, in: Work, Employment and Society (July). doi: https://doi.org/10.1177/09500170211031458.

Shinozaki, Kyoko (2015): Migrant Citizenship from below: Family, Domestic Work, and Social Activism in Irregular Migration, New York: Palgrave Macmillan.

Stothard, Michael (2021): Grocery-Delivery Startups Flink and Getir Announce $800m in Fresh Capital in One Day, in: Sifted, 04.06.2021. https://sifted.eu/articles/flink-getir/ [06.09.2021].

Tassinari, Arianna/Maccarrone, Vincenzo (2020): Riders on the Storm: Workplace Solidarity among Gig Economy Couriers in Italy and the UK, in: Work, Employment and Society 34(1): 35-54.

van Doorn, Niels (2017): Platform Labor: On the Gendered and Racialized Exploitation of Low-Income Service Work in the 'on-Demand' Economy, in: Information, Communication & Society 20(6): 898-914.

van Doorn, Niels (2020a): At What Price? Labour Politics and Calculative Power Struggles in on-Demand Food Delivery, in: Work Organisation, Labour & Globalisation 14(1): 136-49.

van Doorn, Niels (2020b): Stepping Stone or Dead End? The Ambiguities of Platform Mediated Domestic Work under Conditions of Austerity, in: Baines, Donna/Cunningham, Ian (eds.): Working in the Context of Austerity, Bristol: Bristol University Press: 49-69.

Weise, Karen (2021): Amazon's Profit Soars 220 Percent as Pandemic Drives Shopping Online, in: The New York Times, 29.04.2021. https://www.nytimes.com/2021/04/29/technology/amazons-profits-triple.html [11.01.2022].

Woodcock, Jamie (2021): The Fight Against Platform Capitalism. An Inquiry into the Global Struggles of the Gig Economy, London: University of Westminster Press.

<title>"Processed Food on the Urban Data Highway. Food Delivery Services as In_Visible Infrastructure in the Production of Urbanity" </title>
<meta name="EmergeError">

<!– Akteurinnen für urbanen Ungehorsam

<div class="Introduction">

<p> Urban space has increasingly been infused with digital infrastructures, built upon algorithmic app architectures and shaped by information systems and collected data not everybody has access to.[1] One of these city-making platforms in Germany is the food delivery service Lieferando. Embodied by its riders, it visibly occupies the streets, influencing our everyday cityscape through bright orange uniforms, a mass of moving advertisement columns. What stays invisible, however, is an infrastructure of constantly processed information behind the platform, delivering app-generated user data and behavioral profiles that are not only used to make profitable predictions but that mainly serve the private interests of a few CEOs and shareholders (Shaw/Graham 2017; Zuboff 2018). In this contribution, we will discuss how this information asymmetry – upheld by the 'reign' of the Lieferando algorithm that structures gig work[2] processes but also our 'taste' of the city – literally 'cycles' around the consumer's awareness: hidden behind the brightly colored

---

1   A big and heartfelt thank you especially to our interview partners and all the people who supported us in the creation of this work.
2   Gig work within the so-called *gig economy* characterizes a digital and platform-based form of employment. It is mostly temporary, often unstable (or flexible, depending on perspective), and very precarious since the working conditions do not offer social or any kind of security to the employee (Woodcock/Graham 2019).

riders, Lieferando continuously tries to digitally delegate and produce – and reproduce – urbanity in a profit-oriented way. Thus, it eliminates social urban spaces of encounter, exchange, and participation. We will show how invisible information inequalities and 'data wealth' are monopolized and materialized within the city. Our findings are based on a six-month-long period, from October 2019 until February 2020 (right before the Covid-19 pandemic hit Germany), of ethnographic research on in_visibilities of gig work as a new urban infrastructure. Wondering how platforms influence urban everyday life, our research collective conducted six qualitative interviews with two male riders, two members of a city-based workers' council, a gastronome working with the Lieferando app, and a frequent client. Adding to the interviewees' insights are participatory observations and mappings that ask: in what way do delivery services contribute to the capitalization of urban space (production)?

Emerging from the interviews with Lieferando riders is a visible "human pipeline" (Tonkiss 2015: 388): a cycling assembly line mostly consisting of the seemingly "disposable" (Doherty 2017: 192) and ever interchangeable bodies of riders forming the corporation's last mile. As an infrastructural platform, Lieferando not only invisibly takes over urban operations and services, but, as Jathan Sadowski (2020: 450) describes, is also "remaking cities in [its] own image". Its app interfaces are functioning as urban digital gatekeepers by black boxing accessibility of and participation in data. Therefore, the platform increasingly shapes our perception and guides our way through digital urban realms on its own terms. Although Lieferando's mechanisms of invisibility mask the true purpose of its infrastructure, moments of visible crisis unveil resistive potential. Repurposing the invisibility of digitality for their own cause, rider coalitions build similar information infrastructures, exchanging practices of resistance and knowledge to overcome the everyday control of their work by *algocracy* (Ivanova et al. 2018). "The normally invisible quality of working infrastructure becomes visible when it breaks" (Star 1999: 382), Susan Leigh Star notes. This moment of an emergent breakdown of usually automated, mediating, circulating, and connecting elements of the ordering platform becomes apparent in crisis: cold food on our doorsteps, a rider's dead cellphone battery, bodily injuries, failing employment rights of the gig workers, and, at last, protesting bodies on the street. By standing up and being seen, rider coalitions point to the failure of a food delivery infrastructure that attends to the needs of a few while costing many a stable job, corporal capital, and personal data.

<title>"Processed Food on the Urban Data Highway. [...] </title>

We argue that these urgent matters, the emergent emergencies of a glitch or error in invisible data infrastructures, are a (often literally) painful but necessary moment of crisis to resist the urban rule of digital platforms. The following analysis, first, shows the authority of the Lieferando app, controlling the riders' every move. Despite being alienated, at the mercy of the algorithm, and only temporarily employed, riders nevertheless manage to escape their incapacitation. Through collective coalitions and protests, they expose critical platform structures and their material impact on an 'urban stage': the streets. Second, by revealing the slow decline of heterogeneous spaces of urban encounter, taken over by home delivery services, our research indicates a change in urban (social) architectures. Reinforcing the vanishing opportunities to meet over food, Covid-19, in addition, has made city life a matter of keeping our distance. As a catalyst of crises, the virus makes visible hidden control mechanisms, oppressing algorithms, and powerful opacities, thus temporarily uncovering repressive structures everybody needs to know about: to be able to resist them and to turn the emergency into an emergent infrastructure for all. </p></div>

<div class="Big data is watching you: Moments between algorithmic incapacitation and organized empowerment">

<p> Lieferando is part of the Dutch company Just Eat Takeaway.com Central Core B.V. This company provides a digital, internet-based platform on which restaurants can offer their dishes for delivery and through which customers – who like to eat freshly prepared food at home – can order these dishes online (Lieferando 2021). At the moment, Lieferando has a monopoly-like position in many German cities, supplying just-in-time deliveries in the sector of ready meals (Manager Magazin 2021). The delivery staff, mostly riders, are employed by Lieferando (except for the restaurants that have their own delivery fleet) and embody the human link between the customer and the serving restaurant as a mediating infrastructure. The economic model of the company is based on the use of two apps: the orange-colored Lieferando app for customers, and a turquoise-colored app called Scoober for riders, which distributes and organizes work-related information. As one member of a workers' council describes in an interview, both apps allow the company to accumulate data and make behavioral predictions about their users. It is not apparent to these users which cell phone data and information are extracted, stored, and further used by Lieferando during use of the app and beyond. The general terms, conditions, and the employment contracts do not provide any insight into the algorithms underlying the apps. It is also not easy to obtain information from the company on their structure or how personal data is used. For end users and riders, the principle and data extraction behind the platform services remains intentionally invisible and inaccessible, forming a hidden data and information infrastructure. Their unawareness of the prevailing knowledge and information asymmetry thereby further stabilizes and reproduces the freedom of action of informational capitalists, in this case that of the Lieferando company (Zuboff 2018).

Customers are uninformed about these market mechanisms and often prioritize their own comfort by conveniently ordering online. Moreover, the app-based management of gig work gives riders the feeling of being able to act individually and flexibly on the job. Contrary to this feeling, however, the riders are only able to act within the limited range of action of the app architecture and algorithmic structures, which continuously learn by using artificial intelligence. "You go in a war [sic] with the app, with the system", a Lieferando rider explains during one of our interviews (2020). The riders do not seem to have any agency facing algocracy in their everyday work life, since the algorithmic design takes control over every decision every step of the way (Ivanova et al. 2018). They have no influence on which orders they receive and do not know how they are allocated. Also, the delivery routes that the app suggests to the riders can only be changed by use of their own local knowledge and outsmarting the app. Despite their right to co-determination, the categorization of the data and the design of the algorithm remains largely invisible to institutions such as the many workers' councils, which are a result of ongoing organized union-building processes throughout cities in Germany (interview with workers' council of Lieferando). Being at the mercy of the "app as a boss" (Ivanova et al. 2018: 1), riders are under the control of and seen by the company merely as data resources and material for digital production processes (Zuboff 2018). In its deliberately non-transparent and controlling logic, this seems to primarily serve "informational elites" (Shaw/Graham 2017: 913), as Joe Shaw and Mark Graham suggest in their thoughts on a digital right to the city.

This surveillance capitalist system[3] only becomes visible to end users and riders in a crisis – that is, when the app fails, the delivery is too late, or the rider is injured. To us, the failure of the invisible digital data infrastructure seems a necessary moment of crisis. It is only in these moments that an incapacitating control and information asymmetry (that uses unawareness and invisibility) is uncovered and becomes visible (Star 1999). Thus, we argue, only these (critical) moments enable the use, knowledge about, and empowerment of – and against – this infrastructure. Its crisis becomes the decisive moment of participatory appropriation and/or resistance.

Our research has shown that the faulty, controlling, and failing features of the app lead to dissatisfaction among riders and result in self-sustaining avoidance tactics. Riders develop 'coping' strategies as well as resistant everyday practices to temporarily escape the control of the algorithm. They establish external chats, for example, in which they exchange knowledge, networks, and common tactics in solidarity. Furthermore, they use their personally acquired urban situated knowledge to deliver orders faster as well as navigate through the city efficiently but safely. Here, the street is an assembly line as well as a platform for solidarity and contact: it is the place where the riders meet and recognize each other by their uniforms. Consequently, glitches in the algorithm and automated organization of work are used strategically or are even consciously created by the riders in order to momentarily overcome the reign of the app. Institutions such as labor unions try to make the company's handling of their data more visible to riders and use it as a means of pressure for changes. This hacking of the invisible trackers, viruses, and cookies is necessary in order to expose repressive mechanisms, to oppose them, and to be able to use and resist them (Akteurinnen für urbanen Ungehorsam 2021). Furthermore, this self-created *counter-visibility* also allows riders to gain public recognition, attention, and, hopefully and ultimately, a fair reward for their work since being a delivery rider is a job opportunity that is often the only way to pursue legal employment for, e.g., migrant workers in Germany. Hence, digitization also opens up opportunities that are not available otherwise in our societal structures. </p>

---

3   A concept and term coined by Shoshana Zuboff, who defines it as a market-based, capitalist system that collects personal data by technical means. Resulting from the behavioral information captured, predictions are made about (future) individual behavior, which are used to generate profits (Zuboff 2018).

<div class="Of bits and bodies:
The urban materialization of a virtual infrastructure">

<p> Although the riders remain invisible behind algorithms and numbers within the company, they become brightly visible in the cityscape. At the same time, the colorfully dressed riders also lose visibility in urban space due to them being part of everyday life and routines – they increasingly melt into the scenery. It is only through breakdowns and failing standards and norms – that are inscribed into infrastructures – that the abstract data flows managing the riders become exposed, critically questioned, and made visible in resistant practices (Tonkiss 2015). Therefore, the question arises: what does the delivery of food at any time to any place do to our understanding of the city? More precisely, as we asked ourselves during our research, to what extent does Lieferando influence urban heterogeneity, the coming together of the most diverse people in dense urban space? By collecting data, Lieferando is able to influence which restaurants are at the top of the selections offered in the app, which places are being represented, and which meals are thus available. Can these processes influence the taste of the city's inhabitants over time?

In this article, we want to discuss the impact of food platforms in different ways. Initially, the infrastructure Lieferando materializes through the bodies of the riders, who form the visible pipeline of the platform. Due to the remarkable color of their uniforms, the riders are clearly assigned a specific role in urban space. On the one hand, their bodies are advertising columns for the company, as a member of the workers' council stated; on the other hand, they are ignored as invisible deliverers. Their movements through urban space are related to their tasks as employees. Due to the many interfaces between the human body and urban infrastructure – such as the street – the city and the body can only be understood as an interrelated unity (Schroer/Wilde 2017). Processes and practices shape the materiality of the urban: new behavior can produce changes in the road network, floor plans, and so on. *Materiality*, thus, should be understood not only as a surface but also as the process of materialization that, over time, sets boundaries and definitions (Butler 2015). Food delivery functions like a technical infrastructure while, at the same time, the individual bodies of the riders are exposed to the boundaries and divisions of the urban space. They form new dispositions within it.

Furthermore, food delivery services change the (social and material) urban architecture within cities. Lieferando replaces the need to cook at home.

Cooking is outsourced to a restaurant and customers are no longer required to go to this restaurant, because the rider brings the food to their doorstep instead. This could lead to developments of greater outsourcing of self-catering or maybe even changes in apartment floor plans, such as smaller or kitchenless apartments. First and foremost, it leads to changes in the floor plans of restaurants. A gastronome told us in an interview that only small changes have been made since their restaurant started working with Lieferando. However, if a restaurant really wants to profit from cooperating with Lieferando, it needs to reorganize. The sales of a restaurant depend on the location. This will change, though, if more and more food is ordered online. A restaurant would then no longer need a representative space, e.g., a sitting area.

On the opposite end, and during another interview, a customer talked about experiencing delivery restaurants as *non-places*. Non-places are defined here as places that do not seem to actually exist, because the customer never sees them, except in the form of a digital menu. Additionally, the ordered food is eaten in the customer's own home. There, they can escape from the outside world and make themselves comfortable, just as they like it. *Social cocooning*, a complete retreat into privacy, describes the activity of ordering food as a free time activity well (Duden 2020). Even though the trend of cocooning may primarily serve the desire to isolate oneself, it nevertheless seems to create a need for social interaction at a digital meeting place, such as sharing ordered food on social media. This symbolizes a transfer of urban meeting places to the virtual world. Both the rider's and the customer's body then become the interface between physical meeting places as well as the virtual realm, and thus also the location of border dissolution (Schroer/Wilde 2017). The individual actors are connected to each other through the digital infrastructure. They are not in personal contact with each other; there is always an instance in between that is algorithmically disciplining and controlling their agency. The one-sided digital monitoring of the riders' routes and processes illustrates – and, at the same time, materializes – these unequal relationships between the actors.

A lot has changed during the pandemic. Quarantine has become the new cocooning and, during lockdowns and in times of physical distancing, restaurants seem to rely more on online platforms and delivering food. Food delivery services may even help people who cannot leave the house. Nevertheless, there is a delivery monopoly on who delivers food and collects the data on the taste of the city. How did the circumstances change in light of a global pandemic?
</p>

<div class=Covid-19 as a catalyst: When one crisis hits another >

<p> During the pandemic, the growth of delivery services has multiplied (Dhillon/Wu 2021). Unfortunately, though, this seems to happen at the expense of social life, encounters, and the working conditions of those who deliver. As a consequence of local lockdowns and contact regulations, social cocooning, as already mentioned, has now become a must. In times of physical distancing, we are limiting our mobility and demanding the same from others in return. The access and use of mobility have shifted. Delivery platform services have become connectors to the 'out there'. Nowadays, the 'luxury service' of ordering food at any place at any time online has unfolded into a system-relevant infrastructure in Germany, so classified by the Federal Employment Agency (Bundesagentur für Arbeit 2020). Thus, food delivery riders belong to the so-called 'heroes' of the pandemic. A key question remains: who takes care of those who are taking care?

Currently, food delivery services seem to be more than a delivery infrastructure: they even have the intention to be a *caring* infrastructure. However, riders do not 'sacrifice' themselves voluntarily (and heroically); it is their job to deliver food – a job their existence depends on. Only rarely do they have the choice not to expose themselves to the virus. Rather, they are at a higher risk due to encounters with different households. The question, in fact, is more about staying or quitting; or being fired. Miserable working conditions and constant time pressure go along with the fear of being infected and being unable to work (Robinson et al. 2020). Riders report that there are hardly any opportunities to wash their hands on the routes or that they are not able to keep a proper distance in stairwells (Altenried/Niebler/Wallis 2020). Also, solidarity among the riders, e.g., sharing knowledge in public space, is denied by the current regulations of having to maintain a physical distance. Even pre-Covid-19, the platform's business model was based on systematically avoiding taking responsibility for its employees. Usually, companies have to provide for permanent workers – even in cases of crises such as the pandemic. In practice, working *contactlessly* refers less to the frequency of contact between riders and restaurant staff or consumers and more to the already limited social contact between the company and its employees. What about showing solidarity through tips? Tips have declined. Adding to the fear of direct contact, customers have also been faced with reduced working hours (Macho 2020). Less orders also means less tips and thus less additional income to compensate for low wages.

Although Lieferando has established an online tipping feature, voices are being raised that this money has never reached the riders because of technical issues (Movassat 2020). Getting food means ordering online, watching the rider come closer on a map. Today, it also means a delivery from a masked and 'faceless' person. While the customer expects a quick and perfect delivery, the algorithm – together with the pandemic – has consumed the personal interaction even more. Additionally, the restaurant's visibility is shifting from the public space to the enhanced visibility of digital platforms, shaped by their own rules. The restaurant as a salesroom, as a place of encounter, no longer plays a role in the process. Will gastronomic structures be changed permanently after the pandemic?

Several restaurants have long resisted the delivery monopoly. In times of the pandemic, platform cooperation might be a last resort for their business to survive, even if that means being confronted with non-transparent cost structures, one-sided decision-making power, and uncertain future prospects. The knowledge of this inequality seems to – literally – be a price they have to pay in order to serve the basic need for existential visibility and digital presence.

While restaurants have to find new solutions to be seen, other actors are becoming more visible. In addition to monitoring behavioral performances of riders, the stay-at-home customers are also tracked. Through ordering food via the app, the customers themselves are the *deliverers* of data. Who is at home where, and how many people are located in which district? Food delivery reveals more than just food preferences; it is also a 'behavioral data supply chain'. The pandemic paves the way even more for what Shoshana Zuboff calls a new phase of capitalism: "surveillance capitalism" (Zuboff 2018).

It is important to emphasize that the source for the critical conditions described above is not just the infrastructure itself. In pandemic times such as these, delivery services help us to ensure that as few people as possible leave the house, thereby supporting the containment of the virus. However, we are confronted with the institutionalization of a questionable network of surveillance (capitalism) that comes with this delivery infrastructure, whose invisible data collection, monopolies, and privileges we need to pay attention to. Contrary to the processes observed, the appeal should be to use the current crisis as a 'window of opportunity': as an aim to address the lack of alternative supply services in order to find, develop, and support new possibilities.
</p>

<div class=Conclusion – How (not) to run a city like Lieferando[4]>

<p> To 'deliver' ourselves (and our cities) to tech-solutionist, platform-urbanist infrastructures cannot be – quite literally – the end of the road. As shown, the protesting bodies, creating a counter-visibility on the streets, reveal a system that neither cares for their workers nor their city. The lasting effects of the pandemic and its amplification of already existing inequalities remind us to question what and who stays in_visible and un_heard, and to uncover power structures hidden behind the surface of apps that not only run services but, increasingly, city streets (Sadowski 2020). "City-making is always [...] an enactment of city-knowing – which cannot be reduced to computation" (Mattern 2017) or profit-oriented interests, Shannon Mattern stresses. In light of urban knowledge and collective experiences decreasingly being able to shape and decide upon the design of public spaces, urban researchers and planners have the responsibility to reflect on and call for regulating monopolistic, one-sided, and digitally automated urban production processes. The commodification of the social and the quantitatively predictable optimization of city spaces do not even come close to the complexity of lived urban practices. Moreover, it is necessary to not leave the production of urbanity to algorithms, automations, and artificial intelligence. Rather, we have to get involved, gain insight on how our cities are controlled, and who currently controls them – namely, anti-democratic, private platforms dividing us into "'informational' classes" (Shaw/Graham 2017: 913), ruled by segregating and invisible "informational elites" (ibid.). This is not a rejection of digitalization – on the contrary. However, "[w]e need to shift our gaze and look at data in context, at the lifecycle of urban information, distributed within a varied ecology of urban sites and subjects who interact with it in multiple ways" (Mattern 2017).

Whether we see riders 'hacking' and appropriating the invisible informational infrastructure that feeds on their (personal) data to visibly demand their right to fair working conditions, as seen in the first segment of this chapter; whether, secondly, we notice the materiality of places of urban encounters, such as restaurants, vanishing but gaining visibility through pandemic discourses on their importance; or whether we witness now 'systemically relevant' platforms profiting and taking over the production of cities while exposing their riders to health risks, as shown in the last section: all of

---

4 A reference to Graham et al.'s (2019) scenarios on "How to Run a City like Amazon".

these issues call on us urbanists to question digital in_visibilities, data privileges, and information architectures that shape the city of concrete, code, and content. </p>

<!- References ->

Akteurinnen für urbanen Ungehorsam (2021): Der Digitalität ausgeliefert!? Essenslieferdienste zwischen verkörperten Codes, Un_Sichtbarkeit und städtischer (Re-)Produktion, in: KUCKUCK Notizen zur Alltagskultur 21(1): 28-32.

Altenried, Moritz/Niebler, Valentin/Wallis, Mira (2020): Corona-Krise – Ondemand. Prekär. Systemrelevant, in: der Freitag. Die Wochenzeitung, 25.03.2020. https://www.freitag.de/autoren/der-freitag/on-demand-prekaer-systemrelevant [20.06.2021].

Bundesagentur für Arbeit (2020): Weisung 202003015 vom 30.03.2020. https://www.arbeitsagentur.de/datei/ba146387.pdf [09.07.2020].

Butler, Judith (2015): *Notes toward a Performative Theory of Assembly*, Cambridge, MA: Harvard University Press.

Dhillon, Sunny/Wu, Kevin (2021): *Delivery 2.0: How on-Demand Meal Services Will Become Something Far Bigger*, in: Fast Company, 15.02.2021. https://www.fastcompany.com/90604082/future-of-on-demand-meal-delivery-ghost-kitchens-postmates-doordash-uber-eats [15.02.2021].

Doherty, Jacob (2017): Life (and limb) in the fast-lane: disposable people as infrastructure in Kampala's boda boda industry, in: *Critical African Studies* 9(2): 192-209.

Duden (2020): Cocooning. https://www.duden.de/rechtschreibung/Cocooning [03.01.2021].

Graham, Mark/Kitchin, Rob/Mattern, Shannon/Shaw, Joe (eds.) (2019): *How to run a city like Amazon, and other fables*, Manchester: Meatspace Press.

Ivanova, Mirela/Bronowicka, Joanna/Kocher, Eva/Degner, Anne (2018): Foodora and Deliveroo: The App as Boss? Control and Autonomy in App-Based Management – The Case of Food Delivery Riders. Working Paper Forschungsförderung. No 107. https://www.econstor.eu/bitstream/10419/216032/1/hbs-fofoe-wp-107-2018.pdf [20.03.2022].

Lieferando (2021): Essen Bestellen in ganz Deutschland. https://www.lieferando.de/wer-sind-wir [01.07.2021].

Macho, Andreas (2020): *Kommt das Online-Trinkgeld bei den Fahrern an?*, in: WirtschaftsWoche: Das führende Wirtschaftsmagazin, 20.06.2020. https ://www.wiwo.de/my/unternehmen/dienstleister/lieferando-kommt-das-online-trinkgeld-bei-den-fahrern-an/26656680.html [20.06.2021].

Manager Magazin (2021): *Just Eat Takeaway: Lieferando-Mutterkonzern boomt noch stärker als erwartet*, in: Manager Magazin, 10.03.2021. https://www.m anager-magazin.de/unternehmen/handel/lieferando-just-eat-takeaway-boomt-noch-staerker-als-erwartet-a-0d5b6208-e02b-4921-8b0b-4119921 dc9a2 [01.07.2021].

Mattern, Shannon (2017): A City Is Not a Computer, in: *Places Journal*. doi: https://doi.org/10.22269/170207.

Movassat, Niema (2020): https://twitter.com/NiemaMovassat/status/1282659 610734845959?utm_source=pocket_mylist [15.08.2021].

Robinson, Laura/Schulz, Jeremy/Khilnani, Aneka/Ono, Hiroshi/Cotton, Shelia R./McClain, Noah/Levine, Lloyd/Chen, Wenhong/Huang, Gejun/ Casilli, Antonio A./Tubaro, Paola/Dodel, Matías/Quan-Haase, Anabel/ Ruiu, Maria Laura/Ragnedda, Massimo/Aikat, Deb/Tolentino, Natalia (2020): View of Digital inequalities in time of pandemic: COVID-19 exposure risk profiles and new forms of vulnerability, in: *first monday* 25(7). doi: https://doi.org/10.5210/fm.v25i7.10845.

Sadowski, Jathan (2020): Cyberspace and Cityscapes: On the Emergence of Platform Urbanism, in: *Urban Geography* 41(3): 448-52.

Schroer, Markus/Wilde, Jessica (2017): Stadt, in: Gugutzer, Robert/Meuser, Michael (eds.): *Handbuch Körpersoziologie Band 2: Forschungsfelder und Methodische Zugänge*, Wiesbaden: Springer VS: 319-33.

Shaw, Joe/Graham, Mark (2017): An Informational Right to the City? Code, Content, Control, and the Urbanization of Information, in: *Antipode* 49(4): 907-27.

Star, Susan Leigh (1999): The Ethnography of Infrastructure, in: *American Behavioral Scientist* 43(3): 377-91.

Tonkiss, Fran (2015): Afterword: Economies of Infrastructure, in: *City* 19(2-3): 384-91.

Woodcock, Jamie/Graham, Mark (2019): *The Gig Economy: A Critical Introduction*, Cambridge: Polity.

Zuboff, Shoshana (2018): *Das Zeitalter des Überwachungskapitalismus*, Frankfurt am Main: Campus Verlag.

Ordinary Invitations in Spaces of Everyday Life
Arriving in Neighborhood Life through Analogue Platforms

Yvonne Franz

Conceptualizing neighborhood life as *platforms* by using the platform analogy

> *Benches, blackboards, soccer courts, street signs, even the space in front of a building, conveniently located for cleaning a bike or chatting to a neighbor on the street...*

Have you ever noticed the various *platforms* within an urban neighborhood? Platforms that invite people within that space to take a moment's rest, to observe life, and to engage in everyday happenings? This paper is an invitation to dive into urban neighborhood life by thinking about the non-digital neighborhood platforms in public spaces. It is an invitation to become aware of the various opportunities to actively participate and contribute organically to creating livable, social, vital urban public spaces. Please, join the imaginary neighborhood walk while reading this paper. Enjoy and discover ordinary (but fruitful) facets of everyday life in the neighborhood.

In characterizing specific neighborhood spaces as *ordinary*, the intention is not to imply that they are somehow simple or useless. Rather, referring to them as ordinary hints at the way in which they are frequently undervalued by people using (or not using) these spaces. Or people may not even be consciously aware of them. Let us think of these ordinary, public micro-spaces (Amin 2002) as invitations (see Koch/Latham 2013: 17). Invitations to do something, to make contact, and perhaps even socially interact (or not) with others. This paper aims at expanding our understanding of such invitations, seeing them as non-digital neighborhood platforms with an element of analogue, spontaneous, and casual social interaction at their core.

The *platform* analogy drawn upon in this paper is influenced by recent debates on *platform urbanism*, which emphasize the digitalization of our lives in cities, where "[d]igital platforms mediate specific services for everyday life in cities, lead[ing] to new relations and interaction between service providers and users [...]" (Bauriedl/Strüver 2020: 274). As implied by this description, most analyses have focused specifically on digital services, such as Airbnb, Uber, or food and grocery delivery services. This paper seeks to contribute a complementary non-digital, 'analogue' dimension to our understanding to neighborhood platforms. Non-digital neighborhood platforms might serve as 'enablers' for social interaction but should not be pre-defined as *being social* in the sense that social media or sharing platforms usually tend to self-represent. Dominant social media platforms such as Facebook or Instagram have become important tools in placemaking and branding neighborhoods and communities (Breek/Eshuis/Hermes 2021). Additionally, specific digital neighborhood platforms also exist. Prominent international proponents include Neighbourly[1] or Nextdoor[2]. At the local level, FragNebenan[3] and ImGrätzl[4] are two recent examples of neighborhood platforms operating in Vienna, Austria. These cases of digital neighborhood platforms both have an overarching aim of *sharing*, enabling individuals and businesses to give back to the community in the form of time or other resources (e.g., rooms, tools, knowledge). However, (potentially huge) differences in visual appearance, financial construction, and spatial scope, as well as the organization of activities in and for the neighborhood create specific (market) niches. Such platforms enable sharing practices by linking needs and interests through a digital platform. The enabling element might be seen as a key characteristic of both digital and non-digital neighborhood platforms. While the former aim to enable social interaction through digital technology, non-digital neighborhood platforms deploy their materialized existence in micro-spaces within the neighborhood.

This article starts from the position that urban neighborhoods represent focal points of everyday life. Practices of everyday life occur largely through

---

1   See https://www.neighbourly.com/.
2   See https://nextdoor.com/.
3   See https://fragnebenan.com/.
4   See https://www.imgraetzl.at/.

unplanned, superficial, fluid, and temporally limited interactions, similar in character to *arrival infrastructures*, which support newcomers (Meeus/Arnaut/van Heur 2019). Neighborhoods can be seen as the built environment in which people form public spaces, allowing for contact, interaction, and more. These platform-like spaces might be considered as entry points from which one might socially *arrive* in a neighborhood, or from which one might *depart* when staying feels unpleasant or uncomfortable rather than inviting. Encounters may or may not occur in these public spaces, but the very possibility exists by virtue of their existence. There is the invitation to become part of the neighborhood, not just as a passer-by, but as an active participant in the form of conversation, activities, or other involvement. As such, arriving in a neighborhood also means making social connections and participating in everyday life.

Arriving in a neighborhood through platforms

To capture the full picture of everyday life, considerations of platform urbanism should not be limited to the digital platforms that 'organize' neighborhood life. We might also consider neighborhood platforms that exist in public spaces within the material world (specifically, within urban neighborhoods) that can be entered both bodily and cognitively. Materialized platforms are tangible features in the public space. They enable individuals to change the situation in which they are located in real-life, creating the possibility of spontaneous interactions. Such an understanding is built on the assumption that visible, material platforms can serve as enablers for action or interaction, which can variably be pleasant or unpleasant – or, indeed, eliciting no reaction at all. These interactions might take the form of a conversation, fleeting eye-contact, or shared laughter over funny neighborhood goings-on mutually observed by two or more people. These examples already indicate an awareness of ordinary but socially connecting interactions. They might be more meaningful compared to the 'ordinary uses' of neighborhood spaces, which oftentimes are merely viewed as passing-through spaces in which people move from A to B.

In this context, the notion of *arrival* is significant, both in terms of newcomers to a neighborhood, but also for long-term residents seeking to become more involved in their community or more 'connected' to people and places. Terms and concepts emerging around the *arrival city* (Saunders 2012) are mostly linked to processes of migration and diversification. Driven by new schemes of international migration and super-diverse neighborhoods, current academic discourses on arrival spaces and arrival infrastructure capture the character of flow, fluidity, and relationships in the urban context at specific points in time (Meeus/Arnaut/van Heur 2019; Schrooten/Meeus 2019). Since Saunders' book, *Arrival City*, was published in 2012, an interest (mostly academic) has evolved concerning the process of arriving in a city and the possibilities and limitations that this entails. While Saunders looks at arrival from the perspective of international migration, other authors, like Hans et al. (2019: 515), expand the notion of arrival city into the concept of *arrival spaces*, understood as those parts of an arrival city that are shaped by international migration. Such spaces include diverse types of migrants, high fluctuation in numbers within these groups, and a high concentration of *structures for opportunities*. Possibilities for arrival in urban spaces can be assessed in terms of the availability of inexpensive spaces for people to inhabit.

The notion of *arriving in the neighborhood* is connected to spaces and structures, which invite and enable one *to arrive*. However, the arrival process is not only relevant for migrants, but also for ordinary residents. The examples of materialized non-digital platforms showcased in this paper shed light on public spaces in urban neighborhoods in which all residents and visitors may arrive, free of charge or at minimal expense, in their everyday lives – irrespective of peoples' length of stay. The examples are manifold both in appearance and potential to stimulate social interaction, but they all include the potential for spontaneous, fleeting encounters. Such interaction might simply entail making brief eye-contact or exchanging a friendly greeting with someone who already seems at home in the neighborhood, but even these minute interactions can contribute to a sense of belonging (see Blokland/Nast 2014). Analogue platforms in the neighborhood might be seen as spaces of encounter (Valentine 2008), open to all newcomers in urban neighborhoods, but also for long-term residents. As spaces of encounter, non-digital neighborhood platforms enable the development of social interaction, relations, and networks, as well as of negotiation of conflict and power (im)balances – all considered crucial elements in cohesive urban (neighborhood) development.

Finding 'non-digital social platforms' in urban neighborhoods

In this paper, the notion of *non-digital social neighborhood platforms* is based on a visual approach that selects *platform spaces*, viewing them as anchor points from which to reflect on their potential for social interaction within a neighborhood. The identification and selection of spaces for analysis in this paper was inspired by Boot (2017: 144) who applied a visual workshop and developed further *streetology* – a framework invented by the Dutch designer Reineke Otten. The aim of streetology is to analyze patterns of everyday life from a visual perspective. Specifically, this approach entails looking at pictures, treating them as stand-alone pieces taken out of context and seeing the process as an opportunity to identify new contexts which might have remained invisible if the picture had shown more visual information on the environment. By repeating the analyses of decontextualized elements in public spaces, new contexts may occur, as well as patterns that can be found in other situations.

As such, the following identification and presentation of non-digital social platforms in the public spaces of urban neighborhoods in Vienna (Austria) is completely subjective. However, reflective interpretation that builds upon the background of current debates in society, planning, and academia is added. This explorative approach – designed as imaginary neighborhood walk – might serve as starting point, contributing an important (analogue) dimension to the concept of *platform urbanism*.

How should one read the imaginary neighborhood walk that follows below? It starts easy with looking at the picture of the presented platform and identifying its use, location, and spatial context. Ask yourself questions, such as: what does it look like? Where is it positioned, and what else might be in the direct environment? How do you imagine the local context? Would you find this platform in your own neighborhood? Then, juxtapose your thinking on these questions with the 'Platform for' explanation provided. Now, as invitations include communication, the platform is speaking to you while you read the 'self-description' given by the platform itself. Next, you might begin an inner conversation with yourself concerning whether you would accept or refuse the invitation issued by the neighborhood platform. If you like to compare your own reaction to another (imaginary) one, read the inner conversation by the passer-by. It is a hypothetical formulation, and you may (or may not) find yourself in this conversation. Do you know why you would react similarly to the passer-by – or completely differently? Finally, in case you wonder what is needed to create such non-digital neighborhood platforms, the explanations on 'character' and 'requirements' may stimulate reflections on both simplicity and complexity of non-digital social neighborhood platforms. Surprisingly, sometimes it merely seems to require ordinary material to create more than ordinary spaces.

"Arriving on platform...": Selection of arrival platforms in urban everyday (neighborhood) life

"Arriving on platform 'INFORMATION': Local activities ahead."

Platform for: Central point of information on neighborhood activities provided by local management. Invitation to participate in activities and initiatives to get to know other locals and the possibility of co-creating your neighborhood.

Information-board to passer-by: *"Hi there, would you like to know what is going on in your 'hood'? Pretty sure, you do not realize how many people take care of your living environment. Well, although not everyone feels attracted to becoming active in the participation process, just give it a try and you will see that your demands and ideas will be heard. In any case, you will be surprised that 'knowing about' activities in your neighborhood already makes a difference to how you will perceive your living environment."*

Inner conversation from passer-by: *"Well there. What's the worst that could happen? I have to walk the dog, anyhow. Why not join the neighborhood walk next Friday afternoon? Maybe there is someone who can explain why the building next to mine is still empty and underused. This does not feel right in a city where so many people are searching for housing. But I have no idea what is going on there, and who leaves a building empty? If no one knows anything, well, I at least have enjoyed a neighborhood walk and put my interests and concerns out there."*

Character: Materialized, visible, provision of information.

Requirement: Material infrastructure, awareness of the intended action, i.e., "read about news from the neighborhood"; someone who takes the time to stay informed; someone who takes the time to read information.

Figure 1 Invitation to inform yourself about activities in the neighborhood and to eventually participate in these

(Franz 2021)

"Arriving on platform 'MEDIATION': Productive conflict management ahead."

Platform for: Various uses and appropriations of public space by different interest groups, which are mediated by intermediaries who balance out different demands, uses, and interests in the public space.

Graffiti wall to passer-by: *"Hi there, I know, this place looks quite ordinary. You often walk through without even noticing how precious this space in the city is to kids and young people. Can you imagine the scarcity of space available to them? Obviously, con-*

flicts are pretty likely if you have limited space and many interests. Playing basketball while skaters and scooters wind around the surface and others would like to take a rest is not always fun. In that case, mediators are trained social workers who can balance out interests through communication. And guess what: it is always about communication. Suddenly, multi-uses of the space at the same time become possible."

Inner conversation from passer-by: *"Look at this, the painting could use some fresh color. Why is there a painting at all on this wall behind the bike racks? Someone is obviously taking care of this park. I did not even recognize a park. It is more like an ordinary space. Well, anyhow, if someone takes care of it, there must be some people using it."*

Character: Subtle sign of existence; existence of human-spatial interactions; communication-based park mediation.

Requirement: Users of public space; human resources; training and skills in mediation; reason for interaction with different interest groups and users in the public space.

Figure 2 Invitation to think about different demands of park users and how to mediate those interests

(Franz 2021)

Ordinary Invitations in Spaces of Everyday Life 225

"Arriving on platform 'SERVICE': Extension of horizon ahead."

Figure 3 Invitation to think about counter-hegemonic positions in society and to learn (about) skills in the neighborhood

(Franz 2021)

Platform for: Stickers and announcements at first sight; information, representation and (counter-)practices on second sight.

Traffic sign to passer-by: *"Hey, wait a second. I know, it is not very inviting to read the pole of a traffic sign. But it is worth it. Just look at me: people and initiatives with all kinds of different interests put their messages on a sticker. Besides making me aware* *of different perspectives and interests amongst people using this neighborhood, there is even more: have you ever wanted to learn a foreign language? Read this advertisement on the pole. There is a native-speaker nearby offering to share her linguistic skills with people like you."*

Inner conversation from passer-by: "Come on, why should I stop here and look at the pole of a traffic sign? It is a busy pedestrian street and there is scarcely enough space to pass others by. And I really do not think that putting stickers on public inventory is an appropriate way of decoration. But I like the announcement of the language course. Last time, I noticed announcements for babysitting. It is quite nice to learn about the skills people from this neighborhood are willing to share. Even if I do not call the language trainer, I have learnt a little bit about the people from the neighborhood."

Character: Improvised and informal; randomly allocated in the public space at eye-level; invitation to read without expectations as to whether a reaction occurs or not.

Requirement: Urban furniture, written information, and messages.

"Arriving on platform 'COMMUNICATION': Unexpected conversation ahead."

Platform for: Designated sitting place for having a conversation; intends to enable communication amongst people from the neighborhood; could prevent loneliness by instigating contact with others one does not know; might lead to an unpleasant or uncomfortable conversation with random people; possibility of creating a sense of 'public familiarity' once a conversation has begun.

Chair to passer-by: "Hi there, would you like to have a nice conversation? Possibly with someone you do not yet know, who may live nearby, though you might have never met otherwise because you have no common friends or interests. However, you obviously share a sense of curiosity. So, welcome, take a seat, and enjoy the anticipation of seeing whether someone will sit next to you."

Inner conversation from passer-by: "Well there. What's the worst that could happen? Maybe I should just sit down and see? Though maybe no one will pass by and sit down? Also, not everyone knows that these chairs are designated to invite conversation. But why should I assume this? Anyway, it might be nice if I move the chairs to catch the sun *while waiting for some conversationalist. I will give it a try and sit down for a couple of minutes. If nothing happens, at least I will have enjoyed observing the neighborhood in the sunshine."*

Character: Materialized, visible commitment: "If I sit down, I'd like to talk."

Requirement: Material infrastructure; awareness of the intended action, i.e., 'to sit down'; for someone else to sit down; conversation.

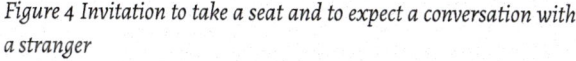

Figure 4 Invitation to take a seat and to expect a conversation with a stranger

(Franz 2021)

"Arriving on platform 'SELF-REPRESENTATION': Just being yourself ahead."

Platform for: Sitting, resting, and conversing in the midst of the neighborhood; intends to expand available public space by reducing space for parking lots. Instead, space for social interaction is provided by offering an inviting place for all kinds of ordinary appropriations, such as whiling away a lunch break, quietly reading a book, or meeting friends outside. The active use of this space creates a sense of urban vibrancy in a residential neighborhood with limited public space available for active use.

Parklet to passer-by: *"Good afternoon, what a lovely sunny day! Please, take a seat in the shade. It is free of charge and no one is here at the moment. Some people from this neighborhood have lovingly cultivated this area and would be really delighted to see it become a well-used micro public space. It is way friendlier in this big city if we share the outside space and make contact with one another, don't you agree? What a treat to hang out outdoors without the obligation to consume anything, just being yourself."*

Inner conversation from passer-by: *"Such a colorful place amidst the greyish, black, and white cars on this street. I feel instantly happier just looking at this inviting sitting area. I was going to go home, but I would probably just end up reading some news on my smartphone anyway. Why not do it here, outside? Nobody minds whether if I sit here or not, so I may as well do it. And I could call a friend to come over and join me for small talk."*

Figure 5 Invitation to take a seat and to share a micro public space

(Franz 2021)

Character: Do-it-yourself design; accessible, low-commitment sitting area; visual limitation to parking lots next to it; recreational and cooling due to some greenery; consumption free.

Requirement: Designated space in the public space (former parking lot); legal permission; self-organized people to establish, build, and finance the place; regular maintenance to avoid deterioration; people who use the space in their daily life practices.

"Arriving on platform 'MOBILITY': Micro mobility ahead."

Platform for: Various modes of (mainly) micro mobility including e-scooter and bicycle sharing systems as well as tools (e.g., tire pump, repair tools) to maintain their own bike; mobility-related information and orientation within the neighborhood.

Pole to passer-by: *"Hi there, do you need a quick ride? You find here all sorts of options to move from here to somewhere. Of course, you might prefer to walk. But what about using a bicycle or e-scooter? Rent it here and return it elsewhere. Got it, this might seem too complicated as you do not know whether there is a similar mobility hub at the place you want to go. But I see, you do have your own bike with you. Put some fresh air into your tire. You see, you can also use this super convenient tire pump over here. And if you need some help with a repair, why don't you ask just this young guy returning an e-scooter?"*

Inner conversation from passer-by: *"Well, this comes as a surprise: all kinds of support to use sustainable modes of transport in one place. I have never seen that before. The planners of this place even included a map to orientate myself in the small streets of this neighborhood. This is much more convenient compared to the small digital map on my smartphone. The tire pump really comes handy to put some fresh air into my tires. I will use it right away and will be even faster on my bike arriving to my next meeting. I am wondering if I am the only one using this professional tire pump. Next time I come by this place, I will use the little repair pillar to check my bike frame and fix some screws."*

Character: Visible and inclusive due to its various services for different modes of micro mobility; empowering due to its support for self-servicing and maintaining own bike or scooter; central mobility hub to use bike or e-scooter sharing.

Requirement: Designated space in the public space (former parking lot); cooperation with micro mobility providers; commitment to principles of sustainable mobility and sharing; financial means to build and maintain this mobility hub; people who use these services.

Figure 6 Invitation to maintain own means of micro mobility or to participate in sharing micro mobility

(Franz 2021)

"Arriving on platform 'SHARING': Circular economy ahead."

Platform for: Exchanging books and contributing to a sharing economy; spending some time exploring the books on offer; associate with other book readers and lenders.

Public bookcase to passer-by: *"Hey, dear friend. When did you last read a book? Look at me, I am filled with all sorts of books. From novels to children's books, to cookery books and dictionaries. I am sure you will find at least one book that interests you. And guess what? You will not only enjoy a good read for free, but you will also be contributing to a more sustainable future. Wondering why? Well, you do not need to buy a book which will remain in your bookshelf at home, lonely, and only read once. You return it to this bookcase so that someone else can enjoy it after you. If that person also returns the book, we will have managed to create a circular lending system. And I am really proud that I have become a much more active space instead of a boring shop window nobody paid attention to. So, please, help yourself!"*

Figure 7 Invitation to lend and read a book, and then to share the book again

(Franz 2021)

Inner conversation from passer-by: *"Books. I have so many books at home that are not used. I mean, you read a book once, maybe a second time years later, or you give it to a friend who appreciates a book recommendation. But, in general, they take up quite a lot of space in my home. And I do not want to throw them away. This bookcase could be a good opportunity to pass along at least some of the books from my home. It is nice to imagine someone else taking pleasure in reading it. It seems like a subtle way of sharing resources with strangers, who are in fact not so strange after all, since we share a common interest in books."*

Character: Vehicle to create micro activities amongst people; stimulation of attractive ground floor use; do-it-yourself design; cost-free sharing.

Requirement: Bookcase accessible in a sheltered public space to save books from wet conditions; bottom-up initiative to build a public bookcase; substantial financial investment; people who donate books; people who borrow books.

Arriving in the neighborhood, or ready for departure? Reflecting on the potential for new relations and interaction

Did you enjoy the imaginary neighborhood walk? Do you feel elevated, maybe because you recognized some analogue platforms which also exist in your own neighborhood? Were your responses similar to the platform invitation, or similar to the hypothetical inner-conversations from the passer-by? Building on these experiences, we now think about the connection between the invitations issued through analogue platforms and to make (active or passive) use of this (new) awareness to create new relations and interactions within our own neighborhood (Bauriedl/Strüver 2020). Fig. 8 aims to systemize the non-digital social platforms in urban neighborhoods based on their potential to create, actively or passively, (new) relations and interactions (x-axis), as well their invitation to arrive in or to depart from the neighborhood (y-axis).

While the information-board (example one) and the graffiti wall (example two) might invite passers-by to learn about and reflect upon the neighborhood, the character of these interactions remains quite passive. One might 'merely' read or think about the role of activities that go on in the neighborhood but, in being better informed, this might nonetheless support the individual's arrival in the neighborhood. The parklet that serves as a sitting

Ordinary Invitations in Spaces of Everyday Life   233

Figure 8 Reflecting on the potential for new relations and arrival in the neighborhood

(Franz 2021)

island (example five) might elevate an individual's arrival in the neighborhood by supporting self-representation in everyday life and facilitating them in becoming familiar to others from the neighborhood. Use of the conversation chairs (example four) and the public bookcase (example seven) both involve a visible activity (i.e., to sit down or to take a book and return it later). Both examples also entail an element of communication and 'tangible intention', indicating an interest in having a conversation or sharing same interests. As such, both platforms may have the highest potential for interaction and for creating new relations. The traffic sign (example three), as well as the mobility pole (example six), provide knowledge about existing services in (and maybe even outside of) the neighborhood, as well as repair tools and micro mobility services to even leave the neighborhood (and later return). Nevertheless, both service platforms remain at the individual level and might only allow for interaction (through support) and new relations in the neighborhood in a passive sense.

However, why are there no examples for analogue social platforms in urban neighborhoods included in the upper left segment of Fig. 8? Platforms which actively invite one to leave (rather than remain within) the neighborhood, and to socially interact elsewhere? Perhaps, those platforms might not exist. Alternatively, they may seem so radical in appearance that we ignore, avoid, or reject them. More likely, however, they do exist and actually represent our tangible and self-created social network existing of stronger ties to friends, families, colleagues, and others. But those ties probably do not create spontaneous interactions for new relations or opportunities to arrive in the neighborhood.

Drawing on the imaginary neighborhood walk in this paper, we might ask: what makes analogue platform urbanism distinct from digital platform urbanism? Obviously, both impact upon everyday urban life by providing and mediating services through platforms (Bauriedl/Strüver 2020). However, the difference may lie in the details. Digital platform urbanism emphasizes the technical aspects in the 'new organization' of everyday life, where so-called *service providers* interact with *users* through digital platforms. This requires a distinct practice of active engagement with others. There is no reason to use a digital platform unless one is interested in the consumption of a specific service. On the contrary, analogue platform urbanism differs in intention, character, temporality, and economic value extraction. The service provided on the platform is represented as an invitation to interact socially. This invitation might be accepted or refused; yet, in both cases it cannot be guaranteed that social interaction will (or will not) take place. What happens will happen as analogue platform urbanism consists of material platforms in the public space being used (or not used) by human beings.

The materialization of the platforms might be planned by civic or even public actors. Also, the location and maintenance of these in the public space represents intended practices. However, the actual use of the platforms and the resulting interaction between human beings can only be enabled. Such interactions are unplanned, occurring spontaneously with high fluidity (in the sense of its non-binding nature) between *users* and *service providers*. The *social value* of analogue platform urbanism cannot, however, be priced, sold, or bought.

Recapitulating the seven examples in this paper and thinking about them together as social platforms shows that the appearance and character of non-digital social platforms in urban neighborhoods are manifold. They are all tangible invitations to participate in neighborhood life, but their variety may differ between neighborhoods within a city, as well as across cities and countries. Nevertheless, they most likely exist everywhere and, in a sense, provide evidence of a travelling concept of neighborhood practices performed through platforms. We may learn from these practices by reflecting upon our role as residents in neighborhoods, but also on the role of planners in supporting the co-creation of *ordinary spaces* and the role of policymakers in thinking differently about infrastructure. A more differentiated understanding of all sorts of urban infrastructure not only concerns the question of accessible infrastructure and how to organize their services efficiently through digital and analogue urban platforms. It is also about the pronunciation of an invitation to engage in (neighborhood) life. Everyday.

References

Amin, Ash (2002): Ethnicity and the multicultural city: living with diversity, in: *Environment and Planning A* 34(6): 959-80.

Bauriedl, Sybille/Strüver, Anke (2020): Platform Urbanism: Technocapitalist Production of Private and Public Spaces, in: *Urban Planning* 5(4): 267-76.

Blokland, Talja/Nast, Julia (2014): From public familiarity to comfort zone: The relevance of absent ties for belonging in Berlin's mixed neighbourhoods, in: *International Journal of Urban and Regional Research* 38(4): 1142-59.

Boot, Isis (2017): Sensing the city from within: Tracking traces in the public space, in: Franz, Yvonne/Hintermann, Christiane (eds.): *Unravelling Complexities. Understanding Public Spaces. ISR Forschungsbericht* 44, Wien: Verlag der Österreichischen Akademie der Wissenschaften: 139-46.

Breek, Pieter/Eshuis, Jasper/Hermes, Joke (2021): Sharing feelings about neighborhood transformation on Facebook: online affective placemaking in Amsterdam-Noord, in: *Journal of Urbanism: International Research on Placemaking and Urban Sustainability* 14(2): 145-64.

FragNebenan (n.d.): https://fragnebenan.com/ [16.12.2021].

Hans, Nils/Hanhörster, Heike/Polívka, Jan/Beißwenger, Sabine (2019): Die Rolle von Ankunftsräumen für die Integration Zugewanderter. Eine kritische Diskussion des Forschungsstandes, in: *Raumforschung und Raumordnung* 77(5): 511-24.

ImGrätzl (n.d.): https://www.imgraetzl.at/ [16.12.2021].

Koch, Regan/Latham, Alan (2013): On the Hard Work of Domesticating a Public Space, in: *Urban Studies* 50(1): 6-21.

Meeus, Bruno/Arnaut, Karel/van Heur, Bas (2019): Migration and the infrastructural politics of urban arrival, in: Meeus, Bruno/Arnaut, Karel/van Heur, Bas (eds.): *Arrival Infrastructures. Migration and Urban Social Mobilities*, Cham: Palgrave Macmillan: 1-32.

Neighbourly (n.d.): https://www.neighbourly.com/ [16.12.2021].

Nextdoor (n.d.): https://nextdoor.com/ [16.12.2021].

Saunders, Doug (2012): *Arrival City: How the largest migration in history is reshaping our world*, New York: Vintage Books.

Schrooten, Mieke/Meeus, Bruno (2019): The possible role and position of social work as part of the arrival infrastructure, in: *European Journal of Social Work* 23(3): 414-24.

Valentine, Gill (2008): Living with difference: Reflections on geographies of encounter, in: *Progress in Human Geography* 32(3): 323-37.

PLATFORM CAPITALISM IN NEOLIBERAL TIMES

Echo Chambers of Urban Design
Platformization in Architecture and Planning

Cordula Kropp, Kathrin Braun & Yana Boeva

Digital information and computation are about to change the worlds of urban design.[1] Cities and buildings have assumed a two-fold existence in analog and virtual spaces. Everyday moves, spatial practices, and individual decisions leave their traces in both. What was once planned as a one-off building project can now be stored, modified, recombined, and reproduced again and again. Every path, every decision, every building is now a potential object of optimization. Henri Lefebvre (1991) has described the social production of space as a triad emerging from the entangled and contradictory interactions of spatial practices, socio-political concepts, and utopian visions, materializing in the form of buildings, monuments, streets, and cities, shaping and being shaped by social agency and power. In the 21st century, these spatial practices, concepts, and visions are increasingly being absorbed by a new form of digitally mediated space production. In the following, we consider the emergence of echo chambers of digitally conceived and perceived cities that could lead to an era of platform urbanism driven by large technology companies. However, this digital production of space seems strangely detached from previous planning principles. Yet, the critical questions of political economy, "'Who produces?', 'What?', 'How?', 'Why and for whom?'" (ibid.: 69) can still help us decode the emerging patterns of platform urbanism. To do so, we contend, it is useful to take recent analyses of digital capitalism and, specifically, the role of platforms into account.

Until recently, debates on digital capitalism rather focused on citizens' use of mobile phones and the world wide web, their individual clicks, and volatile preferences than on solid urban structures and the built environment.

---

[1] Partially supported by the Deutsche Forschungsgemeinschaft (DFG, German Research Foundation) under Germany´s Excellence Strategy – EXC 2120/1 – 390831618.

The promises of the networked smart city moved infrastructure systems and their control and surveillance apparatuses into the focus of digital capitalism (Kitchin 2014; Zukin 2020). City governments started to invest in digital tools and platforms, making the digital transformation of urban infrastructures and services a rewarding long-term business for hardware- and software vendors. The latter could "quietly stay in the background" and steer urban flows following an underlying "informational diagrammatic of control" (Marvin/Luque-Ayala 2017: 84). These developments laid the foundations for an urban policy characterized by entrepreneurialism, privatization, and austerity, and following the mantra "spend less; grow more; cede control" (Sadowski 2020b: 449).

The next step, we hypothesize, could be the digital transformation of structural urban development, a highly robust business field for the coming decades. Private corporations and start-ups have already created new platform markets for an urban tech economy to build on, "from fintech for banks and other financial institutions to proptech for real estate and construction companies and property managers to healthtech for hospitals and insurance companies" (Zukin 2020: 944). Under these conditions, a variant of platform capitalism based on building data from urban planning, architecture, and construction is emerging, which may profoundly impact cities. Its data-driven planning strategies reconfigure not only the actions of city dwellers, urban infrastructures, and services but also the socio-material reality of buildings and places we live in.

In the following, we outline the role digitalization, platform capitalism, and planning data may play in the future of urban design. In a first step, we sketch out the conditions of urban design in times of techno-utopian narratives and "corporate sociotechnical imaginaries" (Hockenhull/Cohn 2021) translated into platform urbanism. Next, we draw on critical political-economic analyses of platformization and platform capitalism and indicate how these are reconfiguring actor and power relations in architecture and construction. We then describe how building information modeling (BIM) in architecture and planning is driving this version of digitalization through government policies and empowering technology providers and software vendors, particularly Autodesk, to gain influence in the world of building data. The goal is to better understand how platform capitalism's logic is gaining traction in architecture, construction, and urban design and what this may mean for cities in the future.

Cities in an age of techno-utopian narratives

"Smart umbrellas light up to alert you that rain is in the forecast. Smart vehicles take over the drudgery of driving during rush hour. Smart, virtual assistants obey your every command, learn your preferences and routines, and automatically adjust accordingly", writes Jathan Sadowski (2020a: 1) in his examination of digital capitalism. Urban life, in particular, is being reconfigured by pervasive communication and sensing technologies collecting data from an ever-growing array of mobile shopping, navigation, and socialization apps. Alison Powell analyzes how the "move, from technologies of access to technologies of data" is driving the vision of a "big data optimized city" (2021: 5). Digital platforms brokering transport, accommodation, music, dating, gastronomic, and other services as well as energy and healthcare provision, municipal traffic planning, and city administration offer to meet all our needs in ever smarter and efficient ways. Typically, the providers, mostly ICT companies, but also municipal governments and some digital activist groups, promise many things at once: more efficient infrastructures, accessibility, customized offers for individual needs, more convenience, individuality, safety, and sustainability.

The basis for all their aspirations and applications, from delivery and mobility services to e-participation and urban planning projects, is the ubiquitous gathering and processing of data. Yet, data alone, especially unclassified data, do neither map social realities nor can they be easily turned into values. They have to be cleaned, ordered, and analyzed to work out statistical patterns. Municipal authorities can rarely do this by themselves; mostly, they lack the necessary tools, resources, and skills. Instead, they outsource these tasks to private companies, losing direct access to the insights generated and the opportunity to stand up for democratic values of equality, transparency, and a focus on the common good (Brauneis/Goodman 2018). The data analytics they need is provided by IT firms offering to optimize the operation of public infrastructures and the delivery of urban services. Data analysts, however, do not reinvent the software each time but take many thousands of lines of code from existing program libraries and other data workers', data brokers', or data scientists' work and apply them to the municipal tasks, according to their own values and assumptions or the perceived interests of their internal and external contractors. At the same time, the traces of previous priorities and classification practices persist in code and computational rules and continue to shape the outcomes.

Tracing their origins to the beginnings of post-war defense applications, organizational IT systems, and urban operating systems, Simon Marvin and Andrés Luque-Ayala draw our attention to the "potentially transformative implications for how the city is imagined, planned and governed" (2017: 86). Software programming based on logistic rationalities, for example, has been shown to reconfigure organizational functions, agents, and relationships by shaping and governing actions following a "variety of strategies of *functional simplification* and *reification* by which it lays out its prescriptive order" (Kallinikos 2007: 7; original emphasis). Computational capacities that enable the functional and informational integration and coordination of heterogeneous urban spheres and dimensions meet older cybernetic thinking of the city as a complex system to be digitally synthesized and controlled (Marvin/Luque-Ayala 2017). They are flanked by the renewed conviction that computer modeling of processes and operations is not only an efficient but a unique approach to managing the dynamics of urban complexity.

Predictive algorithms take over planning responsibilities in city politics and administration in many cases. In the last decade, technology companies with their techno-utopian narratives of superior smart cities have pushed far into the realms of urban planners and architects, raising the question "how 'smartness' and the production of normative knowledge through datafication, platformisation and algorithms shape urban everyday life" (Bauriedl/Strüver 2020: 268). Their narratives draw a picture of better information and control, efficient management, technical synergies, tailored solutions, and "a more livable future" (Woethzel et al. 2018) in general. These visions are promoted by technology and consulting companies "connected to strong advertising, publishing and marketing industries" (Zukin 2020: 942). At the same time, they show a longstanding connection to scientific concepts of cities as communication systems and ideas of "dashboard governance" (Mattern 2015), propagated by governments. Together, such opinion-leaders are advancing techno-utopian imaginaries of smart, autonomous technologies that could and actually should replace human planning, knowledge, desires, and decisions.

However, behind the algorithms and calculations are people and networks, namely the data analysts, programmers, tech gurus, platforms, and corporations, whose ideas and interests are inscribed into the new production of space. Their mostly invisible work makes economic efficiency, technocratic ideals, and datafication the goals of public planning (Powell 2021). Tools and technologies to achieve these goals permeate the heterogeneous fabric of modern networked urbanism and its sentient infrastructures (Graham/Thrift

2007; Kropp 2018; Wilde 2021). This is why techno-utopian fantasies about smart cities are not just discursive beliefs and visions but are strongly entangled with sociotechnical systems and assemblages (Amin/Thrift 2017; Powell 2021). They result in specific regimes of urban development and design. These are built on the techno-utopian promise of making the complexity of cities manageable through data-based 'evidence', connectivity, algorithmic governance, and a more rational selection of optimized solutions from the endless shelves of rapidly iterated virtual combinations. As a result, cities are becoming a major business domain of large tech companies such as Alphabet, Alibaba, or Autodesk, allowing them to consolidate their economic power and digital dominance in the built environment.

Building information modeling, platforms, data, and a new political techno-economy

Building information modeling (BIM) could play a key role in opening the gates towards platform urbanism through facilitating the digital transformation of architecture and construction. BIM is a digital method for planning and construction that adds semantic information about geometry, materials, components, costs, or simulations to 2D- and 3D building models, and shares these through an interface for multidisciplinary collaboration. According to its proponents, mostly governments, consultancies, and pertinent software providers, BIM will solve the construction sector's efficiency, productivity, coordination, and quality problems, in addition to reducing 'cost and carbon', as it is often said. Whether and for whom the promised benefits actually materialize remains to be seen. For now, it is not clear to which extent this potential has, in fact, been realized and what, if any, monitoring mechanisms have been established to check.

In what follows, we explore the potentials and implications of BIM for transforming urban design and the social production of space in light of data-driven, digital platform capitalism (Gillespie 2010; Srnicek 2017; Staab 2019; Sadowski 2020a). We draw on empirical material from in-depth interviews with architecture, engineering, and construction professionals in Germany, carried out in 2019 and 2020 (and translated form German), along with document analysis and a literature review.

The rise of platforms as the core of digital capitalism has nurtured a new regime of techno-capitalist production and accumulation, with the commercial digital platform as its core model (Srnicek 2017; Staab 2019). Digital platforms are techno-economic and cyber-physical arrangements that enable, mediate, structure, and constrain economic or social activities by bringing together different actors (Kenney/Zysman 2016). Although non-proprietary platform models are possible, the dominant type is proprietary. One can distinguish between technology platforms and market platforms, noting that many platforms show attributes of both (Gawer 2014). BIM can be seen as a technology platform in that it entails a modular technological architecture composed of a core and a periphery that allows to create value by generating and harnessing an economy of scope. However, it also shows characteristics of a platform as a market that mediates transactions between planners or clients and producers of building components, such as doors, windows, walls, stairs, or others who can offer their products for sale through BIM software.

Digital platforms expand through self-reinforcing network and feedback effects (Srnicek 2017; Mayer-Schönberger/Ramge 2018). The result is an expansive winner-take-all logic, pushed further through aggressive acquisitions, often beyond the original domain and the creation or takeover of digital infrastructures, such as clouds or payment services. A further characteristic is the tendency of platform firms to enter the 'old' economy and challenge incumbent firms through disruption (Montalban/Frigant/Jullien 2019: 808f.). In this vein, Google, Facebook, Autodesk, and others invested in off-site construction start-up Factory_OS, and Alphabet subsidiary and Google's sister Sidewalk Labs launched Delve, a generative design tool powered by machine learning for urban development.

BIM: Promises of data-generated modeling and policies

Data-generated 3D building information models allow to represent and store the design results and process in a model. It takes the form of an "editable, re-executable design history" (Aish/Bredella 2017: 69), which can be re-winded, edited, and re-executed several times in different ways leading to varying project-related results. At the same time, BIM models allow the extraction of large amounts of data on costing, materials, collaborative relationships; semantic details of the model, results of design work, and the operations performed on the model create various data that can be rearranged, exchanged, reused, and transferred to further projects and actors.

BIM thus constitutes a data-based sociotechnical infrastructure that profoundly changes the nature of design processes (ibid.: 66). Decision-making about materialities and forms, for example, were previously left to designers' experience and expertise, but now often are implicitly shaped by product libraries from financially strong construction companies defining designers' and clients' scope of options. As the range of project parties and the types of data stored are expanding to include maintenance, facility management, and demolition, BIM is evolving from a way of cooperative modeling to a way of digital management. At the same time, interoperability issues, common standards, cloud services, and the question of who controls these become ever more critical.

Worldwide, the diffusion of BIM is strongly promoted by governments. The last few years have seen a proliferation of policy programs, strategy papers, conferences, and reports produced by a variety of actors such as associations of architects, software providers, consulting firms, governments, international governmental and non-governmental organizations[2]. In the architecture, construction, and engineering (AEC) sector, governments act in various capacities: as major clients of construction projects, as promoters of national competitiveness, as regulators, and policymakers. As clients, they see BIM as an instrument to better control risks, improve time and cost efficiency as well as quality and performance of public construction or infrastructure projects, and optimize admission procedures. In their capacity as promoters of the national industry, they see it as a means to increase its productivity and competitiveness in global markets. As regulators and policymakers, they can prescribe the use of BIM for segments of the construction sector or by creating the conditions for a general diffusion of BIM, be it through guidance, regulatory frameworks, mandates, training programs, or common standards.

In Germany, for instance, the 2015 Road Map for BIM stipulates its use for all public projects procured in Germany from the end of 2020 onwards (BMVI 2015). On a supranational level, the EU BIM Task Group launched a handbook (EU BIM Task Group 2017) that guides public procurers when introducing BIM. Environmental objectives are mentioned only once and in passing as

---

2   For an overview of government BIM policies in the EU, see (McAuley/Hore/West 2017; Panteli et al. 2020). Other authors of programmatic policy documents include the World Economic Forum (2017), the EU BIM Task Group (2017), buildingSMART international and its various national chapters, consulting firms like McKinsey (2017) or The Boston Consulting Group (2016), and others.

"[a]dapting to a sustainable built environment – one that supports the challenges of climate change and the need for a circular economy" (ibid.: 16). The main policy objectives are greater productivity, sector growth, faster production, better value for public money, and "an open, competitive and world-leading digital single market for construction" (ibid.: 2).

Often, these policies are championed by an industry-led initiative of larger planning and construction firms and software producers. BuildingSMART, one of the largest international BIM standardization initiatives, is an alliance of companies, government bodies, and institutions, which promotes the use of open (not to be confused with non-proprietary), sharable building information based on the Industry Foundation Class (IFC) platform (Laakso/Kiviniemi 2012). IFC defines a standard for data exchange in the construction industry and thus a basis for interoperability between different BIM and computer-aided design (CAD) software. Software producer Autodesk has been a founder of buildingSMART and is now a member of its Strategic Advisory Council, together with software solutions providers Nemetschek Group and Trimble and other multinational corporations. On a global level, the Global BIM Network consisting of public- and private-sector representatives and multi-lateral organizations advances the knowledge and capacity of national policies and programs. Within the network, software provider Autodesk leads "a global team advancing policies to support Autodesk's business" (Friendly 2021).

As many governments have pushed to make BIM a standard, we view it as an obligatory passage point (Callon 1986), forcing all parties involved to adopt its rationalities, pushing and enabling particular ways of practicing design and construction, and foreclosing others.

BIM and urban design automation

A key role in disseminating BIM and spreading the principles of digital capitalism has been assumed by Autodesk, especially with its BIM product Revit. Several companies and research laboratories have been involved in BIM development, but Autodesk and Revit significantly define its popularization and broader dissemination. Autodesk acquired Revit in 2002 and turned it into a $20 billion industry-standard today in BIM. Since then, it has held a dominant position in the global BIM market and increasingly defines digital formats, interfaces, and standards for 3D building models worldwide. Autodesk has made Revit the prime BIM platform and locked in most BIM users worldwide. Exact numbers are hard to obtain, but anecdotal evidence suggests that as much as 90 % of US and 80 % of UK firms working with BIM use Revit (Davis 2020). As an architect and structural engineer working for an international engineering office told us: "When people say BIM, three-quarters of them mean Revit." (2020, interview) With their Construction Cloud Connect, a combined cloud-application programming interface (API) solution, Autodesk further bridges companies, processes, and data. In 2020, it announced to push for a one-stop AEC cloud solution by investing in the development of the Revit API and Autodesk Forge, a cloud-based software development platform, as their primary future strategy (Davis 2020). The need for interoperability of data models for project partners to this standard decreases the chances for architects and developers to employ non-proprietary software applications. Even if they do, Revit remains an obligatory passage point, as a computational designer explained to us: "Yes, we are forced to use Autodesk products as well. However, we do not work with it. We work partly with it by creating interfaces. […] And of course, we have written such interfaces to several software [applications]. So, also to Revit." (Computational Designer 2020, interview)

In sum, we see a set of techno-economic moves, strategies, and arrangements that show an inherent tendency towards concentration of economic power and a turn from technologies of access to technologies of data (Powell 2021: 5), through which Autodesk has gained a nearly monopolistic position in the world of BIM. Starting from offering software solutions for collaborative work in project design, management, and construction to integrated interfaces for digital object libraries where third-party manufacturers and subcontractors offer their services or building components for purchase, the software company has assumed functions of a marketplace in the construction industry. Their arrangements allow generating and gathering design, construction, and collaboration data via software logs and cloud connections that can be exploited for secondary use and turned into rent-generating assets[3]. BIM tool producers can also offer data analysis and evaluation that can be fed back into design and planning, thus facilitating design automation in general.

By now, Autodesk and Google have started expanding into the business of urban development. In November 2020, Autodesk acquired the Norwegian technology start-up Spacemaker for $240 million. Spacemaker is a cloud-based artificial intelligence-supported software for urban development that

---

3 For the concept of assets and assetization, see (Birch/Muniesa 2020).

Figure 1 Spacemaker and Co's promise of AI-based urban planning

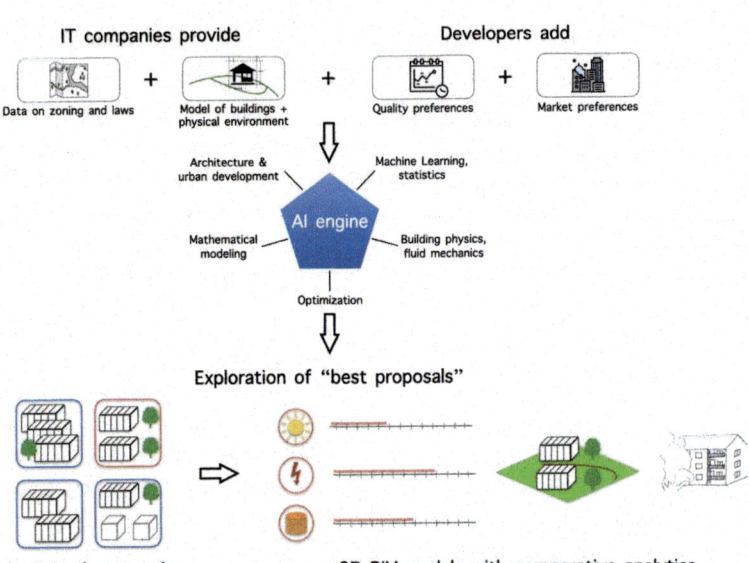

(Kropp/Braun/Boeva on the account provided by Kyle 2021)

promises to deliver the 'best possible' urban planning solution for a site through quick iteration of design options along with specific input criteria (Baumgarten 2021; see Fig. 1). Autodesk proclaims on its website that it helps to "maximize developers' long-term property investments and realize the full potential of the site" (AP News 2020), to increase project value, and the ability to consider sustainability options. Shortly before, Sidewalk Labs launched Delve, a similar generative design tool powered by machine learning for urban development, and there are some others. The algorithms for these cloud-based AI platforms are fed and trained with data from existing BIM models in order to support urban planners, architects, and developers in their data-driven and thus seemingly evidence-based urban design decisions:

> "As architects create 3D models in their Autodesk program of choice, they can input their project data, parameters, and constraints into Spacemaker's criteria form. From there, the system will analyze the existing 3D model and written data to process alternate layouts and configurations. The best

possible site plans are then selected by A.I. and displayed in a sidebar in the user's Autodesk program of choice, along with additional statistics and tips." (Oriaku 2021)

Spacemaker and Co believe that the continued growth of cities is creating significant pressure to build faster, denser, and more sustainably. At the same time, urban planning is becoming increasingly complex, time-consuming, and burdened with regulations, but the resources of public urban planning authorities have been cut everywhere. Against this backdrop, the companies promise to reduce complexity and save "millions of dollars by using the software early in the development process" (Kyle 2021). Value creation will be generated by "the quick iteration of thousands of design operations" generated from the "synthesis of publicly available data sources such as physical, regulatory, environmental, and other forms of inputs used in the designing of large-scale real estate developments" (ibid.).

Since Spacemaker was founded in Norway, the company initially benefited from accessing a rich source of built environment data supported by Norwegian government agencies and focused on multifamily housing. These restrictions made it a challenge to extend its functions "universally across geographies" and to other building types, making "new forms of data and tweaks to the machine learning [..] necessary" – a challenge "not necessarily technical, and relatively easy to overcome" (ibid.). It comes as no surprise that automatically generated design options have been criticized as "urban design echo chambers", working with data from previous urban construction and development projects in a way that once available "layouts are endlessly reproduced, never challenged, questioned, or evolved" (ibid.). Since all the data originate from BIM projects, we can speculate that they typically fall into the segment of high-priced or serial construction projects (Sundermeier/Beidersandwisch 2019; Braun/Kropp 2021).

Platform urbanism, its echo chambers, and the challenges of responsible urban design

So far, design processes have unfolded as somewhat unpredictable, multilayered interactions between architects, developers, clients, sketches, models, calculations, materials, and technologies (Latour/Yaneva 2012), sometimes involving public participation. In the future, automated generation of design options could take over large parts on the assumption that this will optimize planning processes, reduce costs, and make spatial planning calculable and predictable. To the extent that the tools for design automation will be owned by platform companies such as Autodesk or Alphabet, the logic of platform capitalism is beginning to transform both cities and the AEC sector, with BIM acting as a data provider and obligatory passage point and government policies as gate-openers. The implications of the "emerging dynamics between the production of space and value, catalysed by the integration of digital platforms and urban environments [...] happening] under the auspices of global tech companies" (Sadowski 2020b: 448) are not yet fully visible, but certainly, the relationship between technology, capital, and cities will once again change. While platform urbanism has so far been oriented to the movements and decisions of city dwellers as users, if only to achieve value with ever new and customized offerings, in the sociotechnical developments and corporate imaginaries presented here, the citizens' routines, desires, and actions may easily fall out of the sight. Cities may be optimized based on building data and machine learning along earlier decision-making of municipal governments, developers, and investors, legitimized by the argument that the best out of hundreds of – automatically generated and assessed – options has been selected.

The techno-economic moves and shifts bound up with this transformation will most likely affect who will gain and who will lose, with consequences for the building culture. In the realm of design software, this reconfiguration includes a further concentration of economic power with the tendency towards a near-monopoly by US-software provider Autodesk, further stabilized by securing control in the realm of cloud infrastructures and interoperability standards and a shift of focus and investment from architectural design to software solutions for urban construction and site development; all this will be benefitting primarily real estate owners, investors, developers, and construction companies. We can expect large construction firms to act as early adopters, securing themselves a comfortable starting position in a first-mover-takes-the-most game, and the encroachment of tech giants and domain outsiders such as Alphabet into architecture and construction, turning buildings and cities into machines for data extraction. At the same time, the hidden internal logic of BIM data generation, structuration, and processing may have its own "informational diagrammatic of control" (Marvin/Luque-Ayala 2017: 84). In various fields, it has already become apparent that the rule of algorithms is associated with a change in considering, classifying, and setting priorities (Coletta/Kitchin 2017; Gillespie 2014). These changes tend to benefit those who already dominate the given power constellations because their previous decisions are reflected in the available data. Accordingly, an impoverishment of perspectives and a focus on profit interests can be expected for the field of urban planning (Simpson/Brandlhuber/Grawert 2019).

IT companies and governments alike tend to present BIM as a panacea for all ills befalling the construction industry, from stagnating productivity via skilled labor shortage to its devastating environmental impact. Whether all these benefits will actually materialize in equal measure or whether the imperative of building ever more, cheaper, and faster will prevail over sustainability will be seen. So far, to the best of our knowledge, there is little systematic research on the actual impact of BIM mandates in terms of economic concentration processes, an environmentally sustainable building culture, or the delivery of livable and affordable housing. However, we see types of actors benefitting from the ongoing techno-economic shifts that are not precisely known for prioritizing environmental sustainability, affordable housing, or more livable cities over data extraction and their own economic profit. Without accounting for the logic of platform capitalism, BIM policies will most likely, even if unwillingly, facilitate platformization and assetization in architecture and construction and in the future also in urban planning. The grand challenges posed by the environmental crisis and the need to provide adequate and affordable housing are likely to rank second at best. It would be worthwhile to study the respective policy processes and see whether urban planning actors are problematizing the social and environmental risks and side effects of automated city design. Already today, there are city council members, state legislators, and community organizations that oppose the government's tendencies to satisfy Big Tech companies. At the same time, the less human and financial resources are available to develop suitable concepts, the more promising the use of artificial intelligence in urban planning appears. In any case, it is crucial to critically interrogate this digital transformation in light of the techno-economic dynamics and the reconfiguration of urban power relations it is enmeshed with.

Algorithmic rationalities and data-based operations tend to establish standardized ways of processing inputs and conducting operations. As a result, a city's complexity may be drastically simplified and limited in its ability to adapt to local *spacing* and synthesize the interplay between urban objects, structures, and actions (Löw 2018). As Marvin and Luque-Ayala explain, drawing on experiences with digital resource planning, it may turn out that

"presumptions of the software package cannot be overridden; evaluation is restricted to a limited number of criteria; cognition processes rely on the identification and deployment of common elements across experiences; and finally, the black-boxed nature of the technology itself – the software – protects it from deliberate manipulation or transformation" (2017: 89).

Moreover, more wicked problems such as reconciling growth and sustainability are unlikely to be solvable with transmitted data and current AI: "A correlation between input and output is not enough. More important is the justification of choices, based on theory and policy accountability." (Komninos/Panori/Kakderi 2019: 4) Instead of thinking in terms of techno-managerial optimization and automation, there are important urban planning decisions to be made to respond to the major challenges of climate change, biodiversity loss, demographic change, and ongoing urbanization. The development of responsible city design is better advised not to rely on data about what already exists since what exists is neither socially just nor sustainable, but to look for a much more profound basis upon which to make decisions (Carmona 2009) and to develop entirely new ways of living and building in order to foster the required urban transformations (Hölscher/Frantzeskaki 2021).

Anyone who sees urban planning and construction as a purely managerial task for optimizing technical parameters runs the risk of seeking the solution only in faster, bigger, more, thus making the necessary transformation in urban design, architecture, and construction even more difficult. In current techno-utopias, the city is imagined as a hyper-optimized, efficient, and smoothly functioning place. However, this is not necessarily a sustainable and inclusive place that allows for a responsible and fair distribution of resources. As Arno Brandlhuber and Olaf Grawert point out in a conversation with Deane Simpson (2019), the current trend toward algorithmic (post)planning is leading to an increasing loss of decision-making authority in urban planning for architects and planners. While those should be guided by the democratic values of liberty, equality, and fraternity, the new defining power of smart city paradigms and their proponents seem to pursue more individual goals (ibid.). Thus, platform urbanism threatens to make urban planning and society disappear into algorithms and computational design capacities, ushering in a silent, unnegotiated revolution of guiding principles.

Lefebvre criticized industrial capitalism for boiling down the interactions of spatial practices, socio-political concepts, and utopian visions to a dualist antagonism between an abstractly conceived, organized space "defined by [..] echoes, repercussions, mirror effects" (1991: 39) and the lived, fluid spaces of everyday life, such that "lived experience is crushed, vanquished by what is 'conceived of'" (ibid.: 51). As a result, the dominant production of abstract space tends towards repetition and homogeneity. Lefebvre considered social class struggles as the only force capable of maintaining differences in face of the "homogenizing efforts of the state, political power, the world market, and the world of commodities". But how can these differences be mobilized when the production of abstract space takes place in the digital worlds of algorithms, data, and clouds? While in the 1970s, repetitious spaces were "the outcome of repetitive gestures (those of the workers) associated with instruments which are both duplicatable and designed to duplicate: machines, bulldozers, concrete-mixers, cranes, pneumatic drills, and so on" (ibid.: 75), nowadays, these effects are produced by *informational diagrammatics of control*. Yet, it is still capitalism, assetization, and the ideas of abstract government that rule urbanism for the benefit of value creation.

References

Aish, Robert/Bredella, Nathalie (2017): The evolution of architectural computing: From building modelling to design computation, in: *Arq: Architectural Research Quarterly* 21(1): 65-73.
Amin, Ash/Thrift, Nigel (2017): *Seeing like a city*, Cambridge/Malden: Polity Press.
AP News (2020): Press Release: Autodesk Completes Acquisition of Spacemaker, Provider of AI and Generative Design-enabled Urban Design Platform. https://apnews.com/press-release/pr-newswire/technology-business-corporate-news-building-construction-products-and-services-ecddf6bcd1fc686186cbee147b51e259 [24.02.2022].
Baumgarten, Elias (2021): Bedrohliche Chance? Autodesk kauft Spacemaker. http://direct.swiss-architects.com/de/architecture-news/meldungen/bedrohliche-chance-autodesk-kauft-spacemaker-1 [15.01.2022].
Bauriedl, Sybille/Strüver, Anke (2020): Platform urbanism: Technocapitalist production of private and public spaces, in: *Urban Planning* 5(4): 267-76.

Birch, Kean/Muniesa, Fabian (2020): *Assetization. Turning things into assets in technoscientific capitalism*, Cambridge: MIT Press.

BMVI – Bundesministerium für Verkehr und digitale Infrastruktur (2015): *Stufenplan digitales Planen und Bauen*, Berlin: Bundesministerium für Verkehr und digitale Infrastruktur.

Braun, Kathrin/Kropp, Cordula (2021): Schöne neue Bauwelt? Versprechen, Visionen und Wege des digitalen Planens und Bauens, in: Braun, Kathrin/Kropp, Cordula (eds.): *In digitaler Gesellschaft. Neukonfigurationen zwischen Robotern, Algorithmen und Usern*, Bielefeld: transcript: 135-65.

Brauneis, Robert/Goodman, Ellen P. (2018): Algorithmic transparency for the smart city, in: *Yale Journal of Law & Technology* 20: 103-75.

Callon, Michel (1986): Some elements of a sociology of translation: Domestication of the scallops and the fishermen of St Brieuc Bay, in: Law, John (ed.): *Power, action and belief: A new sociology of knowledge?*, London: Routledge: 196-223.

Carmona, Matthew (2009): Sustainable urban design: Principles to practice, in: *International Journal of Sustainable Development* 12(1): 48-77.

Coletta, Claudio/Kitchin, Rob (2017): Algorhythmic governance: Regulating the 'heartbeat' of a city using the Internet of Things, in: *Big Data and Society* 4(2). doi: https://doi.org/10.1177/2053951717742418.

Davis, Daniel (2020): *Architects versus Autodesk*, in: Architect, 27.08.2020. https://www.architectmagazine.com/technology/architects-versus-autodesk_o [15.01.2022].

EU BIM Task Group (2017): Handbook for the introduction of Building Information Modelling by the European Public Sector. http://www.eubim.eu/downloads/EU_BIM_Task_Group_Handbook_FINAL.PDF [15.01.2022].

Friendly, Andrew (2021): Governments can help fix construction woes with global BIM. https://redshift.autodesk.com/global-bim/ [15.01.2022].

Gawer, Annabelle (2014): Bridging differing perspectives on technological platforms: Toward an integrative framework, in: *Research Policy* 43(7): 1239-49.

Gillespie, Tarleton (2010): The politics of 'platforms', in: *New Media and Society* 12(3): 347-64.

Gillespie, Tarleton (2014): The relevance of algorithms, in: Gillespie, Tarleton/Boczkowski, Pablo J./Foot, Kirsten A. (eds.): *Media technologies: Essays on communication, materiality and society*, Cambridge: MIT Press: 167-94.

Graham, Stephen/Thrift, Nigel (2007): Out of order: Understanding repair and maintenance, in: *Theory, Culture & Society* 24(3): 1-25.

Hockenhull, Michael/Cohn, Marissa Leavitt (2021): Hot air and corporate sociotechnical imaginaries: Performing and translating digital futures in the Danish tech scene, in: *New Media and Society* 23(2): 302-21.

Hölscher, Katharina/Frantzeskaki, Niki (2021): Perspectives on urban transformation research: Transformations in, of, and by cities, in: *Urban Transformations* 3(2). doi: https://doi.org/10.1186/s42854-021-00019-z.

Kallinikos, Jannis (2007): *The consequences of information. Institutional implications of technological change*, Cheltenham: Edward Elgar Publishing.

Karvonen, Andrew/Cugurullo, Federico/Caprotti, Federico (eds.) (2019): *Inside smart cities. Place, politics and urban innovation*, London/New York: Routledge.

Kenney, Martin/Zysman, John (2016): The rise of the platform economy, in: *Issues in Science and Technology* 32(3): 61-69.

Kitchin, Rob (2014): The real-time city? Big data and smart urbanism, in: *GeoJournal* 79: 1-14.

Komninos, Nicos/Panori, Anastasia/Kakderi, Christina (2019): Smart cities beyond algorithmic logic: digital platforms, user engagement and data science, in: Komninos, Nicos/Kakderi, Christina (eds.): *Smart cities in the post-algorithmic era: Integrating technologies, platforms and governance*, Cheltenham: Edward Elgar: 1-15.

Kropp, Cordula (2018): Intelligente Städte. Rationalität, Einfluss und Legitimität von Algorithmen, in: Bauriedl, Sybille/Strüver, Anke (eds.): *Smart City. Kritische Perspektiven auf die Digitalisierung der Städte*, Bielefeld: transcript: 33-42.

Kyle, R. (2021): Spacemaker: Merging AI technology with Urban Planning and Design. Digital Innovation and Transformation. MBA Student Perspectives. https://digital.hbs.edu/platform-digit/submission/spacemaker-merging-ai-technology-with-urban-planning-and-design/ [15.01.2022].

Laakso, Mikael/Kiviniemi, Arto (2012): The IFC standard – a review of history, development, and standardization, in: *Journal of Information Technology in Construction (ITcon)* 17: 134-61.

Latour, Bruno/Yaneva, Albena (2012): Give me a gun and I will make all buildings move: An ANT's view of architecture, in: Harrison, Ariane Lourie (ed.): *Architectural theories of the environment*, London: Routledge: 80-89.

Lefebvre, Henri (1991): *The production of space*, Oxford: Blackwell.

Löw, Martina (2018): *The sociology of space. Materiality, social structures and action*, Basingstoke: Palgrave Macmillan.

Marvin, Simon/Luque-Ayala, Andrés (2017): Urban operating systems: Diagramming the city, in: *International Journal of Urban and Regional Research* 41(1): 84-103.
Mattern, Shannon (2015): Mission control: A history of the urban dashboard, in: *Places Journal*. doi: https://doi.org/10.22269/150309.
Mayer-Schönberger, Viktor/Ramge, Thomas (2018): *Reinventing capitalism in the age of big data*, New York: Basic Books.
McAuley, Barry/Hore, Alan/West, Roger (2017): *BICP Global BIM Study – Lessons for Ireland's BIM Programme*, Dublin: Construction IT Alliance (CitA) Limited.
McKinsey Global Institute (2017): Reinventing construction. Full report: A route to higher productivity. https://www.mckinsey.com/business-functions/operations/our-insights/reinventing-construction-through-a-productivity-revolution [24.02.2022].
Montalban, Matthieu/Frigant, Vincent/Jullien, Bernard (2019): Platform economy as a new form of capitalism: A Régulationist research programme, in: *Cambridge Journal of Economics* 43(4): 805-24.
Oriaku, Ali (2021): *When the machine intervenes: Autodesk acquires urban design AI assistant Spacemaker*, in: The Architect's Newspaper, 08.01.2021. https://www.archpaper.com/2021/01/autodesk-users-can-opt-for-an-ai-assistant-through-new-spacemaker-program/ [15.01.2022].
Panteli, Christina/Polycarpou, Kyriacos/Morsink-Georgalli, F.Z./Stasiuliene, Laura/Pupeikis, D./Jurelionis, Andrius/Fokaides, Paris (2020): Overview of BIM integration into the construction sector in European member states and European Union Acquis. IOP Conference Series: Earth and Environmental Science 410(1). http://oro.open.ac.uk/70998/ [24.02.2022].
Powell, Alison B. (2021): *Undoing optimization. Civic action in smart cities*, New Haven/London: Yale University Press.
Sadowski, Jathan (2020a): *Too smart. How digital capitalism is extracting data, controlling our lives, and taking over the world*, Cambridge/London: MIT Press.
Sadowski, Jathan (2020b): Cyberspace and cityscapes: On the emergence of platform urbanism, in: *Urban Geography* 41(3): 448-52.
Simpson, Deane/Brandlhuber, Arno/Grawert, Olaf (2019): Die Stadt des Plattformkapitalismus, in: *Arch+ Zeitschrift für Architektur und Urbanismus* 236: 50-55.
Srnicek, Nick (2017): *Platform capitalism*, Cambridge: Polity Press.
Staab, Philipp (2019): *Digitaler Kapitalismus. Markt und Herrschaft in der Ökonomie der Unknappheit*, Berlin: Suhrkamp.

Sundermeier, Matthias/Beidersandwisch, Philipp (2019): Trends und Strategien für das Planen mit BIM – eine ökonomische Betrachtung, in: BDB – Bund Deutscher Baumeister (ed.): *Digitales Planen und Bauen. Jahrbuch 2019/2020*, Gütersloh: Bauverlag: 28-49.

The Boston Consulting Group (2016): The Transformative Power of Building Information Modeling. https://www.bcg.com/de-de/publications/2016/engineered-products-infrastructure-digital-transformative-power-building-information-modeling [15.01.2022].

Wilde, Jessica (2021): *Die Fabrikation der Stadt. Eine Neuausrichtung der Stadtsoziologie nach Bruno Latour*, Bielefeld: transcript.

Woethzel, Jonathan/Remes, Jaana/Boland, Brodie/Lv., Kathrina/Sinha, Suveer/Strube, Gernot/Means, John/Law, Jonathan/Cadena, Andrés/von der Tann, Valerie (2018): Smart cities: Digital solutions for a more livable future. McKinsey Global Institute. https://www.mckinsey.com/business-functions/operations/our-insights/smart-cities-digital-solutions-for-a-more-livable-future [24.02.2022].

World Economic Forum (2017): *Shaping the future of construction. Inspiring innovators to redefine construction*, Cologny/Geneva: World Economic Forum.

Zukin, Sharon (2020): Seeing like a city: how tech became urban, in: *Theory and Society* 49: 941-64.

The Financialization of the Housing Market in the Digital Era
Airbnb in Berlin

Katalin Gennburg

Like many other cities around the world, Berlin has faced rapidly rising rents over the past three decades. From 2015 to 2020, rents under new contracts have increased by 21 %, while existing rents have risen by 12 % (IBB 2021: 64). This development has been accompanied by a withdrawal of the state from housing provision, which has its onset in the 1980s, and a far-reaching privatization of municipal housing stocks. This can be understood as a successive shift from a state housing policy to a housing market policy (Egner 2019: 98). Recent attempts to politically regulate the excessive development of rental prices at the subnational level have failed. After a rent cap was introduced by a former center-left Berlin government coalition, it was eventually annulled by the Federal Constitutional Court due to Berlin's lack of jurisdiction. In a so-called *tenant city* such as Berlin, where the share of rented apartments in the housing stock was 84.25 % in 2020, and where there is thus a relatively low rate of home ownership, these developments have socially explosive impacts (IBB 2021: 10). The displacement of the poor population and social segregation in the urban space are among the most widespread consequences of these escalating market dynamics in Berlin.

This process is complemented by the increasing influence of platform companies on the local housing market. Using the example of Airbnb, an internationally operating platform company for the mediation and booking of apartments, this article describes the role of such a company in the housing policy debate. The main thesis of the text is that Airbnb is exemplary for the financialization and digitalization of the housing market, and that it, as a platform, exploits data generated by urban processes and rental practices.

In this context, it is of particular interest that digitalization is not a neutral process in itself; it takes place embedded in consumption-oriented and competitive logics and capitalist accumulation processes and is significantly influenced by technology and innovation policies. This process of exploitation, which takes place in both analog and digital space, is reflected in all spheres of society – including the area of housing.

The question to be asked is how platforms for the supposed short-term rental of homes for vacation lead to a cannibalization of the common rental relationship. In addition, this new kind of platform-mediated private housing is to be negotiated as the herald of the valorization of housing based on algorithms. Further, the use of rental software for tenant tracking indicates that the issue is also of interest in regard to digital surveillance and data exploitation. Finally, policy strategies that can be used to intervene against companies such as Airbnb will be presented at different scales.

Airbnb: From start-up to market power

Founded in 2008 as a start-up, the company has since experienced a meteoric rise: while it was able to list 120.000 accommodations in 2012, by 2019 there were already seven million accommodations available for booking worldwide, bringing in around 187 million bookings in the same year. Airbnb's underlying business model is as simple as it is successful: the company takes up an intermediary position between supply and demand. For example, Airbnb charges rental fees and collects 5-15 % from guests and 3 % from landlords for each rental transacted via the platform. This allowed Airbnb to generate more than three billion euros even in 2020, when tourism plummeted across much of the world due to the Covid-19 pandemic. As a company without a tangible product, Airbnb is almost infinitely scalable and, with 6.300 employees in 2020, Airbnb is, compared to other tech companies, a relatively lean company, which is nevertheless able to operate almost worldwide. Unlike hotel businesses, it has very little cost factors associated with the provision of accommodation and, as a platform, Airbnb must invest solely in server capacity and software development. In recent years, Airbnb has tried to gradually expand its range of services: the company began to operate regular hotels with partners, took over other platforms, such as the last-minute hotel provider hoteltonight.com, and even arranged entire trips. In addition, the company has expanded its platform function by not only mediating accommodation between those seeking and offering it but between tour guides and tourists as well. In some places, Airbnb has even entered the real estate development business. Together with the company Niido, Airbnb developed a joint venture in entire housing estates, with tenants committing to renting out their apartments via Airbnb on a weekly basis. This brings the group a double revenue stream: regular rent and regular income from arranging short-term rentals.

Moreover, there is the data that the company generates through its intermediary services and uses as an important resource that tells us a lot about trends and consumer behavior in the respective cities. In fact, it can be assumed that generating data and sharing it commercially with third parties is, for Airbnb, now equivalent to the actual rental business, and that every rental is about expanding the company's data landscape.

In Germany, too, Airbnb has become an indispensable part of the tourism industry, with the German capital Berlin being the company's main focus. A report carried out by the Federal Ministry of Economics and Technology showed that, in 2017 alone, around 22.500 offers were made in Berlin, with around half of these being entire apartments (BMWi 2017). This amounts to around 0.5 % of Berlin's housing stock at the time, with the rate likely being even higher in neighborhoods popular with tourists, as it can be assumed that there is a spatial concentration of offers in precisely these inner-city, multicultural, socially mixed, Wilhelminian era neighborhoods (Friedrichshain, Prenzlauer Berg, Mitte, Kreuzberg).

Rent madness and housing losses:
Airbnb as a catalyst for urban exploitation strategies

The problem here is that many of the apartments are being misappropriated and withdrawn from the regular rental market, which contributes to a shortage of apartments on the market and, as a consequence, an increase in asking rents in the surrounding area. This is also the conclusion of a report by the German Institute for Economic Research (DIW). The DIW found that an additional Airbnb accommodation increased the asking rents in the immediate vicinity of the accommodation by an average of 13 cents per square meter, whereby the rent increases varied greatly from district to district, with a variance of between eight and 46 cents per square meter of living space per additional Airbnb offer (Duso et al. 2021: 95ff.). For a new 65-square-meter rental apartment, this can amount to as much as €38 per month, depending on the district – which is thus quite relevant to many Berliners.

On a subnational level, the state of Berlin counters the described problem by the so-called *Zweckentfremdungsverbot-Gesetz* (Law on Prohibition of Misuse of Residential Space), which has been applied since 2014. This law aims to prevent the illegal rental of apartments that are not permanently used for residential purposes. The legislation, which was reformed in 2018, obliges commercial landlords to present a registration number, which, in turn, must be obtained by applying for a rental permit at the district offices. In addition, Berliners are allowed to rent out their apartments whenever their function as a primary residence is not endangered, while secondary residences, the rental of which requires a permit, may be rented out for a maximum of 90 days per year. Permanent rentals of a part of a dwelling can be considered if less than half of the living space is affected. Nevertheless, the new law does not make everyone properly register their advertised apartments. A study commissioned by the parliamentary group of the European Left showed that since the law has changed up to 80 % of the advertised apartments in Berlin still did not have the required registration number (Cox/Haar 2020: 2). Due to the European legal situation, landlords can rely on the support of Airbnb, which has so far been reluctant to disclose the data of the respective landlords. Since the exact address as well as the full name of the landlord are only shown after an accommodation is booked, municipal governments are at a loss here without the company's cooperation.

Thus far, however, the company has shown little willingness to cooperate when it comes to taking action against the illegal misappropriation of residential space and, what is more, has used targeted lobbying against any attempts at stronger regulation. In the past, for example, Airbnb primarily invoked an e-commerce directive of the European Union from the year 2000 that explicitly does not hold platforms responsible for the activities of their users. In addition, according to the directive, platform companies must comply with the laws of their place of business. The Airbnb customer service for Europe has been located in Dublin since 2013, an inner-European paradise for tax avoidance and deregulated data mining. This completely outdated directive allows platform companies to evade their responsibility and urgently needs to be addressed.

Ironically, by tolerating the illegal practice of misappropriation, Airbnb works to secure the basis for its own economy: as rents rise in a city, more people rely on renting out their housing, at least partially and temporarily.

Accordingly, if more people rent out parts of their living space as short-term rentals and exclusively by the day or by the weekend, forms of permanent shared living in particular, which are widespread in large cities, but available living space in general as well, become scarce. Political and cultural scientist Rabea Berfelde argues that Airbnb thus offers "an individualized solution to processes of precarization" (Berfelde 2021: 143) and explains that, in the course of the neoliberal restructuring of the welfare state and the financialization of the global economy, infrastructures of social reproduction also increasingly become the object of exploitation logics (ibid.: 138).

If one considers, moreover, that the shareholders of the listed company include the financial giant BlackRock, it all comes full circle. BlackRock also holds shares in large housing companies such as Vonovia and Deutsche Wohnen AG, which benefit from rising rents in Berlin as well. While a September 2021 petition for a referendum on the socialization of listed housing companies with more than 3.000 residential units in Berlin was successful and is now greatly expected to be implemented (Candeias et al. 2022), right to the city activists adopted the call for expropriation in 2019 and demanded: expropriate Airbnb! ("Airbnb und Co. Enteignen!"; Leftvision 2019)

Airbnb as an example of the entanglement of the financialization and digitalization of the housing market

Sociologist Philipp Staab likewise sees a new accumulation regime in the making, describing an increasingly *digital capitalism* in which formerly analog processes are transferred to digital technological systems and platform companies play a key strategic role. For them, the aim is to create economies of scale and network effects to not only develop market power but to become the market in its entirety. According to Staab, this development can be traced back to multilayered socio-economic processes of capitalist reorganization, with in particular the financialization and deregulation of the global economy, which have been ongoing since the 1970s, setting the final course for the path that has led to the digital capitalism of the present (Staab 2019: 50). Conversely, financialization can no longer be understood independently of digital and electronic technologies. In Staab's words, they are not identical, but they are "structurally analogous processes [with] historical [as well as] structural filiations" (ibid.: 99).

One example of the interweaving of digitalization and financialization can be found in the everyday practice of the housing industry. Algorithm-based management programs have become indispensable, especially for listed rental giants with thousands of units, and they play an increasingly important role even among medium-sized property management companies. The programs make it possible to automatically calculate leeway for rent increases and to close potential income gaps. They also provide a glimpse into the future by calculating potential corporate profits, which, in turn, influences the companies' balance sheets and stock market valuations. It goes without saying that the calculation of potential rent gaps does not take into account the interests of tenants and portfolio management but those of shareholders – as has repeatedly been pointed out by critical shareholders of the real estate corporation Deutsche Wohnen AG (Dachverband Kritische Aktionäre 2015).

In the case of housing platforms such as Airbnb, it is also the data generated on short-term rentals and users that influence share and stock market values and thus determine the value of the company. In addition, Airbnb uses digital and algorithm-supported programs – technologies that go by the term *property technology* as well – both to improve the marketing and utilization of vacation homes and to analyze investment opportunities. Furthermore, digital and algorithm-based technologies are increasingly used in the ecosystem of businesses that depend on Airbnb; the start-up AirDNA, for example, offers spatial analyses of price potentials for providers of short-term rentals, through which apartments can be 'managed' profitably like companies.

Airbnb itself is anything but transparent about its collected data when dealing with interested third parties that have no profit interests. This is not surprising, since data mining and trading has become an essential component of market power and a kind of new currency for corporations in general, and internet platforms in particular. One thing is certain: probabilities are calculated using algorithms from the data collected through platform use. These enable precise forecasts of, for example, demand, trends, and estimates of overnight rates. On the basis of these profile assumptions, providers are then offered price suggestions for their accommodation. In this way, accommodation costs are increasingly controlled by the data that the company receives from providers and users, which are simultaneously designed to increase Airbnb's revenues and thus successively raise the general price level, which in turn intensifies general urban rent increases.

Despite the impact of Airbnb's business model on rising rents and housing shortages, these have been a comparatively underexposed issue within the housing movement. Nonetheless, criticism of Airbnb is growing both in Berlin and worldwide because overall the extent of housing destruction by means of vacancies, vacation rentals, or demolition is becoming increasingly visible and is no longer discussed as a niche issue that has to be seen isolated from rent increases in existing apartments. Interestingly, digital activists are now joining forces with housing activists to call for digital expertise in order to achieve more transparency and a common good-oriented development of the city in the digital age. In 2019, for example, the Digital City Alliance was founded in Berlin to combine experiences of the sell-out of the city in the analog space with knowledge about digital politics and to make demands on state politics, including on how to deal with rental platforms such as Airbnb (Digitales Berlin 2019).

Conclusion and outlook: Regulating platform companies – analog and digital!

The task for the political left is clear: to starkly regulate housing platform companies such as Airbnb in terms of data and housing policies. Local governments must have the opportunity to manage tourism in a way that is compatible with the urban quality of life and housing needs of the urban population while, at the same time, counteracting the housing and rent crisis caused by capitalist urbanization.

The city of Vienna, for example, shows that it is possible to enforce rental bans via the platform. In the city's social buildings, short-term rentals are generally prohibited, and the platforms have committed to deleting all illegal listings. What works in Vienna has so far been impossible in Berlin, which reveals the lack of political will to enforce restrictive housing protection laws, especially digitally and via data policies. In line with the actions of digital platforms and the technological possibilities of digital capitalism, it would be politically advisable to consider illegal rental offers on the platform as a violation of rules and to oblige the company to enforce these rules. Only once a platform is made liable for its content can the enforcement of the applicable rules and laws through the rental opportunities on the platform be ensured.

Against this backdrop, the digital market and associated services provided by platform companies must be regulated more strongly at the supranational level and existing legislation must finally be overhauled. For more than two years, the European Commission (EC) has been negotiating the draft legislation of a Digital Services Act to establish a powerful transparency and a clear accountability framework for online platforms (EC 2020). If this is to be successful from the perspective of European cities, it must include at least the following points: first, companies such as Airbnb must be required to disclose landlord data, as well as a general quantitative overview of rentals, and implement city approval procedures in the platform. In this way, it would be conceivable that an advertisement on Airbnb would no longer be possible without the aforementioned registration number at all – technically, an easily implemented change. In addition, platforms must be obliged to take proactive action against illegal offers and not, as is currently the case, only after being requested to do so and after proof has been provided by municipal governments. Finally, the current principle of company domicile must be dismantled to enable legal proceedings in all European countries.

The digitalization and financialization of global capitalism have led to new forms of exploitation in recent years, with the platform economy being a significant expression and constituent of this development. Those who demand housing protection and rental security over a housing crisis and mass vacation rentals must change the rules of the game for digital offerings and platforms. The problems of our 'analog city management' have long been a reflection of digital malaise and the inability of political actors to think in terms of digital politics. Data extractivism of so-called sharing platforms and financial market-oriented real estate exploitation via property technology, as well as rental housing in the hands of hedge funds and shadow banks, are part of the same problem: the sell-out of cities in the digital age and the exploitation of the urban in the age of digital capitalism. In contrast, there is a need for social housing security and rent regulation, a regulatory policy toward platforms, as well as digital and analog city creators who, according to all the rules of the art of programming and in accordance with the claim of technological sovereignty, shape cities democratically and are oriented toward cities as a common good.

References

Berfelde, Rabea (2021): Das Reproduktionsmodell von Airbnb: Wohnraum 'teilen' im Kontext krisenhafter sozial-reproduktiver Verhältnisse, in: Altenried, Moritz/Dück, Julia/Wallis, Mira (eds.): *Plattformkapitalismus und die Krise der sozialen Reproduktion*, Münster: Westfälisches Dampfboot: 130-47.

Bundesministerium für Wirtschaft und Energie (BMWi) (2017): "SharingEconomy" und Wirtschaftspolitik. Gutachten des Wissenschaftlichen Beirats beim Bundesministerium für Wirtschaft und Energie. https://www.bmwi.de/Redaktion/DE/Publikationen/Ministerium/Veroeffentlichung-Wissenschaftlicher-Beirat/gutachten-wissenschaftlicher-beirat-sharing-economy-wirtschaftspolitik.pdf?__blob=publicationFile&v=18 [22.01.2021].

Candeias, Mario/Demirović, Alex/Fried, Barbara/Koch, Rhonda/Sablowski, Thomas/Völpel, Eva/Warnke, Moritz (2022): Believe the Hype! Why socialization can be a compass for renewing the Left in Germany. https://www.rosalux.de/en/news/id/45866/believe-the-hype [22.01.2021].

Cox, Murray/Haar, Kenneth (2020): Platform Failures. How short-term rental platforms like Airbnb fail to cooperate with cities and the need for strong regulations to protect housing. http://insideairbnb.com/reports/Platform-Failures-FINAL-VERSION.pdf [22.01.2021].

Dachverband Kritische Aktionäre (2015): Protest gegen Umgang der Deutsche Wohnen AG mit Sozialwohnungen. https://www.kritischeaktionaere.de/deutsche_wohnen/protest-gegen-umgang-der-deutsche-wohnen-ag-mit-sozialwohnungen/ [22.01.2021].

Digitales Berlin (2019): https://digitalesberlin.info [05.02.2022].

Duso, Tomaso/Michelsen, Claus/Schäfer, Maximilian/Tran, Kevin (2021): Durch Airbnb-Vermietungen steigen in Berlin die Mieten, in: *DIW Wochenbericht* 88(7): 95-102.

EC – European Commission (2020): Proposal for a Regulation on a Single Market For Digital Services. https://ec.europa.eu/info/strategy/priorities-2019-2024/europe-fit-digital-age/digital-services-act-ensuring-safe-and-accountable-online-environment_en [27.01.2021].

Egner, Björn (2019): Wohnungspolitik seit 1945, in: Bundeszentrale für politische Bildung (ed.): *Gesucht! Gefunden? Alte und neue Wohnungsfragen*, Bonn: Bundeszentrale für politische Bildung: 94-100.

Gennburg, Katalin/Hertel, Jannis/Moje, Carolin/Petri, Denis (2021): *Gemütliches Loft mit Aussicht auf Verdrängung. Wie die Vermietungsplattform Airbnb die Stadt Berlin verändert*, Berlin: Rosa-Luxemburg-Stiftung.
Investitionsbank Berlin (IBB) (ed.) (2021): IBB Wohnungsmarktbericht 2020. https://www.ibb.de/media/dokumente/publikationen/berliner-wohnungsmarkt/wohnungsmarktbericht/ibb_wohnungsmarktbericht_2020.pdf [22.01.2021].
Leftvision (2019): Airbnb und Co. Enteignen! https://www.youtube.com/watch?v=cqrVdkxVRO0 [22.01.2021].
Staab, Philipp (2019): *Digitaler Kapitalismus. Markt und Herrschaft in der Ökonomie der Unknappheit*, Berlin: Suhrkamp.

Smart Ambivalences
Social Economy and Capitalist Rationalities Intersecting in the Field of Sharing

Andreas Exner & Thomas Höflehner

Digital technologies increasingly have been discussed in terms of their potential to raise the quality of life and make cities more sustainable. This discussion and related political initiatives have usually been framed as attempts to create smart cities (Toli/Murtagh 2020), which have been criticized with regard to the role of capitalist interests, a bias toward technological and managerial solutions, and the problematic social, political, and ecological effects of hegemonic smart city policies (Bauriedl/Strüver 2018; Elwood/Leszczynsky 2018; Elwood 2021; Richardson 2020). While smart city imaginaries often emphasize innovations in digital technologies while neglecting social processes, some have included the idea of social innovation (Exner et al. 2018; Exner/Cepoiu/Weinzierl 2018). The term *social innovation* denotes social initiatives that respond to new societal needs. An example often cited among such innovations is sharing, which promises to offer economic opportunities, ecological benefits, and social value as a result of efficiency gains (Martin 2016). Many see sharing economies as closely connected to digital platforms, for which reason sharing platforms have become prominent examples of both the sharing as well as the platform economy in general (Sutherland/Jarrahi 2018; Bauriedl/Strüver 2020).

However, their outcomes have been discussed critically (e.g., Rong et al. 2017; Jin et al. 2018; Geissinger et al. 2019). Sharing economies denote a motley array of various types of economic organizations and strategies (Albinsson/Perera 2018) that often reproduce the rationality of capital accumulation (Scholz 2017) but also include non-capitalist practices and enterprises (such as cooperatives). Sharing economies do not necessarily use digital technologies. However, they are often understood as techno-capitalist initiatives that digitally mediate the sharing of different resources for the sake of generating profit. This latter type of initiative, i.e., the digital sharing platform as a capitalist undertaking, exhibits a specific rationality, which is oriented toward profit maximization through wage labor or contractual arrangements between powerful corporate centers and petty producers who are put into the former's service. Uber is just one, but enigmatic, example of this type of economy. The capitalist sharing economy reproduces or even deepens social inequalities and may contribute to the growth in resource consumption that sustainability seeks to curb. It may also undermine political regulation on the urban scale, since capitalist sharing businesses operate on a global level and thus do not necessarily take into account local economic structures, social needs, or problems. Furthermore, they may disrupt local markets through exposing established enterprises to world market competition and associated pressures to reduce costs and create and be able to exploit novel business opportunities without being the subject of local regulations or a partner of local policy initiatives. However, marginalized within the mainstream of sharing economies, certain initiatives deviate from the capitalist type of economic organization (Martin 2016) either in analog or digital space. These sharing economies constitute commons (with or without digital technologies) and manage them through democratic procedures. In this sense, sharing economies also encompass food co-ops, repair cafés, or similar types of non-capitalist initiatives. Non-capitalist sharing economies are social economies (Chaves-Avila/Gallego-Bono 2020; Social Economy Europe 2021) insofar that they put social needs and ecological concerns center stage and work democratically (Birchall 2011). Members or participants freely cooperate and negotiate their different needs. Following this understanding, all social economies are sharing economies (because they share resources, such as organizational infrastructures, as well as responsibility by taking joint decisions through democratic procedures), but only some sharing economies are social economies. This helps to clarify the notion of *sharing economies*, which, by including capitalist as well as non-capitalist initiatives, conceals substantive differences within this economic field. Understood in this way, the social economy draws inspiration from the notion of solidarity economies on the one hand (Exner/Kratzwald 2021), and social entrepreneurship (Teasdale 2011) on the other. It is an attempt to build a conceptual bridge between various sorts of economic organizations that share a concern for social needs and societal challenges and that are self-managed (Fraisse et al. 2016). Consequently, we, in the following, will distinguish *social sharing economies* from *capitalist sharing economies*, which diverge regarding rationalities, social mechanisms, and societal outcomes.

The relation of digital technologies to these two types of sharing economies differs according to the respective social and economic characteristics of the capitalist and the social sharing economy. These characteristics, rather than any inherently technical feature of technologies, shape their meaning and outcomes. This, however, does not imply that technologies, such as digital platforms that are used for sharing goods and services, are completely malleable and subordinate to social ends.

Starting from this premise, we, in the remainder of this article, will present a case study of a project on developing a new urban neighborhood as a smart city that uses digital technologies to enhance the social benefit of sharing economies. In this analysis, we will especially reflect on the intersection of capitalist and social economy rationalities and how they shape digital platform development. Finally, we will draw conclusions on how digital platform development may be shifted toward social economies.

The case of MySmartCityGraz

The Austrian city of Graz is a typical Central European medium-sized town with about 300.000 inhabitants and substantial new urban development areas. The development project SMASH – Smart Sharing Graz (2020-2023) illustrates the ambivalences and the contentious character of social economy innovations in the context of smart city projects and in view of public value through non-profit platforms. The project is financed at a 60 % rate by the Austrian Climate and Energy Fund (KLI.EN 2021) within the program Smart Cities Demo – Living Urban Innovation. KLI.EN interprets the smart city primarily as a means for sustainable development. This emphasis corresponds to KLI.EN explicitly not funding software development projects within this program. SMASH aims to strengthen and further develop social economies in which people or organizations share or exchange objects (e.g., tools, food, books, bicycles), services (e.g., tutoring, taking care of plants, pets, or flats during vacations), knowledge (e.g., for repairs), spaces (e.g., communal spaces that are part of new buildings in MySmartCityGraz) and responsibilities. For this purpose, SMASH pursues a twofold approach. First, it establishes several analog social economy initiatives at concrete physical places that are collectively organized and managed by local residents. Second, it develops a digital social economy sharing platform that facilitates bilateral sharing and the exchange of activities among residents. Both types of actions take place in a new neighborhood called MySmartCityGraz and its surrounding areas. Social economy initiatives and the digital platform are developed together with citizens, civil society organizations, and commercial enterprises. SMASH aims at fostering eco-efficient, socially integrative, and economically smart social economies and thus attempts to integrate neighborhood support, volunteer organizations, and commercial enterprises to create effective synergies. MySmartCityGraz is established on a former industrial area that is in the process of being transformed into an urban, mixed-use district with (in the final stage) over 5.000 new residents, 2.000 new jobs, and a school campus. Residential, commercial, and office space is being developed on an area of 8.2 hectares as part of an overall concept that combines sustainable technologies, flexible mobility solutions, and renewable energies with ideas for promoting neighborhood relationships. The project consortium consists of the Regional Center of Expertise Graz-Styria (RCE) of the University of Graz, StadtLABOR, and Bravestone Information-Technology GmbH. StadtLABOR operates the on-site district management it has set up in MySmartCityGraz and maintains a dense network of stakeholders and residents in the area, while the RCE is linked with civil society groups and social economy initiatives on various scales. These stakeholder relationships are essential for the success of SMASH, together with the practical expertise of the project partners.

The development of the digital social economy platform was prepared by a survey of the sharing practices and needs of residents, supplemented by the systematization of already existing knowledge about local actors and resources as well as targeted inquiries into local organizations. Additionally, workshops with representatives from social economy initiatives served to include external expertise. These activities provided initial ideas for a SMASH Future Conference. To illustrate the possibilities of social economy initiatives, the project team developed ideas for the project area. Motivated by the Future Conference, working groups were founded for analog social economy initiatives, which intend to establish a food co-op and a repair café as physical places that are managed and organized by local residents. Such initiatives are classical examples of social economy initiatives and are also recurringly understood as sharing economies. Regarding our terminological perspective (see above), they are social sharing economies. Furthermore, SMASH started to cooperate with activists of the local exchange trade system STYRRION, which also belongs to this type of sharing economy.

These activities aiming at establishing analog initiatives in physical space are the immediate context for the development of the digital social economy sharing platform within the project. Neither the food co-op nor the repair café is connected with the digital platform yet, and probably will not be integrated, since members of these initiatives have not voiced a need for it. In fact, the food co-op is already fully operating without any connection to the digital platform. At the moment, it seems doubtful that the platform will be able to contribute added value to the food co-op and the repair café. Usually, this type of initiative does not use digital platforms. However, the analog social economy initiatives are crucial for SMASH in political terms. They are the most concrete outcome of the project so far and, as such, embody best the project's understanding of social economies and demonstrate how social economies can be implemented in the neighborhood. In comparison, the functionality of the digital platform, which is important to SMASH's central goal to strengthen social economies also on the level of bilateral sharing and exchange among residents, is as yet less clear and has been fraught by ambivalences that are connected with the actors involved in the development of the platform, and with its technological structure, as we will explain further on.

The platform will offer specific communication and information channels for different target groups. It is designed to provide diverse means of access to ensure the greatest possible interaction and to present general as well as specific information on sharing offers and requests. Basically, the digital platform is nothing more than a digital 'black board' meant to facilitate the matching of supply and demand in a non-commercial way. The link to further technical systems will be openly specified. While this idea is fairly simple, the design process of the digital tool is less straightforward, for it is established at the intersection of capitalist and social economy rationalities that shape the intended digital platform as a contentious field of urban development embedded in broader social relations. In the following, we will analyze these intersections and ensuing ambivalences.

In general, it is difficult to implement social economy perspectives in urban development in Graz because of the profit-oriented operation of private construction, planning and development companies, the political framework of the city of Graz, which is characterized by austerity, and the lack of resources in the urban planning and development departments.[1] The power of negotiation of the city of Graz with investors and profit-oriented developers is severely limited because of the lack of public land. Since the city does not own building plots in relevant areas, it can only influence urban development through the possibilities of local development and zoning plans as well as by means of implementation agreements or mobility contracts with investors. These, however, are against their interest, as they amount to additional expenses cutting into profits. The city administration therefore occupies an ambivalent position between political agenda setting in terms of the smart city on the one hand – which, at least, may provide some leeway to developing social economy initiatives and perspectives – and a lack of means to actually enforce or implement this political agenda on the other.

StadtLABOR also operates from an ambivalent position due to the commercial character of the urban development regime in Graz. On the one hand, StadtLABOR has generated valuable and far-reaching sustainability impulses on different levels of the city in recent years, including certain social economy initiatives. On the other hand, it is a commercial company creating its own opportunities for economic survival in an environment marked by competition for scarce public resources. It depends on public funding, municipal project contracts, and contracts with private investors and is therefore unable to implement radical approaches in view of, e.g., social economies. These constraints favor activities that do not question power relations and overarching capitalist rationalities.

The ambivalences that result from the intersection of capitalist and social economy rationalities also affect the project lead. RCE has been involved in the co-development and evaluation of participation measures of the city of Graz since 2014. These activities were mainly related to the strategic (administrative) level, which allowed RCE to take on an analytical meta-perspective. Within the framework of SMASH, however, the applied character of the project and the dual function of RCE staff to initiate and accompany social processes as well as investigating them from a critical perspective forces researchers into an ambivalent position. By taking on concrete activities and influencing discourses, RCE is no longer perceived as an independent research

---

1   After the elections of 2021, the Communist Party (KPÖ) has succeeded the People's Party (ÖVP) in city government (in a coalition including the Greens and the Social Democratic Party, SPÖ). The change in government may result in a transformation of this framework.

institution by the actors involved, especially by civil society, which occasionally leads to criticism from these civil society actors, who question the involvement of RCE in urban development processes.[2]

The IT developer within the project, the Bravestone Technology-Information GmbH, likewise occupies an ambivalent position. Funded by KLI.EN at a 60 % rate (like the other partners), its core business of developing software is sidelined by the program. This is in accordance with the sustainability focus of KLI.EN, which pursues a broader notion of smart city, one not reduced to technological development. However, this focus probably increases the firm's cost pressures, for which reason it may aim at recovering unpaid expenses through marketing the software of the digital platform that is developed within SMASH after the project has been finished. Moreover, the owner of the firm is also the head of the local marketing and service association of developers in MySmartCityGraz and has personally invested in the construction of new buildings in the area. This gives him the advantage of political backup from the city of Graz, a strategic position in dealing with developers and other investors, and a privileged opportunity to foster the business of his technology firm. However, the accumulation of multiple functions in different social relations confronts the owner of the firm with contradictory concerns attached to capitalist and non-capitalist rationalities, which requires him to mediate between social forces with diverging rationalities. For instance, while, as head of the marketing and service association, he is expected to represent developers' general interests, he should contribute purely as a technical expert without commercial interests in the SMASH project. Moreover, he has individual business interests as both a developer and software expert, which may not be in line with the general interests of developers in the area. Finally, he aims for a good relationship with the city of Graz in order to promote the general interests of developers but is also subject to the economic incentive to reduce obligations put on developers by the city administration, e.g., in creating public infrastructure. The articulation of different rationalities renders the SMASH platform politically ambivalent.

Given these ambivalences, the outcomes of the development of the digital sharing platform are as yet unclear. For instance, social economy innovations, such as online platforms, bear the risk that traditionally analog urban forms of sharing and exchange (e.g., libraries, public leisure facilities, or transport infrastructure) will be displaced, rationalized, or commercialized. They could

---

2   The authors of this contribution are part of the SMASH project team.

also be misused for appropriating personal data by profit-oriented actors. According to Bravestone Technology-Information GmbH, the sharing economy platform should include all MySmartCityGraz residents, who would be obliged to use the platform insofar as their contracts with houseowners and bills are managed through it. In connection with possible further options, such as matching non-commercial sharing and exchange requests and offers among platform users that include both MySmartCityGraz residents as well as inhabitants of surrounding areas (who should be able to register), this would generate a great amount of data that should be used for the benefit of the community and not for commercial purposes. However, since the platform is organized and hosted by investors and developers who are part of the marketing and service association, the risk of further commercial use, e.g., through data mining, cannot be precluded. An additional danger may be neglect of or the crowding out of social relationships. These develop best through personal contact and elaborate processes of getting to know each other face to face (which is particularly effective when a neighborhood is rather socially homogeneous) and require building trust. A negative effect of the digital platform on the development of social relationships would contradict the goals of the project (and KLI.EN), which define the digital platform merely as a tool, even more so because serious and comprehensive sharing and exchange of services, objects, spaces, and responsibilities beyond capitalist rationalities begin where social relationships are created.

Conclusions

Sharing economy platforms are not in themselves conducive or a barrier to social economy initiatives. They may facilitate social processes that can support social economy practices and provide solutions for particular logistical problems affecting them. While capitalist sharing economies appreciate digital platforms mainly because of their potential to establish new markets and reduce financial costs, social sharing economies have another perspective on such platforms. Social sharing economies are primarily interested in overcoming material challenges of fulfilling concrete social needs. Digital technologies may help to achieve this goal, e.g., by matching non-commercial caregivers and caretakers or managing the joint use of resources such as space for storing food or common activities. However, they may also enable the co-optation or misuse of social economy practices through capitalist power relations. This ambivalence results from the intersection between social economy and capitalist rationalities on the socio-technical terrain of a digital platform. This terrain is pervaded by social relations that are connected with contradictory rationalities and associated with a range of different processes as well as social relations that render the SMASH platform politically ambivalent. On the socio-technical terrain of the platform, the rationality of capitalist urban development therefore intersects with the bureaucratic external regulation of the city administration, which attempts to safeguard overall political development goals; national policies of sustainability oriented smart city projects; the specific rationality of broader social movements and academic trends influencing the project proposal through the project lead and the social networks it is embedded in; corresponding goals, imaginaries, arguments, and strategies of networks of the social economy activists who are mobilized by the project; and, finally, the rationality of the local neighborhood development agency, which operates in an ambivalent social space mediating between capitalist investors, city administration, social initiatives, and smart city goals defined on the national scale.

Navigating such ambivalences is not an easy task. According to our experience, shifting power relations toward social economy perspectives may use two different strategies. First, the political goals expressed in a funding program (established by KLI.EN) can serve as a discursive anchor that helps to move the semantic field, and corresponding development practices, toward social economies. In particular, *social economy* or related terms can be used as identity markers that delimit the realm of legitimate project activities. Second, external social economy actors that are successively included in project activities and take on lead roles for certain initiatives strengthen respective positions within the project team. Such external actors bring in expertise and local networks and create a specific social momentum that cannot easily be contained by other actors. For instance, the push for allowing commercial activities using the euro to take place through the digital platform could be warded off by strengthening the link with the complementary currency STYRRION, which is socially embedded and supports local economies in the sense of a social economy perspective. As was explained above, the analog social economy initiatives (a food co-op and repair café) additionally strengthen the political message and impact of the project and thus counterbalance the more ambivalent activities related to digital platform development. Moreover, the experiences with the SMASH project indicate that action research, as conducted within this project, may be important for strengthening social sharing economies.

It is doubtful that these micro struggles are able to shift overall power relations in a city such as Graz by themselves. In fact, the political sea change of the municipal elections held in 2021, which put the Communist Party in power (together with the Greens and the Social Democrats as minority partners), has poignantly demonstrated the importance of macro political struggles. However, activities of a project such as SMASH may be effective in carving out socio-material spaces for social economy perspectives, and may be necessary to inspire, shape, or operationalize the politics of left-wing city governments. They could also influence national smart city policies through demonstrating that digital platforms are not necessarily at the service of profit-oriented actors and may indeed contribute to a more sustainable way of life in an urban neighborhood.

References

Albinsson, Pia A./Perera, B. Yasanthi (eds.) (2018): *The rise of the sharing economy: exploring the challenges and opportunities of collaborative consumption*, Santa Barbara/Denver: Praeger.
Bauriedl, Sybille/Strüver, Anke (eds.) (2018): *Smart City. Kritische Perspektiven auf die Digitalisierung in Städten*, Bielefeld: transcript.
Bauriedl, Sybille/Strüver, Anke (2020): Platform Urbanism: Technocapitalist Production of Private and Public Spaces, in: *Urban Planning* 5(4): 267-76.
Birchall, Johnston (2011): *People-Centred Businesses. Co-operatives, Mutuals and the Idea of Membership*, New York: Palgrave Macmillan.
Chaves-Avila, Rafael/Gallego-Bono, Juan Ramon (2020): Transformative Policies for the Social and Solidarity Economy: The New Generation of Public Policies Fostering the Social Economy in Order to Achieve Sustainable Development Goals. The European and Spanish Cases, in: *Sustainability* 12(10). doi: https://doi.org/10.3390/su12104059.
Elwood, Sarah (2021): Digital geographies, feminist relationality, Black and queer code studies: Thriving otherwise, in: *Progress in Human Geography* 45(2): 209-28.
Elwood, Sarah/Leszczynski, Agnieszka (2018): Feminist digital geographies, in: *Gender, Place & Culture* 25(5): 629-44.

Exner, Andreas/Kratzwald, Brigitte (2021): *Solidarische Ökonomie & Commons*, Wien: Mandelbaum.

Exner, Andreas/Cepoiu, Livia/Weinzierl, Carla/Asara, Viviana (2018): Performing Smartness Differently – Strategic Enactments of a Global Imaginary in Three European Cities. http://www-sre.wu.ac.at/sre-disc/sre-disc-2018_05.pdf [13.02.2022].

Exner, Andreas/Cepoiu, Livia/Weinzierl, Carla (2018): Smart City policies und Medienframes in Wien, Berlin und Barcelona, in: Bauriedl, Sybille/ Strüver, Anke (eds.): *Smart City. Kritische Perspektiven auf die Digitalisierung in Städten*, Bielefeld: transcript: 335-46.

Fraisse, Laurant/Gardin, Laurant/Laville, Jean-Louis/Petrella, Francesca/ Richez-Battesti, Nadine (2016): Social Enterprise in France: At the Crossroads of the Social Economy, Solidarity Economy and Social Entrepreneurship? ICSEM Working Papers 34. Liege: The International Comparative. https://halshs.archives-ouvertes.fr/halshs-01449222/document [13.02.2022].

Geissinger, Andrea/Laurell, Christofer/Öberg, Christina/Sandström, Christian (2019): How sustainable is the sharing economy? On the sustainability connotations of sharing economy platforms, in: *Journal of Cleaner Production* 206(1): 419-29.

Jin, Scarlett T./Kong, Hui/Wu, Rachel/Sui, Daniel Z. (2018): Ridesourcing, the sharing economy, and the future of cities, in: *Cities* 76: 96-104.

Klima- und Energiefonds (KLI.EN)/Smart Cities Initiative (2021): Teilen, Tauschen, Weitergeben und Gemeinschaftlich-Nutzen für eine gute Nachbarschaft und einen nachhaltigen Lebensstil in der My Smart City. https://smartcities.at/projects/smash-smart-sharing-graz [13.02.2022].

Martin, Chris J. (2016): The sharing economy: A pathway to sustainability or a nightmarish form of neoliberal capitalism?, in: *Ecological Economics* 121(1): 149-59.

Richardson, Lizzie (2020): Coordinating the city: Platforms as flexible spatial arrangements, in: *Urban Geography* 41(3): 458-61.

Rong, Ke/Hu, Jialun/Ma, Yuge/Lim, Ming K./Liu, Yang/Lu, Chao (2017): The sharing economy and its implications for sustainable value chains, in: *Resources, Conservation & Recycling* 130: 188-89.

Scholz, Trebor (2017): Platform Cooperativism vs. the Sharing Economy, in: Douay, Nicolas/Wan, Annie (eds.): *Big Data & Civic Engagement*, Rom: Planum: 47-54.

Social Economy Europe (2021): Social economy. A business model for the future of Europe. https://www.socialeconomy.eu.org [13.02.2022].

Sutherland, Will/Jarrahi, Mohammad Hossein (2018): The sharing economy and digital platforms: A review and research agenda, in: *International Journal of Information Management* 43: 328-41.

Teasdale, Simon (2011): What's in a name? Making sense of social enterprise discourses, in: *Public Policy and Administration* 22(2): 99-115.

Toli, Angeliki Maria/Murtagh, Niamh (2020): The Concept of Sustainability in Smart City Definitions, in: *Frontier in Built Environment* 6(77). doi: https://doi.org/10.3389/fbuil.2020.00077.

Platform Urbanization and Citizenship
An Inquiry and Projection

Filippo Bignami & Naomi C. Hanakata

Globally operating platforms (such as social media, commercial, service, e-government, and e-management platforms) are increasingly critical means of communication, exchange, and daily life. Their growing ecosystem and locally specific variations also increase possibilities for data mining and addressing specific user profiles. For many office workers, it is difficult to imagine a work routine without service platforms for business such as Microsoft Power, Google Cloud, or the Apple iOS system. However, platforms are also increasingly forming a firm component within community services and urban development administration, whether that is for, e.g., submitting taxes, obtaining health services, profiling a political campaign, monitoring the use of utilities, or new employment opportunities (Hanakata/Bignami 2022: 1). Recently, numerous new platforms have become available to track the spread of the Covid-19 virus or to report one's health condition or vaccination status. Together, these various ways of communication, monitoring, and control are changing the way people interact, expanding the possibilities of what we can do, but they also highlight the limitations and the character of different political subjectivations of citizens. This shift is particularly perceivable with regard to the urban environment, which is increasingly immersed and governed through platforms. In a critical reflection on the implications of what we call *platform urbanization*, we, in this contribution, discuss structural and political corollaries of this development and the subsequent need to reconceptualize citizenship today. Furthermore, in an attempt to expand conceptually, we, in this article, want to go beyond dominant practices of the present and scan inherent capacities of platform urbanization for possible urban citizenship scenarios. Taking platform urbanization as an inescapable force in contemporary urbanization processes, and by drawing from a heterogeneous set of examples, we want to look at the aptitude of platform technologies to foster an urban condition in which platforms form an immaterial but concrete political condition and explore what it takes to realize a space of inclusion that offers participation empowerment for all.

Outlining platform urbanization

The urban realm is defined by platform infrastructures that are shifting many modes of interaction and production – of urban governance and identity – to a virtual space (Hanakata/Bignami 2022). This fundamental change is more than an increase in technological opportunities, and it is more than a change in the way we live, as proposed in the concept of platform urbanism (Barns 2014). It transforms how people come together and urban space is produced. This multidimensional process affects our everyday lives and the way our urban environment is perceived, co-constructed, and governed, and it transforms the way we can express ourselves (through social media), how we perceive our urban environment (as a replica of an online experience), and how we plan, manage, or predict its future (through digital twins) (Hanakata/Bignami 2022: 2). The concept of platform urbanization attempts to understand both this process as a planetary phenomenon and its various dimensions, which affect each possible territory and individual. It looks at platforms as infrastructures of a global process that increasingly defines everyday life in a physical and spatial way as well as at the socio-economic and political aspects of the urban. It provokes a new relationship between people and their environment through introducing various kinds of digital interfaces that link the two, which calls for a reconceptualization of citizenship. In a process of dematerialization, abstraction, and disassociation, platform urbanization creates a new political arena where the individual becomes a site for data collection as well as a node of connection flows of information, knowledge, and expertise. These are no longer exclusive to the skill set of the individual but feed processes of algorithmic reorganization and augmentation of data aggregation, which also entails a form of exploitation of the individual value and, all in all, a loss of individual skills.

With regard to its territorial dimension, platform urbanization advances without a specific territorial anchorage, and furthermore with no linkages to nation-states, as many of its infrastructures extend seamlessly beyond any boundaries. In fact, they undermine any physically defined entity and propel and consolidate the networks of global flows, extending conveniences of communication and mobility but also of the traces left. Platform urbanization coincides and enables what Slavoj Žižek (2010) calls, with reference to Rancière, the *post-political*. Within a post-political condition, political practice becomes a matter of managing and policing administrative procedures (Swyngedouw 2019). This development, however, is not determined by the technology itself but by those who create, deploy, and control its use. While platforms provide the structures that enable the connection of goods and services (Barns 2018; Leszczynski 2020), their application requires specific skills and access to resources. A certain liberalization of application development by using open sources has become a major trigger for platform innovation. The impact on and making of our urban environment, however, is a matter of scale which is only attainable through power, defined as a dispositional quality and resource concentration commonly in the hands of a relatively restricted and exclusive group of actors. These are increasingly intertwined with digital market actors and occupied with promoting processes of platformization, adopting a techno-driven language of *smart cities*.

Indeed, smart cities incorporate some of the material infrastructures implied in platform urbanization. These infrastructures have propelled the industry of smart technology producers, "pursuing a technological solutionism that often dismisses the multilayered implications" (Hanakata/Bignami 2022: 3) of platform urbanization. Smart cities and smart city technologies, however, reveal one key aspect of platform urbanization, which is the centralized mode of control and governance and the rapid development of algorithmic-driven management in urban environments that increased at the end of the second decade of the 21st century (Huws 2020). Many recent developments have been called out as new platform cities, including, for example, NEOM in Saudi Arabia by NEOM Company; Woven City in Susono, Japan, by Toyota; Toronto Tomorrow in Canada by Alphabet's Sidewalk Lab; Pungol Digital District in Singapore by JTC; and Dholera in India by a large conglomerate of public and private stakeholders. All rely on customized or all-in-one solutions offered by industry partners or big tech companies (Hanakata/Bignami 2022). All of them provide smart infrastructures that are promoted as neutral facilitators for more efficient living (Leszczynski 2020: 192), and focus on practical aspects of a stipulated techno-utopia. As such, they tend to ignore questions of citizenship, labor, mobility, and the overarching techno-political framework, which are all, however, an integral part of platform urbanization. The currently dominant developments of platform urbanization leverage the privacy and data of individuals and make compliance with (basic) personal information provision a requirement for participation and action to commodify human experience and urban life (Zuboff 2019).

Implications on citizenship - an inquiry

Based on the conceptualization of platform urbanization above, it appears that we are fully immersed in an open-ended techno-political framework (Calzada 2021). Further, it appears that we are within a consolidation of institutional, political, and technical systems through the exponential logics of computation on a planetary scale (Bratton 2015). Such logics of computation are both a technological apparatus and a model for a new techno-political architecture. In this article, we also consider how we might recognize and co-construct alternative scenarios and effects, which forces us to revisit and extend the concept of citizenship (Hanakata/Bignami 2021). The idea of a techno-political scenario is particularly appropriated in the context of the urban environment, where processes of platformization and technology constitute, substantiate, or enact political aims in a wider sense, positioning the city in a central role, which provokes a discussion about urban techno-politics (Foley/Miller 2020). In a techno-political scenario featuring platform and urban politics, we can uncover the aspects that are often hidden within complex arrangements of platform infrastructure and economic production. One of such aspects is, for example, a form of truly invasive platform capitalism (Srnicek 2017), including actors and organizations that shape this type of capitalism and are being shaped by it. Platforms are slowly but steadily eroding and replacing political and institutional spaces since the world wide web has become the real "global institution" (Mathiason 2008). As such, we can conclude that 'exercising' citizenship is not just a matter of participating in predefined institutional realms but a matter of creating new and different types of interaction collectivity and/or of transforming participation in urban politics, in community, and society, online and offline.

The making of the urban can be described as a political process. In effect the definition of platform urbanization, as outlined above, is based on a conception of the urban as both a material and immaterial place where the widespread use of platforms influences the modes of production of the urban. This requires a closer examination: platforms, within the urban, are becoming the new 'boundary condition' for citizenship and space (detached from the nation-state) within which the collectivity interacts in a context of the previously mentioned post-politicization (Swyngedouw 2019). Platforms have not only infused social, cultural, and economic life but resignified political life by creating interconnected relations among people, institutions, technology providers, and built environments. They have influenced almost every aspect of politics, and yet their presence in politics remains obscure. Exploring these new "urban techno-politics and how and whose politics are embedded in infrastructure not only make visible the social and the political, it can also create space for opening-up and engaging alternative sets of techno-politics generated by alternative sets of actors and organizations" (Foley/Miller 2020: 316). Such a techno-political scenario is characterized by disjunctions between formal notions of citizenship and the practical realities of how citizenship is grounded. Such disjunctions point to instances in which compromises must be acknowledged (e.g., less freedom and more security through tech surveillance), which often results in the offering of comfortable but partial forms of citizenship (limited to some groups, to some areas, to some behaviors, to some markets, and to some forms of participation). As a corollary, this process further increases already existing forms of differential inclusion (Mezzadra/Neilson 2012), which has a significant impact on the dimensions of (urban) citizenship: organizers and providers of this scenario are few in number and largely formed by oligopolist private (big tech) companies that leverage on restricted and technical know-how. Users and alleged digital citizens often ignore the logics that engineer such new techno-political scenarios. Platform urbanization's techno-political scenarios alter conventional politics and, furthermore, have created new politics without any obvious precedence (Hanakata/Bignami 2022). Platforms have supported the definition of new spaces and subjects of politics, confirming how historical assemblages of territory, authority, and rights linked to nation-states have been reshuffled and reorganized (Sassen 2005; 2016). Moreover, they have added further dimensions to the concept of citizenship.

By bringing these new dimensions of citizenship to the center of concern, we do away with a mere technology-driven understanding of platforms ensuing a conception of citizens as meek, passive data subjects. Instead, we attend to how political subjectivities are always performed in relation to techno-political arrangements and technological urban infrastructures. We also contend with positivist assertions of sovereign subjects corroborated by libertarian vision of platforms. We argue that, if we shift our analysis from how we are being 'controlled' to analyze how to trigger ongoing processes, social practices, and a political performance rather than a static category, we can identify paths of subversive citizenship (Isin/Ruppert 2020). To reach this conclusion, we need to consider citizen subjects not in isolation (as platforms tend to do) but in relation to the actions and institutions they are a part of (as political subjectivation processes tend to do). This includes, for example, claims and performances of citizenship including a reorganization of digital-social rights for a new "cyberspace" environment (Tomasello forthcoming).

The 'outdated' role of nation-states

If the depicted conception of platform urbanization is based on the city as a dominant social and political scenario where platform providers and operators impose their operating logics on society (Hanakata/Bignami 2021), there are additional aspects to be considered. The actual process of so-called globalization is the basic context within which the circulation of technology, capital, people, information, services, and goods takes place. Today, globalization can be understood as an interdependence of technology, institutions, means of production and finance, goods, people, and economic flows, regardless of borders and polities. Due to the strengthening of transnational institutions and interdependencies, the sovereignty of nation-states, still formally and legally valid, is weakening its nomos. Here, we want to refer to Schmitt's (2003) binary differentiation between the physical and the virtual (Bratton 2015) and put it to use, breaking it apart somehow to highlight that the tension between the online and offline world is blurring. Consequently, national identity and membership are also diminishing or complemented with other forms of identity and membership that are coming to the fore, such as, for example, the urban. Gerard Delanty believes that the nation-state has lost its sovereignty due to a number of factors, including the strengthening of international law; the internationalization of political decision-making; hegemonic forces and international structures of safety; and the globalization of culture and global economy (Delanty 2009). Because of these international connections and interdependencies, the nation-state has become an additional category of supranational and subnational entities. Therefore, it can be argued that the conception of the nation-state, as it originated from a post-Westphalian order, is 'outdated' and does no longer play the unique and central role in international relations as it used to, but that other kinds of institutions and forms of governance appear as key actors. Ulrich Beck proposes the following triad: neoliberal state, supranational state, and cosmopolitan state. The latter appears more able to preserve the interests of its citizens from neoliberal hegemony. This is possible since losing autonomy from nation-states can mean pooling sovereignty. In turn, this pooling of sovereignty produces an increase in collective and shared sovereignty to a level capable of solving collective problems that are not national anymore (Beck 2006). Rainer Bauböck understands the concept of urban citizenship as completing, not replacing, national citizenship. He points out three different accounts of urban citizenship, namely: diminutive, which rests on treating urban municipalities as constructs of higher level governments whose borders and competencies are determined by them (optionally including immigrants in local demonstrations, for example); derivative, which gives additional weight to the urban level by regarding it as similar to citizenship in the constitutive polities of a federation (such as regions, cantons, autonomous territories, etc.); and post-national, which cuts the relation between city and state, highlighting the emancipation of urban areas from the nation-state (for example, through forging transnational city networks) (Bauböck/Orgad 2020). In such a multifarious perspective linking the urban and citizenship, the city appears as a crucial entity able to reshape citizenship, extending it both in the sense of political and social functions and in the spatial-organizational sense. The city (as a form of concentrated urbanization) appears as the dominant form, the economically most developed and politically most powerful societies in the world, the center of the above-mentioned flows (of platforms, technology, capital, people, information, services, and goods), a multicultural environment, and the point of meeting and creation of innovations, new identities, political participations, and memberships.

Platform urbanization scenario – a projection

If we take platform urbanization as a key driver of contemporary urbanization processes and as an increasingly defining force within our urban environment and look at its inherent capacity to define our everyday lives and the way we perceive and conceive our urban environment, how can we envision an urban citizenship scenario that flourishes through the intrinsic powers of platform technologies? The following section draws from some case studies as well as our own imaginaries and describes a selection of examples and ideas in an attempt to outline what could be possible if we leverage the capacities of platform urbanization in a way that is inclusive, equal, and politically constructive for all. It is not a matter of heralding non-profit platforms over those for profit, nor to naively divide them into good and bad practices. Rather, it is about identifying ways of leveraging platform capacities that operate in the interest of a participatory and inclusive urban development.

Strengthening of the value and orientation toward commons

Commons are a collective good that increase their value through shared and collective use and consumption in the city. Therefore, they form an important component within the city as a space for encounter, connection, exchange, and difference. This may include open spaces, facilities as well as infrastructures, but also private spaces, such as certain commercial, residential, and industrial estates, and natural resources. Strengthening the value of and orientation toward commons may include leaving the management of commons not in the hands of a selected few digital platform market actors but in the hands of communities based on collectively established social practices and governance mechanisms. This implies a continuous, informal, and open-ended form of political and social co-construction enabling an increased awareness and responsibility. Such sharing and governance practices, however, require an elaborate political negotiation and participatory management system to be successful. Drawing from big data and capable of coordinating and consolidating multiple data sources (and therefore different interests and voices), platform technologies could be employed to facilitate such an open political scenario. This could also allow for a multifunctional and flexible use of spaces, increasing a city's adaptive capacity and a plurality of opportunities. An example of this is Fairbnb (http://www.fairbnb.coop), a cooperative organization and open-source platform that has adopted a responsible home sharing strategy, working with local authorities to verify hosts. Local representations ensure compliance with sustainability standards to protect the community from the side effects of unwanted tourism. Besides, Fairbnb practices solidarity by involving local communities to define the social projects that are a priority for their sustainable development, supporting them with resources generated by 50 % of the platform's revenues, which are used to fund local projects, while the remaining revenues are used by Fairbnb to maintain its network and operations. Another example is Katuma (http://katuma.org), a network that allows people to sell and buy local foods from farmers and participate in a sustainable model with socio-economic benefits for the community via free software and an app. Through this cooperative approach, small-scale producers can agree on prices and define the network collectively.[1]

Enhancing the interlinkage and transfer of knowledge and skills

Similar to commons, the sharing of immaterial capacities within the urban realm forms an important component of the urban identity and the urban as a space for collectivity and exchange. Platform urbanization is already advancing based on increasing the capacity for individualized influence (Leszczynski 2020: 193). This capacity, however, is often quickly co-opted by digital platform market actors and individual voices subsequently commodified and/or rendered by dispossession and antagonistic subjectivation (Cuppini/Frapporti/Pirone 2015). Therefore, platforms should be leveraged to enhance the interlinkage and transfer of knowledge and skills, which may include the support of individual citizens to find a voice and connect to match interests and demands while strengthening a community of knowledge, experience, and skill sharing rather than just increasing the abstracted data capacity of digital platform market actors. This may also include cross-generational assistance in care and other services, from help with daily errands to child care, but it may also include the repurposing of existing expertise to new demands. An example of this was initiated during the lockdown in Germany and is called Corona School (https://www.lern-fair.de/). This online platform connects pupils from all grades and various subjects with university students as tutors and is dedicated to supporting learning opportunities for all regardless of their social,

---

[1] Both examples are case studies of the European Horizon 2020 project PLUS, which is funded by the European Union's Horizon 2020 Research and Innovation program "Platform Labour in Urban Spaces: Fairness, Welfare, Development" (PLUS n.d.), Grant Agreement No. 822638. The project scrutinizes the main features of the platform economy's impact on work, welfare, and social protection in a trans-urban approach. The platform economy is, indeed, emerging as a strategic sector in terms of the application of digital technologies, business investments, and new jobs, both gig- and employment-driven. The project aims at sketching a picture of such transformations, proposing an innovative approach that identifies urban dimension as a fundamental stage for evaluating the political, social, and economic impact of these platforms and for building more inclusive policies. Within the project consortium, there are partners that are themselves platforms that make businesses but are inspired by and managed with a participatory and citizenship-driven approach.

cultural, and financial backgrounds. Similarly, other platforms such as Rentagrandma.com, GrandmaTutors.com, or VolunteerGrandparents.ca also leverage the intergenerational exchange of knowledge and experience. They offer assistance in childcare and domestic chores and aim to create and strengthen an experience that enriches all involved.

Supporting sustainable urban development

Sustainable urban development is one of the key challenges of our time. Efforts to facilitate such practices have long been at the forefront of exploring the possibilities of big data as a means to optimize transport infrastructures, urban microclimates, public amenities, or other urban services. Supporting sustainable urban development in its social, environmental, cultural, and economic dimension is a complex and essential endeavor that is in the interest of all. Participatory design, for example, which deploys technological artifacts, is often heralded as furthering the democratization of urban decision-making. However, participatory design practices often struggle with carrying the voices of all involved actors throughout the process and reflecting them in the enacted result. Making urban data mining not just a technical exercise to varnish city stats and create impressive visualizations but to substantiate complex urban development as inclusive processes is therefore key. An example that provides meaningful insights in this direction can be found in the latest extension of the HafenCity in Hamburg, Germany. The competition requirements for the project already included a digital platform that would allow a comparative evaluation of future microclimates, cost calculations, and energy demand and supply scenarios (HafenCity Hamburg GmbH 2019). It will, however, take some time before its compatibility with social indicators and its capacity to adapt – once the area is developed and populated with residents – can be verified. A further example of sustainable and cooperative urban development can be found in the initiative Bringthefood (https://bringfood.org), which is a non-profit web application to avoid food waste and deliver it to deprivileged people using criteria of proximity. It is adopted by various food banks, operators, and volunteer networks to manage surpluses from restaurants, small and large retailers, and producer organizations.

All these examples present seeds for an urban citizenship scenario that facilitates an open and expanded understanding of citizenship by advancing on the complex network structures and capacities of platform urbanization. They still present the exception but need to set the stage for a new default in how we leverage the continuously diffusing impact of platform urbanization to increase the conditions for a sustainable and inclusive urban condition while avoiding an elitist city narrative.

What would it take to realize this?

In order to realize such an urban citizenship scenario, platforms need to be considered as enablers of individual skills rather than a deprivation of skills. Evidence from a research project on platform labor in urban spaces (PLUS[2]: see PLUS n.d.) indicates that there are some skill areas that can strengthen the awareness and capacity to create and interact more responsibly within platform environments. These skills are developed by and evolved through interrelations between individuals. The political construction of platform spaces not only shapes the understanding and use of platform opportunities but also determines the conception of users (workers, professionals, clients, policy makers, etc.) and their skills within these spaces.

To corroborate the need to improve the skills necessary to participate in platform environments, PLUS provides some helpful insights. Within the project's activities, seven city training workshops were carried out in Bologna, Paris, London, Berlin, Tallinn, Barcelona, and Lisbon. They were mainly carried out online due to Covid-19-related travel restrictions and involved platform workers and key urban actors to better understand which skills needed to be developed to access and participate in platform-mediated communities and spaces. Since there was a focus on platform workers, resulting insights cannot be applied to the average platform user. A generally valid insight, however, is that improving skills that allow citizens to exercise self-determination as digital citizens strengthens the participatory dimension of platforms and creates a more even landscape of platform urbanization. Further project results include the following insights:

---

2   University of Applied Sciences of Southern Switzerland – SUPSI, Labour, Urbanscape, and Citizenship – LUCI Research area, is partner of this project, coordinated by Alma Mater University of Bologna. SUPSI coordinates a work package dedicated to set up a MOOC for platform economy and reflect upon the meaning of skills in this environment through a specific report.

- Technological skills should be developed not only to improve technological literacy *per se* but also to inform about the data that platforms retain about their users and how to access it. The objective of acquiring technological skills is to educate informed platform users who can demand transparency, information, and fairness in data management;
- A better understanding of how platform algorithms work is necessary among users to balance platform power asymmetry;
- A better recognition and transparent transferability of knowledge are necessary to value professional experience (for example, navigating with maps and within city spaces, communication with clients/users, etc.), which, so far, is often contested by practices that replace individual experiences with big volumes of data (big data);
- An awareness of the collective dimension of platform users is important to improve cooperation with others, share experiences, and promote demands through legal actions, protests, strikes, and other forms of unionism. Platform workers need to be able to improve their capacity to engage in and exploit activism to support political demands for training and recognition of skills, whether at the individual level (for legal purposes and advice) or the collective level (coordinated actions, formulating demands, claiming rights, and creating a social network);
- The capacity to interact with platforms knowing their functioning. This can improve the understanding on, for example, how workers' allotments for different time slots work or how task assignments and the mechanisms of salary calculations are chosen, in order to allow workers to make effective and informed time planning;
- Developing further employable skills through platform infrastructures is key to facilitate the transition to sectors outside the platform economy. This includes the capacity to transfer skills acquired in the field.

Deeply affected by platform urbanization, citizens need to be aware of their rights and duties and find ways to participate in a social and political redefinition of their roles. This allows them to understand and critically deploy platform infrastructures and to gain political, economic, or social capital (Ignatow/Robinson 2017). To do so, citizens need to have the capacities to participate in and contribute to communities of shared interests while critically navigating through the discursive contexts of platform urbanization.

To improve and develop the above listed skills, it is also necessary to alleviate the condition of individuals as passive data subjects and act within platform environments in order to recognize their political power within a ubiquitous techno-political environment.

Literature regarding the definition and analysis of the concept of skill (as well as of competence, knowledge, and attitude) is vast. However, discussions around this concept tend to focus on its technical and professional dimensions and the knowledge associated with the techniques of the working procedures, developed via training and/or experience and assessed and certified by formal or institutional actors. In the context of platform urbanization and the extended conception of (urban) citizenship, we consider skills as a co-constructed and cooperative approach. Evaluating, identifying, and developing skills should not solely be seen as objective top-down processes but as the result of an active social and political practice. Adopting this perspective on skills opens up a path on which citizens are not just data producers and consumers but active agents in the 'construction' of an extended condition of citizenship within the condition of platform urbanization. The trajectory of platform urbanization offers a powerful scenario to co-construct and politically deploy the concept of skills, addressing the fact that most of the skills exploited in this condition are neither defined nor formalized, recognized, trained, or certified.

Platforms are reshaping the urban and the modes of its production. To grasp this requires an extended understanding of (urban) citizenship. The aim is to clarify and improve awareness of such a changed nexus between individuals and collectivity, and correctly identify the connection between the technical and political characteristics of such a link. A pivotal role is played by the individual as the leading enabler of this nexus, which needs to be defined at an urban level to become concrete and widely understandable, since such a nexus needs to find a practical ground to come to fruition (Soares Carvalho/Bignami 2021). Citizenship grounded in the urban improves the uniformity of rights and responsibilities linked with political involvement and, therefore, might potentially mitigate the political impacts of social inequalities (Nyers/Rygiel 2012) that platforms are generating in the urban realm. As such, it seems essential to go for an extended notion of citizenship that is able to crisscross the uncharted trajectory of such a techno-political framework, which embraces online and offline lives in a flurry of unbalanced and unequal (but attractive to the users) scenarios. As a corollary, a new political participatory sphere (see example above) can emerge and allow citizens to participate in and understand new dimensions of citizenship by working, negotiating, and cooperating together. The sheer diversity of actors and positions within this sphere offers opportunities to develop an extended understanding of citizenship that could allow people (of course, in given conditions) to see beyond their own immediate perceptions or individual techno-optimism. It supports a greater awareness of both individual and collective benefits. Interaction in this new political participatory sphere can help transform dispositions among citizens, instilling greater respect and enhancing their propensity to go beyond the surface of platforms and commitment to respond. Yet, part of that depends on the openness and capacity of the urban institutional actors. In other words, we are in a post-political scenario (as depicted above) where entrenched inequalities contribute to the muting of dissenting voices and where little willingness or capacity exists to redress these inequalities and address the specific concerns of the new framework. This is when other spaces outside the classical political and capitalist arena become critical. Actual political spaces, in the context of platform urbanization, are both material and immaterial 'sites' on which to gain confidence and consolidate positions, and from which to act on the urban environment through unedited forms of political (or, better, techno-political) co-constructed action.

The inquiries and projections of this contribution do not stand alone but form part of a growing field of critical inquiry regarding the techno-political framework in which our urban environments are evolving. They shall be understood as signposts of much-needed, proactive thinking in alternative scenarios that critically confront as well as leverage the capacities inherent in platform urbanization. We believe that we are only at the beginning of fully understanding what it might mean to speak of an augmented urban experience, digital citizenship, or platform urbanization, and what these terms might entail for an extended discussions of cities and citizenship alike – also beyond debates about the role of smart cities, around which much current literature on platformization and the urban still pivots.

References

Baker, Mona/Blaagaard, Boletta B. (2016): Reconceptualizing Citizen Media: A Preliminary Charting of a Complex Domain, in: Baker, Mona/Blaagaard, Boletta B. (eds.): *Citizen Media and Public Spaces: Diverse Expressions of Citizenship and Dissent*, London: Routledge: 22-26.
Barns, Sarah (2014): Platform Urbanism: The Emerging Politics of Open Data for Urban Management. American Association of Geographers Annual

Conference, 2014. https://www.researchgate.net/publication/327621979_Platform_urbanism_the_emerging_politics_of_open_data_for_urban_management_American_Association_of_Geographers_Annual_Conference_2014 [27.05.2021].

Barns, Sarah (2018): Platform Urbanism Rejoinder: Why Now? What Now?, in: *Mediapolis. A journal of cities and culture* 3(4). https://www.mediapolisjournal.com/2018/11/platform-urbanism-why-now-what-now [02.01.2022].

Bauböck, Rainer/Orgad, Liav (eds.) (2020): *Cities vs States: Should Urban Citizenship be Emancipated from Nationality?*, San Domenico di Fiesole: European University Institute.

Beck, Ulrich (2006): *The cosmopolitan vision*, Cambridge: Polity press.

Bratton, Benjamin H. (2015): *The Stack: On Software and Sovereignty*, Cambridge, MA: MIT Press.

Calzada, Igor (2021): *Smart City Citizenship*, Cambridge, MA: Elsevier Science Publishing.

Cuppini, Niccolò/Frapporti, Mattia/Pirone, Maurilio (2015): Logistics Struggles in the Po Valley Region, in: *South Atlantic Quarterly* 114(1): 119-34.

Delanty, Gerard (2009): *Cosmopolitan imagination*, New York: Cambridge University Press.

Foley, Rider/Miller, Thaddeus (2020): Urban Techno-Politics: An Introduction, in: *Science as Culture* 29(3): 309-18.

HafenCity Hamburg GmbH (2019): Grasbrook. Wettbewerblicher Dialog Stadtteil Grasbrook. https://www.grasbrook.de/wp-content/uploads/2019/11/Upload__Grasbrook_Auslobungsbroschuere.pdf [14.04.2022].

Hanakata, Naomi C./Bignami, Filippo (2021): Platform Urbanization and the Impact on Urban Transformation and Citizenship, in: *South Atlantic Quarterly* 120(4): 763-76.

Hanakata, Naomi C./Bignami, Filippo (2022): Platform Urbanization, its Recent Acceleration, and Implications on Citizenship. The Case of Singapore, in: *Citizenship Studies*: 1-21. doi: https://doi.org/10.1080/13621025.2022.2077568.

Huws, Ursula (2020): The algorithm and the city: platform labour and the urban environment, in: *Work Organisation, Labour & Globalisation* 14(1): 7-14.

Ignatow, Gabe/Robinson, Laura (2017): Pierre Bourdieu: Theorizing the digital, in: *Information, Communication & Society* 20(7): 950-66.

Isin, Engin F. (2017): Performative Citizenship, in: Shachar, Ayelet/Bauböck, Rainer/Bloemraad, Irene/Vink, Maarten (eds.): *The Oxford Handbook of Citizenship*, Oxford: Oxford University Press: 500-23.

Isin, Engin F./Ruppert, Evelyn (2020): *Being Digital Citizens*, London/New York: Rowman & Littlefield.

Leszczynski, Agnieszka (2020): Glitchy Vignettes of Platform Urbanism, in: *Environment and Planning D: Society and Space* 38(2): 189-208.

Mathiason, John (2008): *Internet Governance. The New Frontier of Global Institutions*, London: Routledge.

Mezzadra, Sandro/Neilson, Brett (2012): Between Inclusion and Exclusion: On the Topology of Global Space and Borders, in: *Theory, Culture & Society* 29(4-5): 58-75.

Nyers, Peter/Rygiel, Kim (eds.) (2012): *Citizenship, Migrant Activism, and the Politics of Movement*, New York: Routledge.

Platform Labour in Urban Spaces (PLUS) (n.d.): https://project-plus.eu/ [08.04.2022].

Sassen, Saskia (2005): The Repositioning of Citizenship and Alienage: Emergent Subjects and Spaces for Politics, in: *Globalizations* 2(1): 79-94.

Sassen, Saskia (2016): Expulsions: Brutality and Complexity in the Global Economy, in: *Trajectories* 27(3): 62-84.

Schmitt, Carl (2003): *The Nomos of the Earth in the International Law of the Jus Publicum Europaeum*, New York: Telos Press.

Soares Carvalho, Ana Paula/Bignami, Filippo (2021): Social development through (global) citizenship education: the Brazilian case, in: *Intercultural Education* 32(4): 464-75.

Srnicek, Nick (2017): *Platform capitalism*, Cambridge: Polity Press.

Swyngedouw, Erik (2019): The Perverse Lure of Autocratic Postdemocracy, in: *South Atlantic Quarterly* 118(2): 267-86.

Tomasello, Federico (forthcoming): From industrial to digital citizenship: rethinking social rights in cyberspace, in: *Theory and society* (submitted).

Žižek, Slavoj (2010): *Living in the End Times*, London/New York: Verso.

Zuboff, Shoshana (2019): Surveillance Capitalism and the Challenge of Collective Action, in: *New Labor Forum* 28(1): 10-29.

Biographies

Akteurinnen für urbanen Ungehorsam is an interdisciplinary city research collective currently focusing on geographies and embodiments of invisible digital infrastructures and urban gig work. While we combine experience and expertise in fields such as architecture, communication design, and political and urban studies, our toolbox is based on critical feminist thinking as well as ethnographic research methods. With it, we tackle questions of cities in crisis, forms of dwelling, and ideas of future urban life. Currently, we do this mainly in and around Hamburg, Germany, as well as online.

Sybille Bauriedl is professor of geography with a focus on political ecology at the Europa-Universität Flensburg, Germany. Her research projects deal with local energy transition, platform urbanism, smart mobility, geographies of coloniality, and climate justice. She is a member of the German academy for territorial development, is engaged in interdisciplinary networks of energy geography and feminist geography, and is involved in the right to the city movement in Hamburg.

Rabea Berfelde is a PhD candidate in the Department of Media, Communications, and Cultural Studies at Goldsmiths, University of London. Her doctoral thesis, based on field research in Berlin, analyses the reconfiguration of labor and urban space under financialized digital capitalism.

Filippo Bignami is senior researcher and lecturer at the University of Applied Sciences of Southern Switzerland – LUCI (Labour, Urbanscape and CItizenship) research area. He holds a PhD in political and social sciences. Among scientific appointments, he has been external scientific consultant for the United Nations International Labour Organization (UN-ILO) and project-visiting professor at the Asia-Europe Institute, State University of Malaya, Kuala

Lumpur, Malaysia. His main scientific interest and expertise is in citizenship, social, and political theories, including applied studies on citizenship policies and education, urban transformation, and mega-events. He has coordinated many European and international research projects in this field.

Yana Boeva is a postdoc researcher at the Department of Social Sciences and the Cluster of Excellence *Integrative Computational Design and Construction for Architecture (IntCDC)*, University of Stuttgart. Her current research explores the transformation of design, architectural practice, and different user perceptions through computation and automation.

Kathrin Braun is research coordinator at the Center for Interdisciplinary Risk and Innovation Studies and postdoc researcher at the Department of Social Sciences, University of Stuttgart. She is a political scientist by training and her research focuses on Critical Biopolitics Studies, Science and Technology Studies, and Interpretative Policy Analysis. She is also co-editor of *Critical Policy Studies*.

Emma Dowling is tenure track professor for the sociology of social change at the University of Vienna, Austria. Previously she has held positions in the UK and Germany. Her research interests include social change and social justice; the financialization of the social; welfare state restructuring; labor, emotions, and affect. Her most recent work asks what our economy looks like when viewed from the perspective of care, charting the material conditions that shape its configurations. She is the author of *The Care Crisis – What Caused It and How Can We End It?* (2021, Verso Books).

Yannick Ecker is researcher and PhD student at Martin-Luther-University Halle-Wittenberg, Germany with a focus on urban geographies of precarization and digitalization. His research engages with the impacts of platformization on the production of space, social justice as well as gender arrangements and labor regimes. He has studied Urban Geographies at Humboldt-University, Berlin and is a former junior fellow of the Elisabeth-List-Program for Gender Research at University of Graz, Austria.

Andreas Exner is operational manager of the RCE Graz-Styria – Centre for Sustainable Social Transformation, University of Graz. Participating in and coordinating transdisciplinary research projects on alternative economies and urban development, he focuses on social ecological transformation, including publications on Solidarity Economies and the Commons.

Yvonne Franz is an urban geographer at the University of Vienna. Her research interests lie in the fields of neighborhood development, urban arrival spaces, migration, housing market transition, and social innovation. She is also member of the interdisciplinary research platform *The Challenge of Urban Futures* and the co-director of the postgraduate course in Cooperative Urban and Regional Development at the Postgraduate Center, University of Vienna.

Katalin Gennburg is a directly elected member to the Berlin House of Representatives for the district Treptow and the party DIE LINKE. due to the elections in 2016 and 2021. She is the spokesperson for urban development, environment, and tourism for the parliamentary group of DIE LINKE. and studied Metropolitan Studies at the TU Berlin. Her topics include: right-to-the-city movements, land and real estate policy, and the reclamation and repoliticization of public space and the public sphere, particularly in a digital age.

Kiley Goyette is a doctoral candidate in human geography at the University of Toronto, Canada. Her current research focuses on direct and indirect platform mediation in the tourism accommodation and cleaning industries, with a focus on cleaning work for short-term rentals.

Naomi C. Hanakata is an assistant professor at the National University of Singapore and co-founder of a research and planning practice based in Singapore. Her work focuses on the research and development of adaptive planning strategies to deal with uncertainties and dynamic urban futures in urban development and planning. Addressing challenges of planetary urbanization, decarbonization, decentralization of resources, and digitalization in spatial production and planning practice are central in her work towards sustainable and equitable urban futures.

Thomas Höflehner is a geographer and sustainability researcher and works as a postdoc researcher at the RCE Graz-Styria – Centre for Sustainable Social Transformation, University of Graz, Austria. His research focuses on inter- and transdisciplinary transition initiatives, integrated neighborhood development, participatory urban and regional development as well as cooperative innovation and change processes.

Marisol Keller is a PhD candidate and member of the labor geography group at the University of Zurich, Switzerland. Her autoethnographic research on the gig economy focuses on the social, spatial, and temporal working arrangements emerging in platform-mediated labor in Switzerland. She is also engaged in the community *Work* of the Digital Society Initiative at the University of Zurich which brings together scholars across disciplines to examine how technological advances and other forces are changing the world of work.

Vicky Kluzik works as a research associate in the Biotechnologies, Nature, and Society research group at the Institute of Sociology at Goethe University Frankfurt. Her research and teaching interests span from social theory, political economy, science and technology studies (STS) to cultural geography, with a specific focus on feminist and postcolonial theories to examine contemporary political, economic, and ecological crises in an interdisciplinary manner.

Astrid Krisch studied spatial planning and currently works as a researcher with a focus on critical infrastructure studies at TU Wien and Vienna University of Economics and Business. Her research projects deal with different forms of established and newly emerging infrastructure systems, social-ecological transformations, climate change research, urban and regional development policy, and urban governance. Currently she is working on her PhD, where she investigates the connection of infrastructure development and urban planning from an institutionalist perspective.

Cordula Kropp is professor of sociology with a focus on science and technology studies at the University of Stuttgart, Germany. Her research projects deal with sustainability-oriented, sociotechnical transformation processes and their participatory and risk-sensitive organization, especially in infrastructure sectors such as mobility, energy, water, and architecture. She is a lead PI in the cluster of excellence *Integrative computational design and construction for architecture (IntCDC)* in Stuttgart and member of the Sustainability Advisory Board in Baden-Württemberg, Germany.

Boris Michel is professor of digital geography at the University Halle-Wittenberg, Germany. His main research interests are in critical cartography and counter-mapping as well as urban studies. One current research project is interested in the relation between urban platform capitalism and open geodata. He is a co-founder and co-editor of the open-access journal *sub\urban*.

Barbara Orth is a research associate and PhD candidate at the Department of Geography at Free University (FU) Berlin. Her dissertation work explores digital platforms as migration infrastructures, particularly in the realm of reproductive services. Prior to joining FU, she conducted research on queer support structures in Berlin's labor market and labor market access for refugees and asylum seekers. Barbara holds a BA in International Relations, University of East Anglia and a MSc in Refugee and Forced Migration Studies, University of Oxford.

Maartje Roelofsen is a postdoc researcher in the Department of Economics and Business at the Universitat Oberta de Catalunya, Spain. Her work has been concerned with the digital transformations of urban space, home and everyday life, tourism, and hospitality labor.

Susanne Schröder-Bergen is a research associate and doctoral candidate specializing in political geography at Friedrich-Alexander-Universität Erlangen-Nürnberg. Her research interests include the critical cartography and political economy of global open-source map and knowledge projects such as OpenStreetMap.

Anke Strüver is professor of human geography with a focus on urban studies at the University of Graz, Austria. She conducts research on urban everyday life with a focus on embodiment related to health, mobility, food, and digitalization. She is also head of the research group *urban HEAP (urban health and everyday activities take place)* and the RCE Graz-Styria – Centre for Sustainable Social Transformation, University of Graz. The center's work comprises six fields of action, all of them based on connecting social justice with ecological sustainability in urban contexts.

Christiane Tristl is a postdoc researcher in economic geography at the University of Bonn, Germany. From the perspective of science and technology studies, social studies of infrastructure, and marketization studies, her research focuses on North-South relations, globally circulating (digital) technologies, the marketization of (public) services, and the increasing influence of private companies in global policymaking.

Henk Wiechers is an urban and regional geographer working on platform urbanism, smart mobility, and local energy transition. He is interested in critical urban studies, political ecology, geographies of homelessness, and the digitalization of infrastructures. In addition to that he specializes in working with ethnographic research methods.

Social Sciences

Mihnea Tanasescu
Understanding the Rights of Nature
A Critical Introduction

February 2022, 168 p., pb.
40,00 € (DE), 978-3-8376-5431-8
E-Book: available as free open access publication
PDF: ISBN 978-3-8394-5431-2

Oliver Krüger
**Virtual Immortality –
God, Evolution, and the Singularity
in Post- and Transhumanism**

2021, 356 p., pb., ill.
35,00 (DE), 978-3-8376-5059-4
E-Book:
PDF: 34,99 (DE), ISBN 978-3-8394-5059-8

Dean Caivano, Sarah Naumes
The Sublime of the Political
Narrative and Autoethnography as Theory

2021, 162 p., hardcover
100,00 (DE), 978-3-8376-4772-3
E-Book:
PDF: 99,99 (DE), ISBN 978-3-8394-4772-7

**All print, e-book and open access versions of the titles in our list
are available in our online shop www.transcript-publishing.com**

Social Sciences

Friederike Landau, Lucas Pohl, Nikolai Roskamm (eds.)
[Un]Grounding
Post-Foundational Geographies

2021, 348 p., pb., col. ill.
50,00 (DE), 978-3-8376-5073-0
E-Book:
PDF: 49,99 (DE), ISBN 978-3-8394-5073-4

Andreas de Bruin
Mindfulness and Meditation at University
10 Years of the Munich Model

2021, 216 p., pb.
25,00 (DE), 978-3-8376-5696-1
E-Book: available as free open access publication
PDF: ISBN 978-3-8394-5696-5

Gabriele Dietze, Julia Roth (eds.)
Right-Wing Populism and Gender
European Perspectives and Beyond

2020, 286 p., pb., ill.
35,00 (DE), 978-3-8376-4980-2
E-Book:
PDF: 34,99 (DE), ISBN 978-3-8394-4980-6

All print, e-book and open access versions of the titles in our list are available in our online shop www.transcript-publishing.com